THE VOICE OF SOUTHERN LABOR

Social Movements, Protest, and Contention

Series Editor: Bert Klandermans, Free University, Amsterdam

Associate Editors: Ron R. Aminzade, University of Minnesota
David S. Meyer, University of California, Irvine
Verta A. Taylor, University of California, Santa Barbara

For more books in the series, see page 180.

THE VOICE OF
SOUTHERN LABOR

Radio, Music, and
Textile Strikes, 1929–1934

Vincent J. Roscigno and
William F. Danaher

Social Movements, Protest, and Contention
Volume 19

 University of Minnesota Press
Minneapolis • London

Published by the University of Minnesota Press
111 Third Avenue South, Suite 290
Minneapolis, MN 55401-2520
http://www.upress.umn.edu

Library of Congress Cataloging-in-Publication Data

Roscigno, Vincent J.
    The voice of southern labor : radio, music, and textile strikes, 1929–1934 / Vincent J.
Roscigno and William F. Danaher.
        p.   cm. — (Social movements, protest, and contention ; v. 19)
    Includes bibliographical references and index.
    ISBN 0-8166-4015-7 (cloth : alk. paper) — ISBN 0-8166-4016-5 (pbk. : alk. paper)
    1. Textile workers—Labor unions—Southern States—History. 2. Radio broadcasting—
Social aspects—Southern States—History. 3. Music—Social aspects—Southern States—
History. 4. Strikes and lockouts—Textile industry—Southern States—History. 5. Textile
Workers Union of America—History. I. Danaher, William F. II. Title. III. Series.
    HD6515.T4R67 2004
    331.88'177'0097709043—dc22

                                                                                    2004002547

Printed in the United States of America on acid-free paper

The University of Minnesota is an equal-opportunity educator and employer.

12 11 10 09 08 07 06 05 04   10 9 8 7 6 5 4 3 2 1

This book is dedicated to the southern mill workers about whom we write, who stood up in the face of hardship for the sake of their children, and to the musicians who sang and played, in doing so breathing strength, community, and spirit into the mill workers' world.

Contents

Preface

Southern textile-worker mobilization in the late 1920s through the mid-1930s reflected a truly amazing moment in U.S. history. Just when unions had virtually given up on southern organizing, and southern businessmen and political leaders adopted the view that southern workers were apathetic or conservative, mill hands took it upon themselves to address years of low wages, grievances pertaining to mill owner control and coercion, and the institutionalization of scientific management and the "stretch-out." Their dignity was on the line, as was, for many, their children's future. Hundreds of thousands consequently walked off the job.

The Voice of Southern Labor addresses not only what unfolded but, perhaps more sociologically important, how it could have unfolded despite limited union organization and the relative dominance of textile elites over the southern political-economic landscape. Such inquiry is central to labor history and analyses, and equally relevant to theoretical perspectives pertaining to social movements, their formation, and their diffusion—perspectives we discuss in the Introduction.

The topic of mill-worker mobilization, and its potential sociological relevance, was the outgrowth of hearing an old southern string band, in the early 1990s, sing a few gritty mill-related songs as the singers (then in their eighties) recalled their "escape" from the mill. They attributed their good fortune to a new, emergent media at the time—radio. Yet, despite their departure, these individuals continued to identify with mill workers and performed oppositional mill music over the airwaves and during live performances. Did radio's emergence throughout the region, and the timing of station foundings, link otherwise dispersed mill communities, and does this help explain how four hundred thousand southern workers struck in 1934? And what in particular was disseminated via the airwaves and during live performances that helped forge workers' sense of identity, oppositional consciousness, and collective, political action beyond the confines of a single mill village? These were the questions we pondered.

We turned to rich historical work on the era, historical data, and firsthand accounts of what unfolded at the time. In terms of notable historical work, *Like a Family: The Making of a Southern Cotton Mill World* by Jacquelyn Dowd Hall, James Leloudis, Robert Korstad, Mary Murphy, Lu Ann Jones, and Christopher B. Daly not only provides wonderful background on life in the southern mill village of the 1920s and 1930s, but also grapples seriously with the complex issue of mill workers' loyalties in the face of a changing, industrializing South. One component of this change was the emergence of radio and traveling string bands of ex-mill workers who linked communities. Another was the connection of mill workers often personally expressed, with a president, Franklin Delano Roosevelt, whom they trusted and listened to intently as he aired radio fireside chats over the southern airwaves.

Other historians, such as Allen Tullos in *Habits of Industry: White Culture and the Transformation of the Carolina Piedmont* and Pamela Grundy in "From Il Trovatore to Crazy Mountaineers: WBT-Charlotte and Changing Musical Culture in the Carolina Piedmont: 1922–1935," provide more detail on mill-worker musicians, their live performances and radio broadcasts, and what this meant for mill workers' sense of culture and community. In preparing this book, these historians (Hall, Tullos, and Grundy) offered suggestions and leads on these topics, and we greatly appreciate their gracious help. Tom Hanchett, of Charlotte's Levine Museum of the New South, similarly proved to be a wonderful resource, providing leads and introducing us to one of the old-time mill musicians interviewed in this book. Other historical work on specific strikes proved incredibly useful as well. Included here are works by Janet Irons, Irwin Marcus, Bryant Simon, John A. Salmond, and George Calvin Waldrep. This work is rich, and speaks to the true complexity of mill workers' lives and the insurgency in which they engaged. It also informs our sensitivity to both the larger structural dynamics affecting mill workers at the time and the complexity, nuances, and even the contradictory tendencies and resistance patterns that were characteristic of mill workers' lives.

To systematically establish the association between radio and mill villages, and to address broader theoretical questions pertaining to social movement diffusion and the impact of media, required significant time and energy in the gathering of data—data that we were unsure at the outset actually existed. This was the most challenging, yet ultimately rewarding, task at hand. We were fortunate in garnering the assistance of a number of archivists and librarians, to whom we are grateful. Among these are archivists at the Federal Communications Commission, the University of North Carolina, Wayne State University, the National Archives, the John Rivers Communications Museum at the College of Charleston, and the University of South Carolina. Librarians at the city libraries of Charlotte, Columbia, Gastonia, Marion, and Spartanburg were also helpful and quite enthusiastic about the project, going out of their way to help locate relevant historical materials throughout the course of the project. From this search came data on mill villages, strike events between 1929 and 1934, and radio station foundings for southern cities during this era.

Establishing a link between mill villages, radio station foundings, and strike events, however, would not be enough, in our view, and would paint an overly determined view of mill workers' lives, mill-owner power, and resistance. And, unfortunately, firsthand accounts are hard to come by because many of these mill workers have passed on. We nevertheless found some accounts, and immersed ourselves in more than a hundred interviews of mill workers at the time, undertaken by the Southern Oral History Project and deposited in the Southern Folk Life Collection at the University of North Carolina archives. These interviews, used throughout this book, speak to issues of work life, family life, and changes in each. Moreover, many of the workers discuss the emergence of radio, the role of music in their personal and family lives, hearing FDR on the radio, and the strikes that unfolded in their own mill villages.

Along with Southern Oral History Project material and letters from mill workers to FDR from the National Archives, we also rely throughout on the transcribed interviews undertaken by the producers of the film *The Uprising of '34*. We are especially grateful to coproducer Judith Helfand for her permission to use this material, which includes firsthand accounts by strikers who took part in and witnessed the strike of 1934, the violence that sometimes unfolded, and the consequences of the strike for mill communities throughout the region. The film itself, first aired on PBS and available for purchase through First Run/Icarus at http://www.frif.com/cat97/t-z/the_upri.html, offers a vivid portrayal of the strike in the words of mill workers themselves.

Because a big component of the project was to identify important aspects of oppositional consciousness and its impact among and between communities, we found it necessary and important to contact and interview surviving mill musicians who made the leap to radio during the era examined and who often delivered live performances for mill communities between radio stints and sometimes even at strike events. In this regard, we owe a great deal of thanks to Alvin Wall, an early southern radio musician and writer of southern music history himself, who was brought to our attention by Cathy Evans, director of the John Rivers Communication Museum. Al has been invaluable, providing us with not only the names and contact information for other surviving musicians, but also an insider's view of early radio. Al's insights helped illuminate for us radio performers' sympathies with mill workers, how ex-mill-worker musicians traveled, and how these musicians would informally congregate to share music and play together.

Early mill musicians turned radio performers with whom we spent time include "Whitey" Grant of the Briarhoppers and the late Homer "Pappy" Sherrill and J. D. McCormick. Other radio musicians from the early 1930s also helped in this project, including Wade Mainer of J. E. Mainer and the Mountaineers, and Gray and Fred Troutman of the Ramblin' Cracker-Jacks. All of these individuals showed us hospitality, spent countless hours with us recounting their own musical past and work histories, and freely discussed issues pertaining to the strikes workers engaged in—issues about which many contemporary southerners have never heard or remain uncomfortable speaking about.

Many of our colleagues at the Ohio State University and the College of Charleston supported us in this project, as did many academic friends and mentors. Some, such as Donald Tomaskovic-Devey, Rick Della Fave, Jeffrey Leiter, and Michael Schulman, planted the intellectual seeds, while others, including Cindy Anderson, Cliff Brown, John Brueggemann, Dennis Condron, Dana Cope, George Dickinson, Nella Van Dyke, Richard Flacks, Bill Form, Chris Hope, Brad Huber, Elizabeth Kaminski, Steve Lopez, Toby Parcel, and Marieke Van Willigan, proved essential in offering encouragement when it was needed. Beyond providing such encouragement, two graduate students, Marc Dixon and Martha Crowley, helped gather some of the materials used here and also provided upbeat, constructive feedback throughout the process.

Especially helpful, from the project's initial inception, were Tim Dowd, Randy Hodson, Craig Jenkins, William Roy, David Snow, Erika Summers-Effler, and Verta Taylor, each of whom took time out of their busy schedules to provide feedback on papers and proposals related to the project, and who enthusiastically responded to this work despite the fact that studying mill workers, oppositional culture, and collective action was somewhat of a departure for both of us. Verta Taylor was particularly important, encouraging us to be both confident and creative in our design and presentation of these materials throughout the course of the project. We also thank Carrie Mullen of the University of Minnesota Press, for her excitement about the project and patience in seeing it through completion, and David Thorstad, Mike Stoffel, and Jason Weidemann for their thoroughness in helping assure a better, more polished product.

The College of Social and Behavioral Sciences at the Ohio State University and the College of Charleston provided small grant money for us to travel and collect data at the beginning phase of the project, while the National Science Foundation ensured, through grant SES-0136837, that we would be able to follow further leads, undertake more interviews, and scour even more archives and libraries. Consequently, this book contains new material and is an extension of some of our earlier work, particularly "Media and Mobilization: The Case of Radio and Southern Textile Worker Insurgency, 1929–1934," *American Sociological Review* 66 (2001): 21–48, and (with Erika Summers-Effler) "Music, Culture, and Social Movements: Song and Southern Textile Worker Mobilization, 1929–1934" *International Journal of Sociology and Social Policy* 22 (2002): 141–74.

We provide a sociological account of what occurred in the southern Piedmont between 1929 through 1934 and attempt to put a human face on what we describe. We do this not simply because it makes for better reading, but rather because acknowledging the creative, constructive, and reflexive nature of human action makes for better sociology. Simply, it brings a sense of agency, and the possibility of agency, into even the most constrained circumstances. We attribute this approach and our interest and focus on hardworking people to our parents, John and Carolyn Roscigno and William and Jewel Danaher. Our parents not only encouraged us throughout but, in many ways, shaped the type of sociologists we have become and the types of sociological questions we ask. Important above all else has been the support, feedback, flexibility, and patience of our partners, Susan Roscigno and Karen Weissman, without whom this book could not have been written.

Introduction

It was on Labor Day in 1934 that I witnessed the closest thing that this country has had to a revolution. The General Textile Strike was one of the largest strikes in American history; it was the culmination of home-grown organizing and protest. For many southern workers it was the first time they had raised their voices as citizens to challenge the control of mill owners.

—Joe Jacobs

The U.S. South experienced a truly remarkable period in labor history between 1929 and 1934. Mill owners were caught off guard first in 1929, when 3,500 workers walked out of the inspection department at the American Ganzstoff Corporation in Elizabethton, Tennessee. Approximately 2,000 workers in neighboring Gastonia, North Carolina, followed suit and walked out making demands pertaining to pay and work conditions. Strikes, not immediately related to those in Gastonia and Elizabethton, occurred soon after in South Carolina. In late March 1929, 800 workers walked out at Ware Shoals Manufacturing company and 1,250 workers walked out of the New England Southern plant in Pelzer. Within three weeks, 8,000 workers had walked out of fifteen plants in the Piedmont area of South Carolina. Strikes followed shortly thereafter in the North Carolina towns of Pineville, Forest City, Lexington, Bessemer City, Marion, Draper, and Charlotte.[1]

This early wave of strike action was quelled relatively quickly through court injunctions against strikers, through the use of state militias in North and South Carolina, and through red-scare rhetoric disseminated through locally owned and controlled newspapers with links to textile industrialists. In one of the most dramatic incidences, occurring in Marion, North Carolina, five workers were killed by local deputies. In another, in Gastonia, North Carolina, the chief of police was killed in a skirmish with strikers. Several workers would eventually be put on trial and sent to prison, and a mill mother and strike leader would be killed by a mill-sponsored mob.

Despite the violence that unfolded and the scars that would be left on mill communities for generations, the voice of the southern mill worker was by no means quieted. On Labor Day 1934, approximately four hundred thousand textile mill workers, most in the South, walked off their jobs. Notably, this major labor walkout, the largest in U.S. history, occurred with little organization by labor unions and in the face of coercive paternalistic practices and state-sponsored violence.[2] Indeed, the United Textile Workers (UTW) did not institute a unionization drive. It had fewer than ten paid organizers in the South at that time and represented only a small fraction of the entire mill workforce.[3] Historical accounts suggest that this was mostly owing to a lack of organizational resources and a vast, hard-to-cover rural area. According to historian Jacquelyn Hall and her colleagues (1987, 304):

> It [the UTW] launched no Piedmont organizing campaign. Agents did not throng to the southern field. Yet within less than a month after passage of the act [National Industrial Recovery Act], union locals had reportedly sprung to life in 75 percent of South Carolina's mills. From an estimated 40,000 in September 1933, UTW membership leaped to 279,000 by August 1934. To the shock of labor leaders, government officials, and businessmen alike, southern workers began "organizing just as fast as we can."

Social scientists shared interest in what was occurring. David Saposs, a sociologist at the time, understood the oppressive conditions southern mill workers were facing and also denoted the general surprise, if not shock, of southern businessmen.

> The most important event which vitally affected the labor movement and stirred the country was the general unrest and strikes in the South, centering chiefly around the textile industry . . . In order to lure industry to the South, the local realtors and chambers of commerce have been featuring the "cheap and contented" 100 percent American labor supply, which, unlike the immigrant workers of the North, was docile and wholly unresponsive to appeals of labor agitators. At any rate the capitalists evi-

dently did not inform themselves but accepted the statements of the local boosters. The shock and attendant consternation were naturally intense when all these elements were rudely awakened to the realization that the 100 percent American cheap labor was neither contented nor docile and manifested its dissatisfaction by striking . . . In general, the strikers were not organized into unions . . . many were so called "leaderless strikes," that is, strikes of textile workers without outside professional leadership or guidance.[4]

This contented 100 percent indeed had a voice—a voice that was expressed whether or not organized unions were present. The discontent and emotions of mill workers were highlighted on a relatively broad, geographic scale by 1930 with the recorded release of Dave McCarn's song "Cotton Mill Colic." As we note later, "Cotton Mill Colic" sold thousands of copies across mill towns, despite a cost that approximated half a day's wages. McCarn's words of dissatisfaction were sung by workers and then strikers in Danville, Virginia, as local deputies and mill owners attempted to outlaw its singing. It was echoed further by "flying squadrons" of striking mill workers, singing from the back of trucks while traveling within and between mill towns of western North Carolina in 1934.[5]

The voice of mill workers was not limited to those with recording contracts, but also included that of the charismatic mill worker, mother, and home-grown leader Ella May Wiggins. During the infamous Loray Mill strike in 1929, crowds pleaded with Wiggins on several occasions to sing her self-penned "Mill Mothers Lament," and she did.[6] Wiggins's powerful and emotionally evocative song would eventually be sung at her own funeral, following her ambush and murder on the way to a strike meeting. It would also become a battle cry for southern mill mothers.

The music shared and its message reached even further across the region by 1933 and 1934 via a new medium—radio—as the Dixon Brothers bellowed their "Weave Room Blues" across the airwaves, and others, with radio contracts, took part in live performances at mill recreation centers, high schools, and dances between their radio stints. Many, beginning with Charlie Poole and his North Carolina Ramblers, had clear roots in southern mill towns. They also had experiences as mill workers prior to radio's emergence. The new medium of radio, in fact, afforded them the opportunity to escape mill life. Some, such as the Tobacco Tags, with ties and experience in the mill, went as far as providing music in 1934 for strike events. "Dancing pickets"—that is, mill workers dancing during strikes to bolster solidarity and block mill entrances—became an important part of strikers' repertoire.[7] Southern mill workers indeed had a voice, constructed through and reflected in songs they created, sang, listened to, and shared.

Beyond the formulation of critical consciousness and solidarity through music, which itself has a long and pronounced historical grounding in southern culture, mill workers' sense of urgency and legitimacy was bolstered further between 1929 and 1934 by President Franklin D. Roosevelt's "fireside radio chats." For many southern mill workers, a national leader was now on their side, speaking to them in their own homes through the new medium of radio. As noted by one mill worker:

> When Roosevelt got elected, well, uh, he, he was, uh, a man that people had confidence in, you know, he said "You have nothing to fear but fear itself." Well, people loved that. And they'd have those fireside chats that they called it.[8]

Mill workers responded back, via personal letters by the thousands—letters that denoted their sense of intimacy with the president and confidence that he, and the federal government more generally, not only understood the conditions in which most mill workers worked and lived but, more important, wanted to remedy the situation.

The Case of Southern Textile-Worker Mobilization, 1929–34

In this book, we embed our understanding of southern textile-worker mobilization within broader sociological questions pertaining to stratification and work, oppositional cultural formation and diffusion, and social movement mobilization. Indeed, the relatively geographically dispersed nature of mill towns in the U.S. South, the limited union organization that existed at the time, and the relatively controlled circumstances in which most mill workers lived and worked present an interesting case through which a number of relevant theoretical questions can be addressed. From where did oppositional culture emerge, and what role did labor unions play, if any? In what ways was music meaningful in workers' daily lives and during protest, and how, if at all, was oppositional music disseminated? What role did political opportunity, or at least perceptions of opportunity, play in workers' sense of efficacy? How can we account for strike activity in some mills but not others? Even more broadly, how might newly emergent media play a role in the diffusion of social movement oppositional culture and perceptions of opportunity? And, are worker grievances toward injustices in the labor process and in the organization of work in and of themselves sufficient for workplace strike action, let alone an industry-wide mobilization?

We address these questions by first turning to literature on social movements, particularly that specifying the preconditions for social movement formation. Rather than focusing purely on grievances, as do more traditional social movement perspectives,[9] recent research suggests that movement occurrence necessitates oppositional cultural framing and political opportunity. Notably, though, few analyses of oppositional culture and its impact on movement formation focus on historical cases. This is perhaps owing to the suggestion that relevant identity and solidarity dynamics are more an attribute of "new," as opposed to "old," social movements.[10] Similarly, only a small handful of analyses have attempted to delineate the mechanism through which cultural information and perceptions of opportunity may be disseminated and altered across geographic space. Our case is informative in each of these regards.

The labor insurgency on which we focus was a pivotal moment in U.S. labor history. It is thus surprising that little social-scientific or sociological attention has been devoted to this instance of southern worker unrest. Instead, labor research typically overlooks the South or treats it as a union-resistant region.[11] This is unfortunate as the ramifications of what occurred extend beyond the particular historical moment in question. Workers' eventual defeat in this instance, in fact, has had consequences for subsequent labor practices, organizing efforts, economic development, and persistent poverty and inequality in the U.S. South up through the present day.[12] Despite a general neglect of the southern case, there is a more general body of research on workplace grievances and labor insurgency from which we draw, and that is informative particularly on questions pertaining to the impact of unions and factors that drive workers to contest.[13]

Sociological Perspectives on Mobilization and Labor Insurgency

We begin with *collective identity* theory, which tends to emphasize the importance of ideological, normative, and cultural processes for inducing individual participation in collective action and for ensuring social solidarity even in the face of harsh countermobilization. Researchers in this tradition, such as Melluci (1985), also assert the importance of alternative belief structures for providing movement participants with a structure of nonmaterial rewards, not necessarily tied to movement success.[14] The relevance of an alternative belief structure and collective identity has been evident in a variety of struggles, including those aimed at promoting racial justice, women's rights, and class-based politics.[15]

Fantasia's *Cultures of Solidarity: Consciousness, Action, and Contemporary American Workers* provides one of only a few social movement studies that make this focus explicit in relation to working-class politics. He highlights the fundamental importance of "cultures of solidarity," defining them as "cultural formations that arise in conflict, creating and sustaining solidarity in opposition to the dominant structure" (1988, 19). Others have denoted similar cultural formations pertaining to labor campaigns, yet the cultural focus typically garners piecemeal or only peripheral attention. More commonly, labor-oriented research and analyses of collective protests by working-class people focus on issues of grievance, union influence, or strike success and failure.[16] Although certainly important, such topics can be informed by an approach that emphasizes movement cultural and identity dynamics. Indeed, if grievances are to resonate, they must be shared and highlighted within oppositional cultural repertoires. If unions are to successfully organize workers and take a leadership role in mobilization campaigns, they must be sensitive to preexisting cultural nuances and identity attributes of the populations they are attempting to serve. Strike success is fundamentally dependent on internal cohesion, solidarity maintenance, and dynamic and responsive cultural repertoires among strike participants.

The application of collective identity perspectives to labor insurgency is not, strictly speaking, new or unique to sociology. In fact, the focus on group formation and solidarity processes resonates with more classical and contemporary theoretical ideas pertaining to "class consciousness" and when, if at all, it may emerge. Indeed, "the most important blank spots in the theory of class concern the processes whereby 'economic classes' become 'social classes.'"[17]

Mann (1973) offers one of the more developed treatments, conceiving of class consciousness as a complex process, occurring in stages, and as something that is often curbed by dominant ideologies, class ambiguities, concessions by elites, or outright defeat. The stages include (1) class identity, whereby one defines oneself as working class, (2) class opposition, whereby one perceives capitalists and their agents as enduring opponents to oneself, (3) class totality, whereby class identity and opposition define the total of one's social situation and the whole of society, and (4) conceiving of an alternative. It is during this final stage, Mann continues, that an "explosive potential" comes into existence, and may manifest itself in terms of a "conflict consciousness," which has as its aim alleviation of the problem, or a more "revolutionary consciousness," wherein the change needed is viewed in terms of overall systemic reorganization. Given the correct progression, the delegitimation of existing ideology, and the existence of an alternative interpretational frame, class consciousness will emerge.[18]

Issues of identity and class consciousness are certainly relevant to our case given that what occurred appears to have been, at face value, a regional class struggle. Yet, we know little about southern workers' own interpretations and collective identity, and even less about their consciousness and stance relative to textile industrialists. In our view, it is incumbent on researchers to demonstrate, rather than assume, that workers see a commonality of experience and purpose as expressed in their cultural expression and in their tactics and strategies of protest. We attempt to demonstrate that southern textile workers of the 1920s and 1930s eventually did come to see the similarity of their plight, in part through oppositional music and the dissemination of information on radio, and that this culminated in strategies of collective action aimed at reformatory change.

In contrast to identity theorists and those dealing explicitly with class consciousness, *political opportunity* theorists focus on the political context in which groups are embedded, and shifting levels of opportunity across time and place. The likelihood of mobilization as well as the degree of leverage exerted by insurgents, it is argued, will be heightened in situations where elites are divided in their defense of the existing order.[19] Where elites are coordinated, in contrast, the reproduction of dominant relations is more likely, as is countermobilization against those engaging in insurgent action.[20] McAdam (1983) emphasizes such countermobilization in his analysis of elite response to tactics implemented by civil rights activists during the 1960s. Barkan (1984) and James (1988) develop the argument by highlighting the role of other actors in the civil rights struggle, namely, the southern racial state, which constrained movement participants, and the federal government, which eventually intervened on behalf of participants once pressured to do so.

Some have extended these insights to labor mobilization specifically. Kimeldorf (1999), Griffin, Wallace, and Rubin (1986), and Montgomery (1987), for instance, stress themes of elite response to labor organization specifically in their analyses of capitalist countermobilization during the 1930s and 1940s.[21] Most subtly, coercion and control through paternalism proved effective as a preventive strategy.[22] More obvious and extreme have been the efforts of capital to divide workers racially, to curtail working-class mobilization with subversive activities and violence, and to control labor organization and labor practices through manipulation of the state and state policy.

For collective identity theorists, then, the central task is to explain how interpretation is altered, collective identity manifested, and solidarity maintained. For political opportunity theorists, the focus is on the degree of elite unity, elite countermobilization, and the extent to which these dimensions of political opportunity enable or constrain the collective expression of grievances within a given historical context. Although undoubtedly useful foci for understanding mobilization generally, there are problematic features of each when applied to our case. How would collective identity theory explain the manifestation of solidarity across this geographically dispersed textile mill population? We are also left wondering about the mechanism through which structural political opportunity, if it indeed existed during the era in question, translated into and shaped political perceptions and the degree of efficacy among mill workers. Important to each of these questions—and indeed a potential bridge between perspectives—is the role of media technology.

The focus on media technology, and radio's emergence specifically, partially bridges the divide between collective identity and political opportunity perspectives by addressing the question of how processes relevant to social movement formation are manifested across space. As an integrative link, however, the study of media and social movement dynamics must be supplemented further by theory that explicitly incorporates aspects of both identity and opportunity into a single framework.[23] One of the most promising contemporary lines of work that undertakes this very task is that dealing with *social movement culture.* Social movement culture, according to theorists such as Verta Taylor and Nancy Whittier (1995), William Gamson (1995), and David Snow (2001), rather than an ambiguous construct, is an influential and clearly defined component of the social movement dynamic composed of normative guidelines and practices that create and reinforce (1) a sense of group identity, (2) an alternative interpretational frame of cause and effect, and (3) a sense of political efficacy. Such a conceptual frame is nicely suited for systematically analyzing influential components of the social movement repertoire, including music. No doubt, extending the focus to other (perhaps simultaneous) forms of creative, linguistic, and/or performance expression, conducive to consciousness raising, group building, and solidarity maintenance, would also be worthwhile.[24]

Diffusion and the Role of Media

One of our central foci is how identity, opportunity, and oppositional cultural dynamics were manifested despite the geographically dispersed nature of mill towns. Such a focus is consistent with those interested in the diffusion of collective action.[25] Such "spillover" spatially requires some form of network structure through which information travels and is shared. Assuming that nonparticipants have the same structural relation to the network as do social movement participants, nonparticipants become potential adopters.[26]

Although information networks may take the form of family, friendship, or transportation ties, media may be particularly important for information flow across geographically dispersed populations.[27] Myers (2000) characterizes this potential influence not as a series of lines connecting individuals, but rather as a concentric area around the network origin defined by the range of the medium's distribution. In our view, this is an important theoretical extension of the previously noted social movement perspectives, as it offers a potential mechanism through which group consciousness and perceptions of opportunity may be altered across place. Chapter 2 focuses on the founding of radio stations within the South, the timing of these foundings relative to the strikes that occurred, and their geographic proximity to, and influence on, mill workers.

It is not enough, however, to assert that media is influential without specifying, a priori, the structural and instrumental ways in which it may shape collective action across an otherwise dispersed population. Media, and radio specifically in our case, can be directly influential when it shapes prospective movement participants' perceptions of political opportunity and sense of efficacy. It is here—in drawing a distinction between political opportunity at a structural level and perceived political opportunity among potential insurgents, and specifying the mechanism(s) through which perceived opportunity may be altered—that political opportunity theory has been limited.[28] By disseminating information on a geographically wide scale, media can be important for molding the political perceptions of a dispersed population. As we suggest in chapter 3, this applies quite straightforwardly to the case of radio and its establishment in the U.S. South. For the first time in U.S. history, a president spoke over this medium to southern workers in the format of "fireside chats," during which national political commitment to the plight of workers and workers' right to collectively organize was communicated despite more local elite repression.[29]

We also believe that on the structural end, the introduction of new media may provide opportunities not directly associated with collective action, but that has the latent effect of transfiguring the leverage and/or autonomy of subgroups. This appears to be true in the case of radio station foundings in the South, which had the unintended consequence of creating a relatively autonomous community of musicians, many of whom were ex-mill workers, that traveled from mill town to mill town, and radio station to radio station. This group, we suggest in chapter 4, represented an important network of information flow between towns in and of itself. Indeed, the mill-specific music that was disseminated, described in more detail in chapter 5, provided some common base of collective experience and solidarity.

Historically, one of the most obvious means through which group identity has been manifested and shared is through language generally, and music specifically. Language and vocabularies of motive, of which music lyrics are no exception, are important facts in social action that are not reducible to individual social psychology. Rather, verbalization, be it through speech or song, is always conversational and dynamic, often political, and potentially consciousness altering.[30] As such, "the language of situations as given must be considered a valuable portion of the data to be interpreted and related to their conditions."[31] We take this suggestion to heart by paying serious attention to the music itself, its use by mill workers in their daily lives and during protests, and the ways in which specific lyrics fostered the three dimensions of social movement culture, outlined earlier.

Although consistent with classical theoretical interest in culture and more recent efforts to develop social movement theory's emphasis on cultural processes,[32] it is surprising that so few analyses systematically consider music as a component of the collective action repertoire and a form of discourse through which collective identity is fostered and movement solidarity is achieved. One exception is Denisoff's (1972) study of American left-wing music, in which he distinguishes between songs that are rhetorical, highlighting discontent, and those that are aimed at recruitment and solidarity maintenance during active, collective protest.[33] Eyerman and Jamison (1998), in their overview of music and social movements, concur and suggest that the articulation of identity through music is central to movement formation. Indeed, music not only adds an authentic air to the plea for social action owing to its emotional appeal, but it builds and reinforces identity and group commitment through ritual and the act of singing collectively.[34] In the southern case, the folk tradition of storytelling through music has had a long and important history.[35] Thus, it is plausible to expect that music, and its dissemination via radio and ex-mill-worker musicians, may have been an influential part of the social movement repertoire for southern textile workers. We make this case in chapter 6, which focuses on the 1929 strikes in Marion and Gastonia, North Carolina, and in chapter 7, which highlights the role of music in the massive general strike of 1934.

Workplace Grievances, Resources, and Unions in the Southern Case

While attention to contemporary social movement theory is essential to the questions we are asking, equally important is recognition that collective action by workers is fundamentally driven by concrete grievances, resources at workers' disposal, and the historical context within which their beliefs and behaviors are embedded. Indeed, attention to such factors can help explain why collective resistance in the form of strike action emerges in some locals, at certain moments, but not others.

It is with this concern in mind that we draw, both implicitly and explicitly, from more traditional social movement research—research that assumes that resources are influential and a sense of relative deprivation is necessary.[36] Southern mill hands, as we denote in chapter 1, certainly had clear-cut grievances pertaining to wages, work hours, health conditions, and the introduction of scientific management—grievances that ultimately drove individual participation in the insurgency that would follow. It remains uncertain, however, that such grievances, in and of themselves, could drive social movement formation without a sense of collective identity, opportunity, or resources. Our analysis builds on the focus on grievances by addressing equally important and necessary dimensions of group identity.

One important component to group identity and class consciousness, as suggested earlier, is clear delineation of group boundaries and, more specifically, workers' recognition of the forces underlying and responsible for their subordination. For workers, including those in the South, dividing lines and antagonism with management and owners would arguably be central to this process. Attention to processes of workplace social relations may also offer analytic leverage in explaining why insurgency occurred in some cases but not others. Recent work on worker dignity and resistance behaviors, such as that by Hodson (2001) and Vallas (1987), supports this point, suggesting that identity and conflict dynamics on the shop floor are equally if not more important than the organization of work, or changes in the organization of work, in determining how or if workers act on grievances.[37]

Finally, attention to resources and the historical context within which mill workers lived and worked provides some understanding of the constraints they faced and the resistance options at their disposal. Populism among southern farmers in the late 1800s and into the early 1900s, despite eventually being defeated through racist rhetoric, legislation, and action, certainly provided a moment and legacy of class awareness and action.[38] Similarly, the southern coal-mining industry had been witness to solid, interracial coalitions of workers in previous decades. Yet, there remains little evidence that mill workers' lives, identities, and eventual actions were shaped by these other working-class mobilizations.[39]

Typically, and beyond historical legacies, resources are afforded to movement actors through social movement organizations. Such organizations, for workers, usually take the form of labor unions. In the case of southern mill-worker mobilization during the late 1920s and 1930s, there was some precedent for the organization of working-class insurgency. The American Federation of Labor's United Textile Workers (UTW) mounted a campaign approximately a decade earlier, but with little success. UTW appearance again, in the late 1920s and early 1930s, along with that of the Communist-affiliated National Textile Workers Union (NTWU), might be interpreted as an organizational call to arms for workers. Upon closer inspection, however, it becomes apparent that union presence was very limited, as were the resources devoted to southern organizing. Indeed, as we show, rather than being forged by unions, workers' grievances were formulated in their lived experiences. Furthermore, their mobilization relied more on their own sense of community and indigenous cultural resources, both of which were inadvertently broadened with the advent of a new medium, radio. Limited union influence and resources, although not particularly detrimental to the formation of the southern mill workers' campaign, would nevertheless eventually play a role in their defeat.

Mill-Worker Mobilization, Historical Specificity, and Sociological Explanation

As the theoretical and historical complexity of our particular case suggests, understanding social movements and collective behavior is by no means a simple task. Rather, like most of the social world, the dynamics of inter-personal relations, loyalties to one's job or one's community, personal histories, and political leanings complicate efforts toward singular or simplistic explanation. The understanding of southern mill workers, their lives, and the strikes they engaged in, presented in this book, is no exception.

We make no claim or assertion about the actions or psychologies of all mill workers at the time, nor do we suggest that the impact of radio, music, or political perceptions can completely account for all cases. Rather, we ground our arguments and analyses in a recognition that the social world of the southern mill worker was complex and sometimes even contradictory in terms of allegiances. Such complexity underlies our background discussion in chapter 1. The migration of mountain folk and farmers to the mill, the paternalism characteristic of many mill villages, work conditions on the shop floor, social status and historical divides across community, and parenting and gender dynamics that were played out in family and work life make the story of the southern mill worker anything but simple. Acknowledging such complexity in social and work life helps us account for periodic loyalty to the mill in the face of oppression, divides in community over union and strike support, the central role of women in the strikes despite tensions with traditional southern notions of gender and parenting, and potential opposition to unions on the one hand but understanding the need for collective action on the other.

Historical detail and recognition of disjunctures and sometimes contradictory processes do not necessarily undermine effort toward systematic and somewhat generalizable sociological explanation. Rather, it grounds expectations and general theoretical propositions within a given historical context, and within the nuances and very real complexities of social life. Although this analytic strategy does reduce the level of determinacy in predicting and/or explaining human behavior, it is appropriate, if not essential, in our view. Actors exist within a structural, historical, and cultural milieu. Their psychologies and behaviors are shaped by these crosscutting social forces. When we acknowledge these facts in our theoretical and analytical models, we not only better capture the dynamic and sometimes fluid character of social life, but we explicitly bring human agency into accounts of social life and mobilization—accounts that are often overly determined.

The historical specificity we provide in this book also helps move beyond explanations that attribute to or assume a general quiescent or hyperconservative stance on the part of working-class people, and southern workers in particular.[40] That nearly a half-million of these workers mobilized during the 1920s and 1930s straightforwardly challenges such a claim. The detail and context we provide regarding the work and family lives of southern mill workers, the daily pressures that they faced, and the structural obstacles to mobilization further highlight anything but quiescence or conservatism. Rather, grappling with day-to-day pressures, worrying about family security, and realizing and experiencing coercive paternalistic pressures in the face of trying to maintain dignity fostered tension and contradictory feelings—feelings that kept some from taking part in the strikes of 1929 through 1934. Indeed, the social, cultural, and structural situation of these mill workers, especially when combined with a historical legacy of mobilization defeat and its impact on divided and torn communities, helps us understand the misgivings and fears that U.S. workers generally, and southern mill workers in particular, carry with them even into the contemporary era.

We thus offer a view that acknowledges variability and agency within the context of serious and very real constraint. We can, nevertheless, draw several important and more general sociological lessons out of this particular case—lessons pertaining to creation, unfolding, and diffusion of social movement culture and its importance to any form or case of mobilization.[41] Our discussion of radio's emergence and importance is especially central in this regard, for the lesson is not about radio per se but rather the potential impact of new media and communication technologies on community and cross-community cohesion. Furthermore, the importance of social movement culture in promoting solidarity, providing an alternative interpretational frame, and forging collective, political efficacy among aggrieved groups cannot be underestimated and can be extended to most, if not all, forms of mobilization.

1

The World of the Southern Cotton Mill

It emerged by the time I'm old enough to really remember it, into a sort of nice thing, in the sense that, in the village itself, you had recreation, you had these meetings of women, sewing societies, library societies, visiting nurses. And everytime somebody would start agitating for unions, say, the first thing the mill management would say is, "See what we're doing for you? Can your union do anymore?" and "If y'all keep persisting, we'll stop this . . ." It kept labor divided, which made union organization more difficult. It also slowed the constant wandering around of labor. And, so, there are mixed motives in this, all the way.

—Albert Sanders

Southern textile manufacturing was rapidly expanding into the 1900s, and offered southern workers their first tastes of industrialization. Indeed, by 1921, southern cotton-producing states accounted for 54 percent of the nation's total yardage of woven cotton goods. This yield increased to 67 percent by 1927, partially the result of the relocation of textile manufacturing operations from the North to the South. The reasons for the regional shift were plenty. Cheap labor was abundant and union activity was virtually nonexistent, the main foci of southern chambers of commerce when attempting to entice northern mill owners. Indeed, wages in southern mills were approximately one-third of those in the North, even after controlling for the cost of living. In addition, southern mill workers worked longer hours.[1]

As a consequence of the swell in available mill work throughout the region, and in North and South Carolina in particular, mill owners increased efforts to recruit small farmers, tenant farmers, and mountain populations for their labor.[2] Some of this recruitment was done via word of mouth. Other mills sent recruitment agents into the field and into the mountains.

> And we went in from the farm. And a lot of people there that hadn't made anything in those three years, country people, good, solid country people went into the mill. They had men that had been in there since about 1914 or '15; they went back in the mountains and got trainloads of people and brought them in there to these new mills.[3]

The principal reason for most migration to mill work was economic. Individuals with deep ties to the mountains, or family history in agriculture, in fact, had an extraordinarily difficult time making the move to what some described as an "urban plantation." Moving to the mill was, for many, a last resort, if not a personal defeat.

> We had to swallow our pride when we lost three crops; we moved in. And soon, everyone in our particular neighborhood there eventually ended up . . . It was a failure in a way.[4]

For those engaged in farming, the pressure to enter the mills was dramatically heightened during the 1920s with the boll weevil destruction of crops.

> My daddy always said that he wouldn't leave the farm, and he particularly didn't want to go to the cotton mill. That wasn't his dream. It was quite different from being your own boss and you—having a boss over you. And he never had that, you see . . . And in 1926, the boll weevils came along. I don't know how long they'd been around, but that's the year that they got my daddy's crop. When my daddy left the country, the only choice he had was to go to a cotton mill, and it broke his heart.[5]

As difficult as the transition to mill work may have been, it did offer some base of financial support for families, and especially for widows with small children. They could find work for themselves in the mill spinning rooms and draw extra income, if the situation demanded, by having their children work.

> And when he [daddy] died, of course, his will with these eight girls and baby boy, was sort of in desperate straits. And so it was she [mama] who decided to pick up and come down to Union County. And they were opening a Union Mill down there. And so she brought the girls down, and put 'em to work in the mill.[6]

Figure 1. Widowed mother and children, who moved from the farm to a mill. The mother, Mrs. A. J. Young, and the five eldest children shown are employed by the Tifton Cotton Mill in Tifton, Georgia. Photograph by Lewis S. Hine. Courtesy of National Archives (photo no. nwdns-102-1h-487).

Longing for the farm and mountain remained a strong emotion, however. This was evident in the efforts of mill folk to keep traditions intact. The preservation of music, variously referred to as "hillbilly," "mountain," or "porch" by mill workers, was especially important in this regard. Although many tunes (e.g., "Turkey in the Straw," "Sally Goodin") were drawn directly from Scotch-Irish mountain and Piedmont culture, newer songs set to established melodies emerged that spoke directly to the migration occurring and the sense of loss that accompanied it. One of the more popular was "Serves Them Fine," whose lyrics provided both the historical backdrop and a clear indication that something was lost along the way.[7] Take, for instance, the following verses:

> Now people in the year 19 and 20,
> The mills run good and everybody had plenty.
> Lots of people with a good free will,
> Sold their farms and moved to the mill.
> We'll have lots of money they said,
> But everyone got hell instead.

It was fun in the mountains a-rolling logs,
But now when the whistle blows we run like dogs.
(CHORUS)
It suits us people and it serves them fine
For thinking that a mill was a darn gold mine.

Now in the year 19 and 25
The mills all stood but we're still alive.
People kept a-coming when the weather was fine
Just like they were going to a big gold mine.
As time passed on, their money did too
Everyone began to feeling kind of blue.
If we had any sense up in our dome
We'd still be living in our mountain home.

Despite misgivings about resettlement, the mill village provided significant economic stability relative to agriculture and sharecropping work. Furthermore, mill owners, in attempting to stabilize their labor forces, provided important services to mill employees and their families. These included housing, medical care, religious services, education, and recreational activities. The emerging "paternalism" helped forge tightly woven communities with loyalty to the mill. On the other hand, it came to be seen and perceived by many as a form of labor control, particularly when workers got out of line or began to contemplate collectively organizing. Consequently, the loyalty that paternalism forged was eroded periodically by day-to-day experiences on the floor of the mill, parenting and work tensions, most notably for women, and the general conditions and poverty in which most workers found themselves.

The Mill Village and Paternalism

The contradictory character of the mill village, and the paternalism that undergirded it, lay in the fact that individuals and families from very similar backgrounds lived in relatively concentrated areas of mill-sponsored housing. Workers were also provided an array of leisure-time activities, and had at their disposal mill-owned stores, schools, and churches. In many respects, what was offered was a welcome relief in the face of a ten- to twelve-hour workday, and compared to living conditions one often found in the more agricultural locales and mountain communities from which many of these workers came.

Historians and social scientists concur that, despite the control functions the mill village structure provided for owners, many workers benefited from the work situation in which they were now engaged and the infrastructure the village provided. The mill village was, in its very essence, a functioning city unto itself with many amenities previously not available in the mountains or on farms. And many mill owners allowed some preservation of past practices by allowing workers to make use of small plots of land to grow vegetables or keep a cow to partially supplement their pay and nutrition.[8] Such action allowed some consistency with the past, but in an increasingly modernized context.

> We'd moved to the mill village. We had electric lights and running water! And I thought that was heaven on earth! That was the happiest I ever was when I didn't have to go draw a bucket of water out of the well, and we could just turn on that faucet, and I just thought that we were rich! I just knew we were rich! It took me a long time to think it that we wasn't as half as well-off as I thought we were.[9]

Beyond the lowest rung of jobs in the furnace room of the mill, or as floor scrubbers, African Americans did not live in mill villages and were, by and large, not employed by mills during the 1920s and 1930s. Rather, in the cases of some mill communities, African Americans lived on the outskirts where they might find employment as house maids and child-care providers for supervisors or those few mill workers who could afford it.[10] The resulting racial homogeneity within the mill village, and the village's social and physical separation from African-American enclaves as well as from more privileged white parts of towns, further reinforced community cohesion and positive recollections.

> Everybody seemed to get along and everybody seemed like they enjoyed working with one another. Just like I said, everybody up there in the room I worked in felt like just one family. We just laugh and joke. We'd say anything. We didn't think nothing about what we said to one another, because nobody paid no mind. We'd all work together and tried to pull together.[11]

Woody Wood, son of a mill supervisor, similarly recalls the tightly woven nature of the mill community, despite the long work hours that mill work required:

> My father hired 'em, and they worked from six o'clock in the morning till six in the afternoon. They had a place to live and, and it was just a better life than they was having on the farm. And wonderful people! It was just one big family in the mill village. But a . . . whoever was in charge had to be in charge.

Community centers and recreational activities such as sewing societies and baseball teams, sponsored by the mill, reinforced workers' sense of community, helped stabilize movement of laborers during the 1920s and 1930s, and fostered loyalties and attachments even further.

> But the whole spirit of community house, a community center, a school interest, a YMCA all working towards the uplift of a mountain group of people to give them pride and self-confidence in there. It all worked into a beautiful job all the way through. And that sort of stuff extended all the way through, from Virginia on down to Alabama, the West Point group down at Langdale and all of that, different groups in there.[12]

One might even say that workers at certain mills developed unique identities— identities that, in their minds, set them apart from those working and living in neighboring mill villages. Mill-sponsored baseball teams, which played during the summer and fall, reinforced such feelings through competition.

> So, if you could get a village where it developed its own personality, it developed its own loyalties—the people at Dunean used to hate the people at Judson, 'cause the people at Dunean thought the people at Judson didn't play fair baseball. You know. I mean, this sort of thing developed.[13]

The control of housing, education, religion, and leisure-time mill village activities, however, ultimately resided with mill owners and supervisors, something that many workers were made keenly aware of when violations of rules, formal or informal, occurred. Company paternalistic policies, in fact, did little to offset the low wages workers were receiving and, for many, came to be seen as an important mechanism of labor control and coercion. Exorbitant interest rates were charged at the mill store, ministers and doctors were on the company payroll, and workers who were not performing to the company standard or who got out of line ran the risk of losing their homes.[14]

It was this dual character of mill village paternalism—on the one hand fostering community and cohesion, and on the other providing a coercive apparatus for mill owners—that set in motion some of the complex disjunctures that would occur within and between mill communities by the late 1920s. Even prior to widespread labor unrest, many workers witnessed, firsthand, the friendly face of paternalism turn sour when mill policy or demands were not met, even if it was a minister that bore the brunt of the owner's sanctions.

> There was a Preacher Anderson that was preaching here at Poe Baptist, and some of the officials of the company didn't like some of the things he

preached. And so they ordered him out of the church and he didn't go too freely, so the last summer he preached the church was locked up by the company. He couldn't get in to preach to the congregation. And he stood on his porch—the house was furnished by the company—and preached to the congreagtion standing out in the yard. He didn't preach anymore; they had to get a new preacher then.[15]

The role of mill-sponsored church minister was not taken lightly by owners. Indeed, they often saw church attendance and religious guidance as a means by which to control delinquency among "mountain folk" and thus stabilize, if not control, life within the community of workers.

Management wanted the workers to be in churches because they felt the churches domesticated the workers and that, um, that they would keep them from getting too uppity, and so that's why there seemed to be a hand-in-glove relationship between the management and, and many of the churches.[16]

It was not, however, only control of religion that impinged upon workers' lives. Mill-owner power was, in certain instances, expressed via ownership of the company store and housing, the supplying of coal and wood for the heating of mill housing, control of the local school, and sponsorship of women's sewing clubs, baseball teams, and any activity that was planned through mill recreation centers. The company store and the credit it offered proved to be especially problematic. Much like sharecropping at the time, the credit extended often functioned to keep workers in debt. Sue Hill, an employee of the Chiquola Mill, noted the cycle of debt that workers had to grapple with:

Superintendent had control of the mill stores, and this is where people had to go and buy their things, their groceries, their clothes. Um, they would be so heavily in debt, um, they would owe their, their whole paycheck to him from week to week. Everything fell back to the mill, the lifeline of everything that those people lived went back to the Chiquola Mill.

Such control, sometimes reinforced via the evictions of families from company-owned homes, by the cancellation of a baseball team's season, and through informal monitoring of what children and adults in the village were doing during their leisure time, was clearly the downside of having the amenities that the mill village afforded. Many workers, in fact, came to see such conveniences not as charity on the part of management and owners, but rather as something that they earned in their work lives. According to a sociologist studying Gaston County, North Carolina, textile operatives in the late 1920s:

> As a rule the mill help does not greatly value or appreciate in either sense of the word the efforts for their entertainment or advancement. First, they do not respond with any feelings of gratitude because they argue that all the money being spent on them is due them anyway as wages and some of them would rather have it in their [pay] envelopes. Most of them feel that they earn it as truly as their cash wages.[17]

Critical assessment of paternalistic policy was no doubt occurring on a regular basis for many mill workers. Such skepticism was eventually brought to the forefront of mill-worker consciousness in 1930, when RCA Victor released a song titled "Cotton Mill Colic" and "Rich Man/Poor Man"—songs penned by Dave McCarn, a textile operative working in Gastonia, North Carolina. The songs themselves speak to the control functions of paternalism and the harsh plight and situation within which most workers in the South found themselves.

Workers sang these and other mill-related songs on the job, despite efforts by some mill owners and deputies to prohibit such behavior.[18] Grievance sharing through song was a practice rooted in mountain folk music, and one that was carried into and through mill towns of the South by everyday workers and early, well-known traveling musicians such as Charlie Poole. Despite efforts by southern elites to steer workers away from traditional or oppositional music by providing music that was more "culturally appropriate,"[19] workers continued to share grievances through song, a fact that became increasingly apparent, and influential, during the 1929 and 1934 strikes.

Despite animosity toward mill-owner policies, and its reflection and expression in song, the paternalistic structure of most mill villages in the 1920s and 1930s continued to generate inconsistencies in mill-worker feelings. On the one hand, many felt that the costs associated with mill-owner control were outweighed by the stability, structure, and amenities that the mill village provided. This was particularly true in situations where the mill was locally owned, where the owner's presence in the mill village was commonplace, and where the owner and supervisors where entrenched in both the local history and the community. Pressing family issues, the employment and well-being of children, and conditions and changes in the structure of mill work nevertheless would present increasingly serious challenges to even the most cohesive and effective paternalistic strategies.

Men, Women, and Babies in the Mill

Mill employment in the South during the 1920s and 1930s was a family affair. Indeed, recruiters often sought families, rather than just men. Priority in the allocation of mill housing often went to those families with multiple members willing to take on employment as weavers, spinners, fixers, doffers, and sweepers. This desire for families was driven, in part, by the sheer need for workers amid heightened mill competition and the desire for a stable labor force. Recruiting families was also consistent with the gendered division of labor of mill work at the time.

The gender-specific nature of mill work, which was most clearly manifested in the bigger mills in places such as Burlington, Charlotte, and Gastonia, North Carolina, along with the small differential in pay between men and women, were not viewed very critically by workers themselves. Rather, such divisions were relatively consistent with workers' traditional notions of appropriate gender roles. Women and girls were largely relegated to spinning and cloth room jobs that required finer motor skills, while men typically occupied mechanically oriented positions, such as fixers, and those requiring more strength.

> They just had women's jobs and men's jobs. The men's jobs were for a heavier or stronger person and all. That's the way it was divided up. The spinning room downstairs was mostly women. They had boy doffers and some help like that, and the winding. Of course, they had a boy bring us bobbins and put them in our trough, we called it, for us to wind, and like that.[20]

Along with more physical jobs were supervisory positions, which, based on available evidence, were entirely reserved for men. Again, however, these divisions of labor were rarely challenged—a fact that is consistent with the hopes of many workers to maintain and carry out customary gender relations at home.

Interview accounts suggest that mill men tended to prefer that their wives not work, if at all economically possible, especially when there were children at home. Mill women, despite incredibly high levels of pride in the quality of their work and enjoyment of the comradery that often occurred with peers on the shop floor, often discussed the difficulty of mill work and expressed hopes of escaping the mill. Such hopes were shared in the song "Factory Girl," which had its origins within the southern textile mills well before 1920. It clearly denotes a traditional means of escape, namely, marriage. The following two verses provide a case in point.

> Yonder stands that spinning room boss
> He looks so short and stout,
> I'm going to marry a country boy
> Before this year goes out.
> (CHORUS)
> Pity me all day, pity me I pray,
> Pity me my darling, and take me far away.
>
> I'll bid you factory girls farewell
> Come see me if you can,
> I'm gonna quit this factory work
> And marry me a fine young man.

Gender divisions of labor within southern mills were thus not in themselves at the core of the protests that eventually emerged. Rather, to the extent that grievances were manifested, they revolved around treatment on the shop floor, poor work conditions, and the *inability* to follow traditional gender role expectations. Indeed, for men, low pay necessitated that their wives, and sometimes children, worked. Mill women, in contrast, struggled to be good mothers in the face of sixty-five-hour workweeks prior to 1933, and then forty to fifty hours a week afterward. Moreover, there is some evidence that women and girls may have faced sexual harassment on their jobs. Although few were willing to discuss what or how such harassment happened, it clearly occurred.

> I remember one night, the Parley Spinning Room, was a huge spinning room—in fact it had two spinning rooms, and the spool room was in the middle, and for some reason or another we had two types of yarn in the spinning and he didn't need it, and he shut down and cut out the lights. And—right there in the mill—the bosses took girls back there during that time; I know what went on.[21]

Such occurrences undoubtedly angered mill workers. Strong emotions on the matter are expressed by one male worker:

> It, it was pretty rough on some of them girls that went in there, ya know. It was a shame they [the workers] didn't take 'em [the supervisors] out and shoot 'em; that's exactly what they ought to have done to 'em, take 'em out and shoot 'em! The way I looked at it . . . But things like that happen in places like this.[22]

Perhaps more pressing than issues of harassment, however, were those pertaining to the care of young children—a burden most obviously carried by mill mothers.[23] Given twelve-hour shifts prior to 1933, it was difficult for many women to provide what they saw as adequate oversight and care of their little ones. If families could afford it, following birth, the woman would stay with her newborn for a month or two before returning to work. Others returned immediately, juggling the baby and work. Because labor was in demand early on, mill supervisors often allowed some flexibility in this regard.

> We had a neighbor, her name was Miss Lamm, and she had a nursing baby, and she worked. She'd take that baby in her roping boxes and she'd take a quilt and she'd lay him in that roping box and she'd work, 'cause they didn't have any help. Now that's how bad they were for help. And they'd let her bring her baby down and keep it in the mill all day long.[24]

More often the case, mill mothers would cover each other's jobs while one ran home to nurse or check on her children, or older siblings would watch the little ones until the mother's shift was over. Some women were able to work the night shift, thus leaving their children alone, sleeping through the night. Those fortunate enough were able to employ African-American women, from the outskirts of the village, to care for their young ones.[25] This was more true in more metropolitan, central Piedmont locales where there was a sizable black population. The least fortunate situations were those in which a widowed or single mill mother could not afford help, and had to choose between work and the care of her children.

> I was working nights and nobody to do for them . . . I asked the super to put me on the day shift so's I could tend 'm, but he wouldn't . . . I don't know why. So I had to quit my job and then there wasn't any medicine, so they just died. I could never do anything for my children, not even keep 'em alive, it seems.[26]

One solution to pressing economic and child-care needs was to allow one's children to take on employment in the mill once they were old enough. Prior to the passage of the National Industrial Recovery Act in 1933, which we discuss shortly, children from eight and nine years old upward, and perhaps even younger, were employed in mills throughout the South. Following the passage of the act, children had to be sixteen to legally work, although many southern mills violated the law and continued to employ young children. Although children usually attended school at first, something that their parents desired, economic need prevailed in most cases. Many left school at a very young age in order to supplement the family income. Most learned to spin or spool by going on the job and watching their parents or a neighbor.

Figure 2. A young spinner, regularly employed at the Globe Cotton Mill in Augusta, Georgia. Photograph by Lewis S. Hine. Courtesy of National Archives (photo no. nwdns-102-1h-490).

Mill children who grew up during this era recollected wanting to go to work, to make money. This decision, however, sometimes came at the cost of poor treatment at the hands of mill supervisors. According to Grover Hardin, who grew up in a mill village and began working as a small child:

> You done what you was told to do, or else you didn't have a job. And that's what would make it hard on the younger people. They couldn't say "Well, I'll quit; I'll go somewheres else." Because their parents was there. They had that to look after. Besides the company's juristiction, you was under your parents'. And you was obliged to obey them, or they just wouldn't listen. They hardly couldn't afford to. It worked in their livelihood.[27]

J. E. Mainer began working in a mill in Greenville, South Carolina, at age nine, and continued doing so until he gained notoriety and then radio and recording contracts as a musician in the early 1930s.[28] In letter correspondence about the origins of his popular song "Hard Times in the Cotton Mill," he recalls especially the poor treatment of children:

> I got the idea of the song from the way people were treated in the mill. at that time I have seen Spiners in the mill. when their work were running

so bad that the spiners could not keep up with their work. and the boss man would jump on them and Cuss them out. and they would go to crying . . . The Boss man back themdays didnt care what they seaid to their help. ive seen seen the Boss man pick up little boys and hold them out the window and the mill were 4 storys High. and they would say to the little fellers. Don't you bleave i will drop you out this window. and they would have the little fellers crying.[29]

The treatment and future of children obviously complicated the situation of mill mothers and fathers, and served as a pressing issue for mill workers throughout the region. Given the relative poverty of most mill families, and the death of children from malnutrition-related sicknesses such as pellagra, the need for extra income was paramount. At the same time, however, there existed a strong desire to forge a better future for one's children and to provide for one's family as a father or mother should, both economically and in terms of oversight and caregiving. Mill workers, both men and women, consequently attempted to abide by traditional gender expectations even in the face of daunting constraints. One mill mother recalls this tension in describing the dreams she had as a young girl.

Figure 3. Sweeper and doffer boys with supervisor at the Lancaster Cotton Mill, Lancaster, South Carolina. Photograph by Lewis S. Hine. Courtesy of National Archives (photo no. nwdns-102-1h-347).

I was going to marry somebody that was rich that I wouldn't have to work, I could have a nice home, and beautiful clothes. Things that most girls dream about. Then after I married, I still had daydreams, and then after I had my children, I still had daydreams. I dreamed about wanting a better life for them than we had.[30]

Tension in work and parenting responsibilities, as we show later, became embedded within grievance frames—especially those grievance frames forged and shared in music prior to and then during the strikes of 1929 and 1934, in songs such as "Mill Mother's Lament," "Factory Girl," and "Hard Times in the Cotton Mill." This is not to suggest, however, that difficulties fulfilling traditional roles of breadwinner or caretaker, or the treatment of children on the mill floor, were the only meaningful grievances workers had. Indeed, the early 1930s witnessed a fundamental shift in the way mill work was structured. Scientific management techniques and the "stretch-out" were introduced in the mid-1920s, and intensified shortly after the passage of the NIRA. As a result, workers found themselves pressed to work harder and faster. The heightened pace of work and the general work conditions in which many found themselves became crucial for the insurgency that unfolded by providing mill workers throughout the region with a common rallying cry, communicated across mill villages and eventually shared with a U.S. president.

Mill Work

Prior to 1933, most adult mill workers worked twelve-hour days, and five hours on Saturdays. Pay was generally low, between twenty and twenty-five cents an hour, and physical conditions in the mill were often difficult, if not outright dangerous. Part of the danger lay in the ever-faster machinery that was brought in, not to mention the inhalation of cotton fibers. Although most at the time were unaware of the long-term consequences of breathing cotton dust, many experienced the beginnings of what would be eventually called brown lung disease.

Didn't know what it was then. Didn't know the word of emphysema or byssinosis, or stuff like that. Never heard those words mentioned. So, I just had the asthma to kind of base my condition on, and it wasn't it at all. Nothing I could take for asthma would do this breathing any good. I could get no air in my lungs, and I slowed up. I was always active, but I got slowin' down till I just didn't have any breath. And it got to where I had to push on the job to stay up there in the mill. And when I'd get a spare minute I'd go over and lay in the windows and get all the air I could.

Well, that got to getting worse and worse. And the second hand I was working for, why, he would come by along and ask me how I was doing, and I'd tell him I was doing pretty well, and I'd say "How are you doing?" and he'd say "Smothering to death!" Maybe I'd be laying in the window and he'd come and lay in with me . . . They had to carry him out a few times, and he didn't last too long after he did come out.[31]

Heat and noise, combined with already inadequate nutrition, also took its toll on many mill workers, both physically and psychologically. According to Vesta Finley:

We used to have some real pale-looking people that worked in that mill. It was hard on them, but I guess it was just the mercy of the Lord that they was able to work. They had to work! But there was a lot of sick people.

Although not extraordinarily common, injuries on the job were by no means rare occurrences. Clothing and hair getting caught in machinery was one such scenario. More common was getting hit or caught by a piece of moving machinery. Such were the cases described by one mill worker.

They had these little rods there that they'd hook on to pull the stockings out. He dropped one down in the machine, and he reached down to pick it up. And there was a big half-moon cam come around, and it only cleared the rod by about that much, and it caught him on the arm here. It come around and caught his arm down in there and just laid it open down there. That muscle all down there was just laid open . . . Things like that. Mash your hand, finger. The worst thing, though, is those hooks. You get them stuck in your hand and you can't get them out.[32]

Despite general problems with cotton dust in certain rooms of most mills, physical injury, and discomfort pertaining to heat, smell, and noise, there was otherwise relatively substantial variation in employer practices when it came to workers resting on the job and taking breaks for food. Some mills allowed workers to take short meal breaks, provided a room to smoke in, or permitted certain workers to periodically sit down while on the job. Others, however, typically required workers to stand for the entire shift and eat, if at all, while working.

Many of these problems understandably led to worker unrest by 1929 and then again, on a larger scale, in 1934. Other factors, however, were also involved. Between these periods, Franklin D. Roosevelt was elected to office and signed the National Industrial Recovery Act in an effort to improve working conditions and quell the insurgency that began to percolate in 1929.

Mill owners responded by intensifying scientific management techniques and introducing what would eventually be called the "stretch-out," a system whereby operatives were forced to work ever-increasing numbers of machines.

Some workers recall with clarity the appearance of "efficiency experts," which began the stretch-out process.

> These little old efficiency experts from North Carolina State College, man, they got to make a show, you know. And they give you about twice as much as you can do, you know. Like this other man give you forty looms, why, he'll say, I'll give you forty-four. That'll make it look good for me, you know. But they ain't thinking about what they're doing to you. You've already got more than you can do. Then they give you more. Well, that looks good to them . . . He's got them running more looms. He's more efficient than this other fellow was. It looks good on him, and it's just killing them other people.[33]

Others observed the physical toll the stretch-out had on mill hands, and began to make explicit their contempt, anger, and moral outrage at what was occurring within the mill.

> Men and women are being killed inch by inch with this terrible system. During the last few yrs. men have been carried away from their work dead or unconscious. I ask you to read of the cruelty of Pharoah to the Israelites to get a comparison. Although the Israelites worked in fresh air while the mill people are shut in and have to breathe the same air over and over again. The time is near at hand where there will be no old people in the mill villages because of the stretch-out system.[34]

Beyond the physical consequences of stretching out workers on the shop floor was the long-term psychological effect speeding up had—an effect that lasted beyond one's shift and even into retirement.

> You can't readjust once you set your pace like that. You don't readjust. You still stay in the same pattern. I mean, it's hard to . . . Well, I don't know. I couldn't. Well, we couldn't because Betty and I, when we go out and eat with people, we're embarrassed still at the way we eat. We're through and setting there waiting and the other people are just getting into their meal. But you just, I reckon you just get in that routine. It's hard to get out of it.[35]

It is important to note that some supervisors and managers disagreed with mill owners about stretch-out implementation and policy, given their sense of kinship with workers. Some pressed workers to follow through with the heightened workload, while others helped workers out wherever they could. As one manager told us:

> I'd run a fellow's machine every once in a while if he'd get behind, you know, and I'd say, "go take a break, I'll run your machine for a few minutes while you go on break." He [the plant manager] come to me and he'd say, "What are you doing?" And I'd say, "This guy, he got behind and I was trying to help him out." He'd say, "We could hire two or three fellows like that for what we're paying you. We don't want you to work on a regular job." It's like they say, though, if you come up through the ranks you feel for people.[36]

Managers more vocal in their opposition to the stretch-out, or who refused to follow through on changes being pushed by ownership, were fired and ran the risk of being blacklisted from mill jobs in the region.

The Mounting of Grievances across Mill Communities

The 1920s and 1930s witnessed changes in the structure and functioning of textile work in the South and the migration of farm and mountain populations to mill villages—villages owned and controlled by mill owners, but that nevertheless provided amenities to which many southern workers were unaccustomed. The paternalistic and relatively homogeneous character of southern mill villages offered a context of community and family on the one hand, but relatively controlled and patriarchal surroundings on the other. Loyalty toward the mill village among workers was forged and was no doubt reinforced by mill-sponsored recreational activities, racial homogeneity, and social distance from more privileged, white parts of towns. Yet, this loyalty was tenuous and was ultimately shaken by the use of coercion by mill owners against employees, by work conditions and injuries, by difficulties in providing for one's family and children, and by changes in the structure of mill work—changes that pushed workers to do more on their jobs, sometimes for less money, and that underscored the need for some form of collective action. According to one worker:

> Well, just oppression, wanting more work out of us. Now you see, they brought out this stretch-out system, they called it. They'd put more work on you for the same pay. More work; they didn't know when to quit. And they got to where people couldn't stand it no longer. That's when they got to hunting somebody to organize them as a union.[37]

Collective response in the form of unionization or walkouts is understandable given the circumstances and grievances described. Yet, grievances were likely not sufficient in and of themselves. As noted earlier, the paternalistic practices of most mill villages fostered solidarity and cohesion *within* particular mill communities, and identification with a particular mill or mill village. Collective organization by workers *across* mill villages, however, was necessary and eventually unfolded. But how? How was identity and a sense of commonality between those residing in distinct mill towns generated? Why were claims of injustice across mill communities now viewed as legitimate? And how did workers, who often expressed loyalties to a particular mill or mill village, justify strike action across mill villages?

In the remaining chapters, we offer answers to these questions by focusing on the advent of radio and its impact on collective identity, oppositional cultural diffusion, and perceptions of political opportunity across and between mill communities during this era. Chapter 2 delineates the timing of radio foundings in the South during the 1920s, ownership patterns, political battles over what was broadcast over the airwaves, and the general impact this had on mill workers, their sense of the world, and their leisure-time activities.

Chapter 3 specifically denotes how radio provided a conduit for mill-worker consciousness and collective, political efficacy between the more fragmented strikes of 1929 and the mass mobilization of 1934 when, in the interim, Franklin D. Roosevelt made use of it to circumvent local power bases and explicitly addressed labor issues. Its influence across mill villages, however, was more than merely political. Chapters 4 and 5 focus on the ways in which the new medium of radio provided relatively autonomous space for ex-mill workers who became musicians. These musicians provided traditional entertainment and music to those still working in the southern mill—music that forged community and identification across mill villages, and that provided both ritualized celebrations and an injustice frame that would ultimately help spur collective action. Indeed, regardless of whether the lyrical content of the music was explicitly oppositional, which it was in some cases, mill workers drew from this music and eventually incorporated it into their protest repertoire.

2

Radio in the Textile South

And I think the radio coming in along about the time I come to Burling-
ton. I remember when, as far as I know, the first radio was ever in this
part of town. This fellow up Webb Avenue worked in the mill up there,
he bought one. It had ear tricks; you'd listen to it. And you'd go up there
to his house and listen to the radio, you'd have to take your turn to hold
that to your ear so you'd hear.

—Jefferson M. Robinette

The radio, first patented by Marconi in 1897, brought information, music,
and a connection to a broader world to those residing in more remote areas
of the United States. Southern mill workers were no exception, and their
lives would be altered forever. Of course, the development of radio was a
decades-long process, but by the early 1920s it had become available to and
extremely popular among the public.[1] It would not be overstating the matter to say that this was the beginning of the radio "craze."

Between 1912 and 1935, stations sprang up virtually everywhere, to the
point where the airways were saturated.[2] Such rapid technological change,
along with the general lack of institutional blueprint for how the medium
should be run and controlled, pushed the federal government to institute
the Radio Act of 1927. This act paved the way for less freedom and more
corporate control of the airways by the mid- to late 1930s. From 1929 to
1934, however, when mill hands were engaging in significant protest, radio
was a relatively autonomous haven for local programming and a device

that disseminated information at unprecedented speed. In this chapter, we examine radio's emergence in the United States and the South, political battles over its use and station ownership patterns, and southern broadcasts specifically and what they meant for textile-mill communities.

Radio's Emergence and Initial Station Foundings: The United States and the South

Although radio had been around since the turn of the century, it had yet to be recognized by most people as more than an experimental gadget. Key to radio's recognition were historical events that were brought to the public over the airways. The sinking of the *Titanic* was one such event. The *Titanic* was equipped with a radio on its maiden voyage in 1912 in order that Morse code messages could be transmitted from ship to shore. Radio's use ultimately led to the rescue of many passengers, and subsequently afforded the general public a sense of its utility. Some, such as David Sarnoff, saw radio's potential extending beyond merely technical use. In a famous memo written to executives at American Marconi in 1916, the newly employed assistant traffic manager foresaw a radio in every American household. "I have in mind a plan of development which would make a radio a household utility in the same sense as the piano or the phonograph."[3] It was several years, however, before others shared Sarnoff's vision.

Around this time, Lee De Forest, the self-proclaimed "Father of Radio," was already promoting voice radio with key broadcasts: one from the Eiffel Tower in 1908, another by Harriet Blatch (his mother-in-law) on women's suffrage in 1910, and still another by the great tenor Enrique Caruso in 1911. These were all milestones in early voice radio. Morse code was still the standard for radio communications, although World War I changed this. During the war, voice communications became increasingly important and, under the guidance of the federal government, radio production became standardized. Key corporate actors were also enlisted in the war effort, creating designs and manufacturing facilities that would spur radio's development in the coming decade.

After the war, President Woodrow Wilson became convinced that communication technology was vital to the interests of the United States. He was instrumental in the formation of the Radio Corporation of America (RCA), which was primarily owned and controlled by General Electric (GE), American Telephone and Telegraph (AT&T), Western Electric, and Westinghouse, with token government representation on the corporate board. These corporations created fair-use agreements among themselves whereby production and sales of radios would be available for public consumption. AT&T was given charge of telephony. The other companies would be primarily involved in the business of selling radio. The reason for this move by the Wilson administration was to oust any non-American corporations from the communications industry for purposes of national security. The principal loser was British-owned American Marconi. There was such a demand for radios by the 1920s, however, that corporate domination of the industry was a long way off. Smaller manufacturers, recognizing the massive consumer demand, often changed radio designs slightly to avoid patent infringement. Radio was the hottest thing going and people all over the country clamored to buy their first set.

The earliest radio stations began as experimental projects or hobbies. Barfield (1996) credits the many "tinkerers" in their garages all over the United States for advancing the radio enough that stations could be formed. The Radio Act of 1912 essentially allowed any citizen who wished to get a license to open a radio station to do so. The first licensed radio stations broadcasting continuously during 1920–21 were primarily owned by companies involved in electronics manufacturing and sales—40 percent by the end of 1922. Colleges and universities established 125 stations by 1928. Newspapers, churches, and department stores also got into the radio game. Sixty-nine newspapers had radio stations at the end of 1922.[4] While early broadcasts tended to promote the sale of radio equipment or whatever product the station supported, educational stations transmitted everything from academic lectures to agricultural reports.

In the South, early ownership patterns mirrored the country as a whole, with heavy reliance on department stores, insurance companies, universities, amateurs, and major electronics manufacturers (e.g., General Electric, Westinghouse), who themselves had links to the newly emerging recording industry (e.g., RCA/Victor) (Garofalo 1997). Many of the early stations were in business to sell the wares of the entrepreneurs who opened them. WBT radio in Charlotte, North Carolina, provides a good example. It was owned by the local Buick dealership, hence the WBT, "Watch Buicks Travel."

Our examination of Federal Communications Commission (FCC) archival records indicates that more traditional industries in the South, such as agriculture and textiles, played no or little role in radio ownership, while colleges, music companies, battery companies, and automobile and insurance dealers did. WBT in Charlotte and WRBU in Gastonia, North Carolina, provide two cases in point. Although located centrally to textile manufacturing, mill owners had no apparent involvement or control in either. Rather, WBT was owned by C. C. Coddington, an entrepreneur and car dealer, while WRBU was owned by A. J. Kirby Music Company.[5]

The timing of radio station foundings in the South generally coincides with the period of worker unrest on which we are focusing. On February 3,

1922, the first license was granted to WGH in Montgomery, Alabama. Within one month, stations were founded in Charlotte, Memphis, Atlanta, Charleston, Richmond, and Morganton. The enthusiasm and interest in this new information and entertainment medium was intense, to say the least, as forty-three operating licenses were granted to various stations across the South by the end of that year. The number of radio stations increased rapidly through the middle of the 1920s, and planed off by about 1930.[6]

Although limited broadcast ranges (twenty to forty miles, on average) initially posed problems, this was partially remedied by the increase in foundings in the late 1920s and early 1930s. Figure 4 shows the growing number of stations during this time period. The increase between 1922 and 1930 was significant, so much so that larger southern cities such as Atlanta, Memphis, and Nashville boasted as many as five stations. Small stations served burgeoning mill towns and rural populations throughout the southern Piedmont, spreading information and leading to a heightened sense of regional if not national community.[7]

Figure 5 maps the concentration of textile-mill manufacturing relative to city-specific radio station foundings prior to 1934. If radio was central to information flow generally, and to perceptions of political opportunity and collective identity for mill workers more specifically, stations needed to have been established in an area geographically proximate to mill concentration. Figure 5 shows a clear and recognizable "radio belt" that cuts through the center of the most dense textile concentration. It is apparent, given these

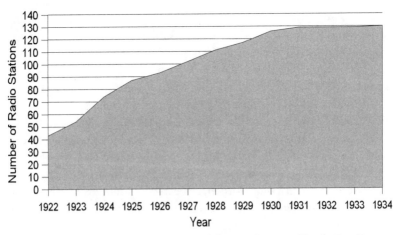

Figure 4. Number of radio stations in Alabama, Georgia, North Carolina, South Carolina, Tennessee, and Virginia, 1922–34. Source: FCC Archives.

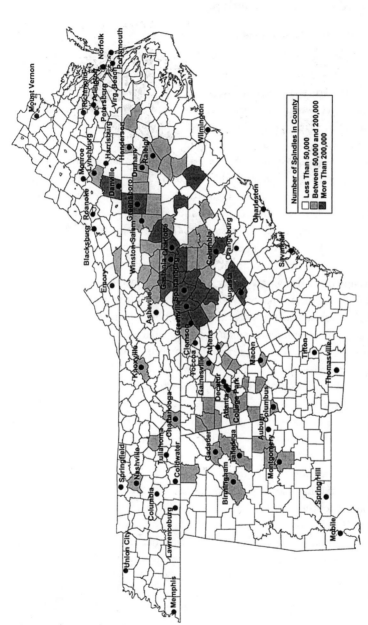

Figure 5. Concentration of textile manufacturing (shaded) and radio station foundings across Southern counties prior to 1935. Sources: Clark's Directory of Southern Textile Mills *(1929),* Davidson's Textile Blue Book, *and FCC Archives.*

patterns, that many southern mill workers during the era in question lived and worked within the concentric rings of radio transmission.

Political Battles: Range, Broadcasts, and Oversight

Two important political issues emerged during the early years of radio, with implications for southern broadcasts. The first had to do with transmission range. Most early stations were low power and, consequently did not broadcast very far. However, as the number of stations and their power increased, problems of overlap among channels became increasingly apparent.

Early stations broadcast at the common 360 meters, but as this band became more populated, interference from other channels became commonplace. This was initially remedied by stations tacitly agreeing to broadcast only a few hours a day. Government involvement was inevitable, though, as the airways became more crowded and competitive. The Radio Act of 1912 essentially established a system to license radio stations. The later Radio Act of 1927 was designed to control the number and power of radio stations.[8]

Among other things, the act established the Federal Radio Commission (FRC) as an organizational body to oversee the granting of licenses, frequencies, and power of stations. The rationale for power regulation was to reduce the chances of interference among stations sharing the same frequency.[9] After the passage of the act, fewer stations broadcast late into the night, giving choice access to stations remaining on the air. Those owned by the large corporations could afford more powerful transmitters and were also given special access to the 400-meter band, where there was less interference. These more powerful stations often boasted of a wide listening area, although reliable regional broadcasting was typically less than ideal.[10]

Limited ranges and poor reception allowed local radio stations, including those throughout the southern United States, to remain important outlets for entertainment and information.[11] Indeed, radio station transmissions in the larger southern cities were not always strong enough to reach the high-textile-concentration counties of western North Carolina and northwestern South Carolina, where worker mobilization occurred between 1929 and 1934. Homer "Pappy" Sherrill, a famous musician from this period, noted that during his first performance on radio in 1929 at WSOC in Gastonia, North Carolina, his parents in Hickory, only forty miles away, could barely hear him through the static.[12]

The second political issue surrounding radio had to do with the nature of broadcasts, and debates over public versus commercial interests. Government oversight was virtually nonexistent at the outset, and the future of the airways as a corporate-dominated media was yet to be sealed. Educational stations, in fact, were the real pioneers during the 1920s, although their influence ebbed in the mid- to late 1930s. Commercialization of the airways, in contrast, was not seen early on as being in the public interest, a fact that even RCA's David Sarnoff accepted. According to historian Robert McChesney (1999, 194):

> Between 1927 and 1934 commercial broadcasting was not considered innately "American" and "Democratic" and therefore immune to fundamental attack. Indeed, the initial public response to commercial broadcasting was decidedly negative, particularly in comparison to later attitudes.

The term "public interest" and its definition were heatedly debated by those in power. The Federal Radio Commission, later to the become the Federal Communications Commission, was established by the Radio Act of 1927 and was given the power to grant licenses and arbitrate disputes. According to McChesney, the FRC reallocations of airways in 1928 "determined the shape of AM radio for the balance of the century" (192). Larger network stations, primarily NBC and CBS affiliates, were given the lion's share of high-power stations and were allowed to broadcast at night. The powerful radio lobby, including NBC, RCA, CBS, and the National Association of Broadcasters, was formed and pushed support for commercial over nonprofit broadcasting. These networks incidently afforded members of government, including Congress, free use of airways. They also adopted commercial advertising to support their operations. When nonprofit stations objected that this was not in the "public interest," the FRC simply responded that nonprofit stations would be likely to spread "propoganda." In contrast, it was suggested that commercial broadcasting had no political agenda, was free of ideological constraints, and thus, in reality, better served the public interest.

Battles over profit versus nonprofit radio broadcasts lasted until the late 1930s and ultimately focused on use of radio as an educational tool. The Broadcast Reform Movement was spearheaded by the Payne Fund in the guise of the National Committee on Education by Radio (NCER). Formed by a coalition of educators from across the country, the NCER opposed the control of radio for purely profit motives. Key among this group was John Dewey, who feared that the democratic system itself would be in trouble if commercial interests took over the airways and controlled what people heard.

The for-profit, commercial broadcasters' main support came from the Carnegie Foundation under the guise of the National Advisory Council on Radio in Education (NACRE). It claimed that the best way to offer educational programs was through cooperation with CBS and NBC. They fought for years to control educational interests on the radio. NCER leadership proved inflexible in their dealings with political leaders and others who could have helped their cause. They tended to make untenable demands that most political leaders viewed as too idealistic. NACRE claimed to share NCER's concerns of presenting unbiased educational programming, although the networks they represented proved intransigent in practice and eventually backed out of agreements to offer prime-time, unbiased programs.

Commercial interests won the fight in the end. In the interim, however, the airways remained relatively open to diverse content and interests, including those of labor. Little federal intervention over broadcast content actually occurred until the mid- to late 1930s, when the Communications Act of 1934 created the FCC. Even then, however, regulation and oversight lagged behind the new and developing technology.[13] As a consequence, stations were relatively free to broadcast what they wanted. Most depended on the programming of NBC and CBS, while simultaneously allocating between one and three hours a day to educational programming and/or live shows that catered to the specific interests of local populations.[14] This was a "frontier" period for radio. The trend was certainly toward domination by networks, yet many stations were either not network-affiliated or had substantial programming that was local.

Southern Radio Broadcasts and Community Participation

Relative weaknesses in early radio station legislation combined with initial ownership patterns were important in determining the relative autonomy experienced by southern broadcasters. Stations tended to be driven more by profit than by political motives and thus catered to the tastes of the listeners.

In the South, radio broadcasts became truly social events, with neighbors and communities congregating to listen. For mill communities, radio's impact extended far beyond entertainment. It fostered for many a broader sense of community and extended mill workers' views and experiences beyond the confines of their mill village. According to V. T. Chastain of Pickens, South Carolina:

> At first WSM, Nashville, Tennessee, was the only station, but later we also got WFBC from Greenville. Reception was pretty good if the weather was good, but bad weather brought static. Programs consisted of country music and boxing . . . Neighbors from all around congregated at our house to see and hear the amazing radio! One man I remember in particular really enjoyed a certain musical rendition, and he told Dad, "Make 'em

play that one again, Wade." Nothing Dad could say would convince him that the musicians were in Greenville and not somewhere, somehow, inside that box![15]

Baseball and boxing were especially popular early on. Fred M. Dowis from Pelzer, North Carolina, where one of the 1929 strikes occurred, recalls:

> The first broadcast I remember came from a loudspeaker hanging on the corner of Griffin's Drug Store in downtown Pelzer. It was one of Jack Dempsey's prize fights. A very large crowd had gathered in the streets and on the sidewalks, standing shoulder to shoulder. I enjoyed an RC Cola and a Moon Pie during the fight.[16]

Political broadcasts were also popular. As early as 1920, the Harding–Cox election results were broadcast over crude early radio.[17] Bell Meban remembers listening to early political speeches:

> I grew up in Franklin Springs, a small village in Franklin County, Georgia. My family did not own a radio for many years, but I was ten years old in 1924 when our teacher took my class to a neighbor's house to listen to President Calvin Coolidge take the oath of office. I had never even heard a radio before and still remember how it excited and thrilled the whole class to hear that ceremony.[18]

Mill workers listened to the radio in a way that no other southern group had.[19] Jenette Caler recalled that "Radio was our lifeline to the world."[20] People often came together as a community to listen. On a summer's evening, people were likely to participate in celebrations on the lawn of their neighbor. Gray Troutman vividly recalls this cohesive impact:

> In the summertime, Daddy'd open up that window there and turn that horn around to the outside and the whole neighborhood would come around. Old folks would sit in chairs, right there in the yard. Those kids would lay on quilts and those babies would be laying around out there in the yard and listen to the Grand Ole Opry or some local bands.

Radio had an immediate impact on southern mill workers' lives. In an analysis of leisure-time activities in three southern mill towns during this era, Hampton (1935, 61) found that nearly 70 percent of mill workers had a radio in their homes. Notably, when asked for their favorite among forty-six leisure-time activities, listening to music on radio was consistently ranked highest by the 123 mill workers surveyed. One noted that "The radio is kept going all the time there ain't no static." While music programming was clearly most popular, others preferred listening to "preaching and talks on the government."

Radio was powerful. It brought voices directly to a person's house or to the local store. The technology amazed many who had spent their lives listening to live voices. Unexpected consequences came out of this new technological marvel. Politicians could use the radio as a tool of persuasion, a fact that benefited them immensely. For example, Herbert Hoover's popularity improved after a speech he made via radio featured him with an uncharacteristically booming voice. His voice was enhanced because of his proximity to the microphone, which made it seem lower and more authoritative, giving the public greater confidence in his political abilities.[21]

Even prior to collective mobilization of mill workers, radio broadcasts became a political forum for local and national leaders. Before the strike action in 1934, Francis Gorman, vice president of the United Textile Workers union, spoke to southern workers over the airwaves, suggesting that their grievances were legitimate and that they were supported by a national (as opposed to local) political agenda.

Franklin Delano Roosevelt was elected president in 1932 and would become a most adept political figure in taking advantage of this technological innovation. His fireside chats, beginning in 1933, were broadcast at a time when the radio had penetrated even the remotest hamlet. For the first time in the history of the United States, a president spoke directly to millions of people. These broadcasts not only allowed Roosevelt to circumvent national and more local political rivals, but it increased his popularity and put him in touch with all people, not simply the advantaged. As we show in the next chapter, working-class people, including mill workers in the South, felt as though Roosevelt was speaking directly to them and their concerns. Indeed, in his July broadcast of 1933, he directly addressed the problems of textile workers, suggesting federal support for their right to organize and the need for workplace reforms.

Although political expression may have reflected concern for the "public good" and certainly bowed to listener tastes, some stations early on tried to influence their audiences socially. Some southern elites, for instance, hoped that radio would provide a modernizing influence on the region and its populations.[22] In its early programming, WBT radio in Charlotte, North Carolina, stressed classical music, reflecting an obsession with European culture and a focus on modernization in the guise of industrialization. Old-time minstrel shows that were very popular in the late 1800s, in contrast, were characterized as vulgar. Elite conceptions of modern, industrialized culture often included a docile and compliant workforce, one that reflected the air of classical, sober art, rather than the rowdy and supposedly crude music of southern "hillbillies."

Radio station owners soon realized that their interest lay in getting and keeping listeners, rather than necessarily changing audience musical tastes. In the textile-manufacturing South, the industrial working class was targeted by programmers because this group was much more likely than farmers to have access to radios. Astute programmers provided musical entertainment aimed directly at the concerns and cultural preferences of their specific broadcast audiences. The rural roots of the southern mill population were key to their musical tastes, and several local programmers were, or became, keenly aware of this and brought various popular musical styles to the airwaves. Throughout the South, "depending on the location, one could usually begin the day or spend the noon hour listening to a program of hillbilly, Cajun, blues, or gospel music."[23]

The music of musicians from the mill villages was in some ways shaped by the more refined tastes heard on early radio and by the listening audiences, particularly audiences that did not want rowdy music. The music of many pre-radio musicians, such as Charlie Poole and his North Carolina Ramblers, was often wild and woolly, dealing with episodes of drunkenness or other unsavory behavior. The music of radio musicians, in contrast, tended to be more amicable, given developed and somewhat complex vocal harmonies. Popularity of music, as measured in consumption, became key. Women and children were primary listeners and women wrote in letters to request their favorite songs. The female audience became a key ingredient in helping define which songs were popular during the period. Moreover, musicians' personal appearances were often arranged by church groups or women's clubs.[24]

"Whitey" Grant of the Briarhoppers recalls that he and his partner Hogan often played for churches and noted that hymns were very popular among his audiences.[25] Religious music was important for giving people hope and helping to create solidarity among those who would later participate in a strike. Performers often conformed to middle-class standards, but underneath were grievances brought on by a hard life. Radio musicians who eventually played at strike events for dancing picketers were the same ones who played for calmer affairs, such as live dances, and who played on radio before the strikes occurred.

Songwriters and musicians were thus alternatively religious and practical, realizing that sometimes religion did not provide workers with needed relief from their problems. Textile worker and musician Dorsey Dixon, for instance, cautioned against drinking in what was to become the famous "Wreck on the Highway," but also admitted that mill work could lead a man to drink in the song "Weave Room Blues."[26] It was these contradictions that existed in the southern mill culture and the variable ability to solve them that set the stage for shared grievances not always addressed by mill owners.

The southern Piedmont boasted the highest number of textile mills and, thus, the largest number of mill workers.[27] Indeed, many local musicians, who themselves had their roots in the Appalachian South or textile mills, would become extremely popular with the advent of radio given that their music often spoke to the concerns and lived experiences of most mill workers. Particularly popular in this regard were "barn dance" broadcasts, featuring an array of music and musicians, steeped in rural traditions.

The barn dance itself, interestingly enough, originated from WLS in Chicago. Soon after, the Grand Ole Opry on WSM in Nashville became a staple for listeners from both the rural areas and southern mill communities.[28] Although barn dances out of Chicago and Nashville reached the textile mills of the southeast, the area had its own barn dance. Sponsored by Crazy Water Crystals, the WBT radio barn dance, out of Charlotte, in the heart of the textile Piedmont, was one such program that brought mill musicians together and garnered considerably popularity among mill hands. These particular musicians also toured throughout textile communities and periodically provided live, in-person entertainment at mill recreation centers, high school auditoriums, and more informally at dances in people's living rooms. Many of the musicians came from the textile mills, still worked in them, or knew someone who did. They quickly became celebrities as a result of their broadcasts, and in the process popularized songs about the mills and the hardships of the workers.

Importantly, broadcasts also offered significant leeway in what musicians played and sang.[29] Musicians were simply told how much time they were allotted and picked their own songs early on. As time went on, much of the music played was spurred on by letter-writing campaigns from listeners. Listeners found that songs like the Dixon Brothers' "Weave Room Blues" spoke to their lives and everyday concerns. Workers appreciated musicians to whom they could relate, just as they appreciated politicians, like FDR, who seemed to be on their side. The radio provided an outlet to disseminate messages, whether overt or not, that tied mill workers and their advocates together across a region and a nation.

Conclusion

The emergence and establishment of radio occurred relatively rapidly in the United States, with broadcast licenses being granted to an array of entities including universities, electronics companies, electric companies, and music corporations. The South was no exception to this pattern, with nearly 130 stations founded by 1930. Although political debates and legislation pertaining to broadcast range and broadcast content pervaded the 1920s and 1930s, this time period reflected relative autonomy for station owners—who were largely concerned with generating local followings. What resulted was an interesting blend of national and local programming in the South—and local programming relied on and tapped into preexistent musical tastes and the recruitment of local musicians, many of whom came from southern mill villages themselves.

The initial novelty of radio, in conjunction with broadcasts of music by home-grown musicians who blended traditional tunes and detailed lyrics that spoke to the work and family lives of most mill workers, fostered community celebration and ritual around its usage. The musicians themselves, the focus of chapter 4, garnered celebrity from their on-air performances and typically traveled from town to town for live appearances between radio stints. These musicians linked mill communities through travels and broadcasts, resulting in a common understanding of mill workers' plight, experiences, and grievances.

Equally important was Franklin Delano Roosevelt. He used radio more than any politician before him, and in a manner uniquely his own. Like radio musicians, Roosevelt too should be seen as a catalyst for workers experiencing an already brewing discontent. As discussed in the next chapter, Roosevelt's fireside chats were revered by listeners. He spoke to the concerns of the people and they responded. Mill hands specifically saw Roosevelt as their friend and as a man who understood them. In the process, he became "the people's president" and fundamentally altered mill workers' sense of opportunity and hope.

3

The People's President

Where we got the idea of writing to Roosevelt was we would hear this over the radio, you know, in that very, very nice voice that he had, "If you have any problems you can always refer 'em to your president." Well, we took him at his word.

—Lucille Thornburgh

Franklin Delano Roosevelt was the first president to use the radio extensively. His rise in politics and his popularity were tied to his understanding that the new medium simultaneously allowed one to circumvent more local power bases and directly reach working-class groups and individuals, many of whom felt great distance and detachment from national leaders. The case of Roosevelt, radio, and southern mill workers is important and informative in several regards. It provides insights on theoretical questions pertaining to political opportunity, and forces us to distinguish between structural opportunity on the one hand, and perceptions of opportunity on the other. Moreover, the focus on the political use of radio specifically helps address how political opportunity or perceptions of it may diffuse across geographic space.[1]

Roosevelt's impact on southern mill-worker consciousness via radio fireside chats was direct, altering perceptions of opportunity and providing some legitimacy to workers' claims of injustice at the hands of mill owners. More indirectly, Roosevelt's creation and support of the Resettlement Administration, the Federal Writers' Project, and the Federal Music Project, along with his own love of string band and southern "hillbilly" music, fostered national and radio interest in the type of music coming out of mill towns—music that was rooted in Appalachian tradition and that often dealt explicitly with working-class grievances and capacity for change. It was the joint impact of presidential support and tacit sponsorship of a solidarity-fostering culture, we suggest, that helps explain why and how southern mill workers walked off their jobs on such a massive scale in 1934 compared to the earlier and somewhat fragmented strikes of 1929.

Roosevelt and Radio

FDR's use of radio, at a time when it was flourishing as the new and best form of entertainment, helps explain his status as one of the first prominent media celebrities, let alone politicians, in the United States. His voice, carried over the airwaves, reached into the living rooms of populations that were largely alienated from national politics. This included those of the rural South, who now had a direct line into the mainstream. According to Filene (2000, 134):

> The attentiveness to the people who had been hardest hit by the depression marked a significant shift in attitude. Hoover had chosen not to focus on America's marginal populations, preferring not to spotlight people whose extreme poverty so clearly illustrated the depths of the country's economic crisis. The Roosevelt Administration, though, made the nation's migrants, sharecroppers, and mountaineers the centerpieces of official culture, emphasizing not their desperation but their character, dignity, and strength.

Not only could Roosevelt reach marginalized, potential voters through the radio, but his very use of it enabled him to circumvent the entrenched interests of big business and the Republican establishment.[2] Newspapers were largely Republican-controlled, but radio was not. In fact, much of control over the radio lay with the FCC; thus radio networks were happy to give airtime to powerful politicians. Roosevelt's radio fireside chats in particular, which began in 1933, allowed him to set a national political agenda in the presence of the public, without direct debate or contentious dialogue with potential opponents.

In the South, Roosevelt's chats were broadcast in the evening, whereas the music of local hillbilly groups typically received airtime in the morning. Regional barn dances, like WBT's Crazy Water Crystals' barn dance, were heard on Saturday night. Most of FDR's fireside chats, in contrast, were heard on Sundays.[3] It was no mistake that Roosevelt broadcast mostly on Sundays. He wanted to catch people at home, just as the barn dances did.

Figure 6. Editorial cartoon by Cy Hungerford, "New Big Stick (Wired for Radio)," depicting Roosevelt's strength and its relation to radio. Copyright 2003 Pittsburgh Post-Gazette *archives. All rights reserved. Reprinted with permission.*

FDR's speeches were short and used common language, just like the songs of the those who played on the barn dances, such as the Dixon Brothers. He even went so far as to use analogies such as baseball that were easily understandable and familiar to mill workers. Take, for instance, a portion of his May 1933 chat "Outlining the New Deal":

I know that the people of this country will understand this and will also understand the spirit in which we are undertaking this policy. I do not deny that we may make mistakes of procedure as we carry out the policy. I have no expectation of making a hit every time I come to bat. What I seek is the highest possible batting average, not only for myself but for the team. Theodore Roosevelt once said to me: "If I can be right 75 per cent of the time I shall come up to the fullest measure of my hopes . . ." To you, the people of this country, all of us, the Members of the Congress and the members of this Administration owe a profound debt of gratitude. Throughout the depression you have been patient. You have granted us wide powers, you have encouraged us with a wide-spread approval of our purposes. Every ounce of strength and every resource at our command we have devoted to the end of justifying your confidence. We are encouraged to believe that a wise and sensible beginning has been made. In the present spirit of mutual confidence and mutual encouragement we go forward . . . And in conclusion, my friends, may I express to the National Broadcasting Company and to the Columbia Broadcasting System my thanks for the facilities which they have made available to me tonight.[4]

Thus, while some were singing about the concrete problems mill workers faced, Roosevelt was telling people what should be done about these problems. Particularly important was the third of his broadcasts, titled "Purposes and Foundations of the Recovery Program," which was aired on July 24, 1933. It dealt explicitly with the need for industrial reform and better working conditions, while also recognizing workers' right to collectively organize if the situation demanded. In referring to the unfolding depression, Roosevelt suggests:

There is a clear way to reverse that process: If all employers in each competitive group agree to pay their workers the same wages—reasonable wages—and require the same hours—reasonable hours—then higher wages and shorter hours will hurt no employer. Moreover, such action is better for the employer than unemployment and low wages, because it makes more buyers for his product. That is the simple idea which is the very heart of the Industrial Recovery Act . . .

Here is an example. In the Cotton Textile Code and in other agreements already signed, child labor has been abolished. That makes me personally happier than any other one thing with which I have been connected since I came to Washington. In the textile industry—an industry which came to me spontaneously and with a splendid cooperation as soon as the recovery act was signed—child labor was an old evil. But no employer acting alone was able to wipe it out. If one employer tried it, or if one state tried it, the costs of operation rose so high that it was impossible to compete with the employers or states which had failed to act. The moment the Recovery Act was passed, this monstrous thing which neither opinion nor law could reach through years of effort went out in a flash . . .

While we are making this great common effort there should be no discord and dispute. This is no time to cavil or to question the standard set by this universal agreement. It is time for patience and understanding and cooperation. The workers of this country have rights under this law which cannot be taken from them, and nobody will be permitted to whittle them away, but, on the other hand, no aggression is now necessary to attain those rights. The whole country will be united to get them for you. The principle that applies to the employers applies to the workers as well, and I ask you workers to cooperate in the same spirit.[5]

This left workers, including those in the South who traditionally felt quite isolated from national bases of power, with the impression that they could count on "the intervention of the federal government as a lever against local elites and guarantor of workers' rights."[6] Roosevelt also urged workers to write in, and they did, in unprecedented numbers.[7]

Beyond direct communication with workers, Roosevelt pushed through legislation that, at least on paper, addressed some of their grievances. As noted in the speech just quoted, he signed in 1933 a bill intended to alleviate the plight of overworked mill hands, the National Industrial Recovery Act (NIRA). This bill seemingly gave mill workers the right to push for decent hours and working conditions through collective bargaining. Section 7a of the Textile Code, noted in this speech, called for a minimum wage, a forty-hour workweek, and the prohibition of child labor. This effort was part of the newly formed National Recovery Administration (NRA). Both Roosevelt and the head of the NRA, Hugh S. Johnson, were opposed to strikes as a means of solving disputes between workers and mill owners. Instead, they were in favor of controlling work hours and child labor in an effort to limit production, drive up profits for mill owners, and improve economic conditions for workers through a trickle down of profits.[8]

Textile workers of the South thus had every reason to think change would be occurring for the better. A president was on their side, speaking their language and about the "Forgotten Man," and he seemed committed to workers' rights and industrial reform. The fact that Roosevelt impacted mill workers' sense of political opportunity and possibility is reflected in their own recollections of hearing him and what it meant. At the same time, however, these very same workers were ill prepared for the ways in which mill owners would respond to the reforms Roosevelt intended.

Roosevelt's Impact on Southern Mill Workers, and Mill Owners' Response

Roosevelt's impact on the nation and on the consciousness of mill workers was immediate, as those in dire need were confident that the new administration would take up the task of turning things around. According to a mill-worker spokesperson at the time:

> The country was troubled. Every group in the society, from the richest, the most powerful, to the common man and the most deprived, were all uncertain as to what the future would be. There was a sense that a new administration was coming in and that would bring a new world into being.[9]

Interestingly, Roosevelt's foray into the presidency was accompanied by a theme song that promised hope and that resounded with Southern textile mill operatives, many of whom voted for him.

> Roosevelt's theme song was "Happy Days Are Here Again"; well, we took him at his word, happy days are here again. And, all the way through, when we went to the polls to vote for him, we were all singing "Happy Days Are Here Again" because Roosevelt's going in.[10]

His real impact on worker consciousness, however, came later with his radio fireside chats.

> And we had a radio. Many people did not have radios. But other people would come to sit around that one radio and listen to the chats that Franklin Roosevelt would give on the radio. And we were happy to know he came out with several supposed to be programs, and NRA was one of 'em. I could see here people talking about this man has a grip on what is needed to help our country.[11]

Roosevelt would reinforce this connection through stops and live, on-the-spot radio broadcasts, throughout southern towns on his way to Warm Springs, Georgia. Poor families, farmers, and mill workers would literally come out of the hills to get a glimpse of their president on these stops.

The impact of Roosevelt's radio transmissions on the consciousness of Southern textile workers was witnessed firsthand in 1933 by Martha Gellhorn, a reporter hired by Federal Emergency Relief Administration director Harry Hopkins to investigate social and economic conditions in the South. In the face of red-baiting during earlier strikes in 1929 in Gastonia,

Figure 7. Mountain folk and mill hands get a glimpse of Roosevelt stopping for live radio broadcast in Newfound Gap near Asheville, North Carolina. Governor Gardner is in foreground. Courtesy of Herbert L. Hyde.

Gellhorn (1934) writes to Hopkins on the conditions of Gaston County, North Carolina, specifically:

> All during this trip I have been thinking to myself about that curious phrase "red menace," and wondering where said menace hid itself. Every house I visited—mill worker or unemployed—had a picture of the President. These ranged from newspaper clippings (in destitute homes) to large colored prints, framed in gilt cardboard. The portrait holds the place of honour over the mantel; I can only compare this to the Italian peasant's Madonna. And the feeling of these people for the president is one of the most remarkable emotional phenomena I have ever met. He is at once God and their intimate friend; he knows them all by name, knows their little town and mill, their little lives and problems. And, though everything else fails, he is there, and will not let them down.

Workers also spoke directly with Gellhorn about Roosevelt, sharing their confidence that the president was on their side.

You heard him talk over the radio, ain't you? He's the only president who ever said anything about the forgotten man. We know he's going to stand by us.

He's a man of his word and he promised us; we aren't worrying as long as we got him.

The president won't let these awful conditions go on.

Roosevelt asked workers to write to him and to Hopkins concerning any labor issues they had, and they did in unprecedented numbers. Among those taking part in the write-in campaign to the president, there was notable representation among southerners.[12] Those who felt excluded previously from the political process, most notably women, felt empowered to share their grievances, discussed the need and desire to collectively organize, and, through their detailed letters, encouraged the powerful to consider the mill workers' plight.

I think management misjudged the southern workers. Th-they didn't know that they were shrewd enough to know that they had laws here and that those laws were being violated. We thought we had these elected representatives in Washington and that if we wrote to them that something would happen. We definitely did.[13]

Notably, many of these letters also appealed for, and made clear that there was a belief among southern workers that there would be, federal intervention.[14] Combined with the demise of child labor, the creation of a minimum wage, and the shortening of the workday to eight hours in 1933, this personal connection fostered a strong sense of closeness to and fondness for the president.

Oh, they loved him. Boy, he pulled them out of the ditch. They loved him to death. Well, everybody everywhere I've ever heard say anything about him—well, it wasn't only in Bynum neither. It was everywhere. Everybody was in the same ditch everywhere.[15]

Prices, sales, and employment increased to the highest level in five years by late summer, although by the fall this prosperity soured. The Depression reached its worst period in the winter of 1933–34 and mill owners, while seemingly supportive of the cooperative message in section 7a, either began to practice old strategies of oppression or, in some cases, instituted new ones. The "stretch-out," for instance, was increasingly employed to circumvent laws limiting working hours. This was the workers' term for the cumulative changes that "set them tending machines 'by the acre,' filled every pore in the working day, and robbed them of control over the pace and method of production" (Hall et al. 1987, 211). Spinners, mostly women, were hardest hit as they were often stretched from 24 to 48 looms, and then from 48 to 96, "without a commensurate increase in pay, often with no increase whatsoever, or even an actual decrease" (Yellen 1936, 299). Thus, workers found themselves working as much in the new eight-hour shift as they had in the shifts lasting two to four hours longer. By further enabling industry to curtail production when mills were producing sufficient product through "short time," the NIRA Textile Code also inadvertently led to a surplus of goods and higher rates of unemployment.[16] In short, mill owners saw the laws enacted under the NIRA as bothersome but easy to manipulate.[17]

In the face of the stretch-out and violations of labor laws, southern mill workers continued to write to Roosevelt, informing him of what was occurring and sure that he and his administration would act on their behalf.

> I am taking it into my hands to write you a letter and tell you how the mills are working against you. I have been doing mill work for 16 years. I know what a man needs to do on their job and what they ought to be paid. In place of the mills putting more men to work they are cutting out men. The mill at which I am working are stopping off part of it and sending the help out and are running part of it over time . . . Send one of your men here to investigate . . . They have speeded up the work until they make the same production now that they did in 11 hours. I am employed at the Ware Shoals Mfr. Co. . . . and asking you not to publish my name.[18]

Textile operatives throughout the South, male and female, wrote to Roosevelt. Of particular concern was the stretch-out, and relative certainty on the part of letter writers that Roosevelt and his administration were on their side, yet unaware that labor policies were being flagrantly violated.

> Dear Sir: Mr. Roosevelt, we know that you are doing everything in your power to help the poor people, but we know that you do not know what all is going on in these mills, and we thought we would let you know, for we think it is our place to do our part in helping you. We have to work so hard in this mill in Belmont, N.C., that we do not get time to stop and eat our lunch, and if we do, our work just tears to pieces and they have to get the machinery up so fast that they make as much production in seven and a half hours as they would in twelve hours, and I think something ought to be done about it.[19]

Roosevelt's rise to national celebrity and the presidency, along with his use of the new medium of radio to reach marginalized working-class populations and to circumvent more local power bases, unquestionably enabled him to bring workplace issues and injustices to the national agenda. Southern textile mill workers were listening. Their support of Roosevelt and their hope regarding his presidency and what it would mean was evidenced by their strong emotional ties to him and their efforts to communicate directly with him via letters. And, despite efforts by mill owners to ignore or work around new labor policies, mill workers remained hopeful and encouraged by a president who recognized their rights. Beyond such direct ties to Roosevelt and a growing a sense of political possibility, Roosevelt's presidency and his New Deal programs also fostered working-class cultural revitalization and appreciation, something that also had implications for the protests that mill workers would engage in.

The New Deal and Working-Class Music

The Works Projects Administration (WPA) and the Civilian Conservation Corps (CCC) were major efforts toward putting the populace back to work during the Depression. New Deal programs were also instrumental in bringing attention to and aiding in the creation of traditional forms of music. The Resettlement Administration, Federal Writers' Project, and the Federal Music Project (FMP) were all involved in actively promoting folk music. The FMP would fund musicians to take part, if they were poor enough. During its peak in 1935, sixteen thousand musicians were taking part in the program.[20]

Rhonda Levine holds that FDR addressed the need for social change and recognition of working-class interests and social reform, yet he allowed elites to maintain power.[21] This was demonstrated in the attitudes of Nikolai Sokoloff, head of the FMP, who preferred "cultured" music rather than folk music. Still, the FMP did fund folk festivals in Virginia and Kentucky. In fact, Eleanor Roosevelt attended Virginia's White Top Folk Festival in 1933. The Roosevelt administration also funded the collection of music by folklorists and, later in the decade, encouraged the use of folk music tunes as the basis of musical composition.[22]

The New Deal era also introduced a new breed of folklorist to work for the government, such as Alan Lomax and Zora Neale Hurston. They recognized folk music as a living, changing entity, thus broadening the scope of what was considered folk music by those officially sent to record it.[23] These teams came to the South and recorded countless work songs, spoke to textile workers about their jobs, and eventually wrote down this material

Figure 8. Poster advertisement for the Federal Music Project.

in songbooks for the whole nation to admire, much as classical music had been recognized up till that point. As Filene (2000, 143) notes:

> With the dislocations of the depression and the rise of fascism overseas, the notion that collection songs could have political utility was tremen-

Figure 9. Eleanor Roosevelt listening to old-time mountain music in White Top Mountain, Virginia, 1933. Courtesy Bettmann/Corbis.

dously reassuring to American folklorists in the thirties, and it permeated their rhetoric. Charles Seeger, for example, urged workers at the Resettlement Administration to select music on the basis of utilitarian as much as aesthetic criteria. "The main question," he asserted, "should not be 'is it good music,' but 'what is the music good for?'" [Head of the Federal Writers' Project B. A.] Botkin shared Seeger's pragmatism, noting in his report on the WPA that the agency's folklore research was premised on a connection between "bread and song." "Throughout," he wrote, "we stress relation between art and life, between work and culture . . . The WPA looks upon folklore research not as a private but as a public function and folklore as public, not private property."

Such sentiments come from those appointed by Roosevelt to oversee the collection and dissemination of the music of the people, and demonstrate the administration's concern for the plight of the poor as recognized in their songs. The administration's focus on public functions and public property sent a message that the government would step up to protect the interests of working people. "Whitey" Grant, a musician from Gastonia, North Carolina, recalls the response of mill workers to Roosevelt's programs:

They loved him. People felt . . . it was like he was a god, and I did too. He done more for the [people] sweating and laboring than anyone we ever heard of.

Hillbilly music, of course, was not necessarily new to Washington, D.C. Al Hopkins and the Hillbillies had played for Calvin Coolidge in 1926. In the same year, Carl Sandburg published *The American Songbag,* a collection of folk songs of all types. It was during the Roosevelt administration, however, that hillbilly music got its due. FDR was captivated by this music of the rural South and invited several folk musicians to perform at the White House. Bascom Lamar Lunsford, a banjo picker from the North Carolina hills, for instance, was invited on several occasions to perform at the White House, in one case for the king and queen of England.

Roosevelt's personal actions spoke to his connection to the common folk. His purchase of a retreat in Warm Springs, Georgia, reinforced this contact and put him all the closer to those working in the textile mills. Although support for folk and hillbilly music was more a personal act of the president's than a major goal of the FMP, Roosevelt's explicit appreciation for such music nevertheless helped legitimize it over the airwaves to a broader public and helped set the stage for its rise in popularity and its broadcast on southern radio.[24]

Conclusion

Roosevelt's rise and then wide popularity in national politics was, in part, molded and fostered by his use of radio. His radio fireside chats entered the living rooms of most people at a crucial economic period, inspiring confidence that, together, the citizenry would ensure and stabilize its way of life. Mill workers of the South were listening as many of the New Deal reforms ran squarely into southern labor practices, including the use of child labor, poor wages, dangerous conditions, and grueling work hours.

Roosevelt's use of radio allowed him to bring these important labor issues to the forefront of the national political agenda, while sidestepping power structures firmly embedded within the southern political economy. The lesson, of course, is that political structures and the opportunity they may afford to aggrieved groups and potential social movement actors are, more often that not, multitiered and not always consistent across levels. It was ultimately the advent of a new communication medium that allowed Roosevelt to circumvent more firmly entrenched local structures, garner leverage in terms of attention and appeal, and communicate his message effectively and more widely.

The processes we have described also speak clearly to the understanding of how altered political perceptions, rather than actual political opportunity, are key and can shape mobilization potential.[25] Worker optimism was heightened, and favorable changes were made with Roosevelt's New Deal. These included shorter work hours, a minimum wage, and the prohibition of child labor. Quickly thereafter, however, southern mill owners, often in concert with local and state political officials (many mill owners themselves), found ways to circumvent altogether, or at least manipulate, the new legislation. Mill workers responded with heightened grievances, shared with Roosevelt through letters, and a sense that any resulting worker action would be legitimate in the eyes of the federal government.

Although Roosevelt's prominence and appeal to working people heightened their sense of opportunity and the legitimacy of potential collective action, the administration's impact on worker consciousness went further. By identifying with, and even sponsoring, working-class culture through the Federal Writers' Project, the Federal Music Project, and the Federal Arts Project, the Roosevelt administration opened up cultural space for the explicit expression of the working-class experience. Folk historians and musicians traveled the country, recording and sharing music from a variety of regions and industries, including music rooted in Appalachian and Piedmont traditions and music of the textile towns of the Southeast. This was important in terms of timing because radio stations in the South were just beginning to book live, local acts and take more seriously the appeal of "hillbilly" bands that sang of work experiences and common complaints of mill folk.

As essential as Roosevelt's direct and indirect influence may have been on the consciousness of southern textile mill workers, equally important was the timing of his impact relative to the strikes that unfolded. A number of southern textile mills experienced strikes in 1929, well before Roosevelt's presidency and popularity. These strikes, however, were scattered and largely fragmented. Roosevelt's rise into the national spotlight, his radio broadcasts, and his New Deal policies largely occurred in 1933 and 1934, prior to the massive strike of 1934. Thus, Roosevelt's visibility, popularity, and policies were important to mill-worker consciousness and collective experience in the 1929–34 interim, a fact that helps explain why the strike of 1934 occurred on a more unified and broader geographic scale.[26]

A critical consciousness was being forged prior to Roosevelt's presidency via music and musicians grounded in the mill experience. The importance of music became widely apparent in the earlier waves of strikes in 1929, most notably in the towns of Marion and Gastonia, North Carolina. Yet, like the impact of Roosevelt, the real and broader geographic impact would be felt into the early 1930s, as the message and plight of mill hands were sung over the airwaves of Southern radio.

4

The Musicians

They listened to a program each day from WIS, I think that's right, in Columbia. Anyway, they listened to a program called the Aristocratic Pigs . . . Fisher Hendley was the head pig, I suppose [laughs]. His signature song was "Weave Room Blues," and he played the banjo, and he would play it every once in a while. He came to Lancaster with the Aristocratic Pigs . . . of course, we all had to go up and see them at the high school there in Lancaster. We all enjoyed it. Back then, ya know, there weren't no TV . . . ya didn't know what they looked like and in order to see them and get a glimpse of what they looked like, you go out when they played those personal appearances. They did that two or three times a week all around the state.

—Woody Dewey

The emergence of radio in the U.S. South and the use of the airwaves by Franklin D. Roosevelt affected the lives, leisure-time activities, and political consciousness of textile mill workers during the 1920s and 1930s. Mill workers' experiences were now linked via a common medium. With this came a recognition that workplace change, family concerns, and poverty where not isolated or unique to their particular village. These issues were now on the national political agenda, and affecting the lives of most across the region.

An unintended consequence of radio lay in the opportunity it afforded to mill musicians to leave mill work and become professional entertainers.

46

The growing popularity of folk art and music, reflected in the cultural re-vitalization component of FDR's New Deal policies, helped in this regard by making the music that mill musicians played more openly acceptable to the mainstream. Local owners and programmers, with institutional free-dom to book and broadcast live, local acts, had to fill the void and looked to mill communities. Radio barn-dance performances in particular offered ex-mill-worker musicians the chance to share their tunes, sing together, and forge a more tightly knit regional community. Indeed, given the geographic dissemination of both traditional mountain music and oppositional music aimed at mill workers in particular, one could conceive of these musicians as inadvertent social movement actors or even "traveling evangelists."[1] Live performances in and across mill villages between radio stints kept them tied to their own backgrounds and the mill experience, while also offering ritual occasions for celebration among mill workers. These were the new celebri-ties of the South. As such, their role in forging a broader sense of commu-nity and experience across the textile South, sometimes subtle, sometimes overt, cannot be overlooked

In this chapter, we highlight the role radio played in transforming per-formance styles, and how musicians' own histories as mill workers affected their music, what they sang about, and their strong emotional connection to those still working in the mill. The music they shared over the airwaves and during live performances became an integral part of mill workers' everyday lives, forged commonality of experience and occasions for community cele-bration, and ultimately provided a blueprint for workers' protest repertoire.

Mill Musicians: Learning to Play and Emerging Styles

In the rural and Appalachian South, musical skills were historically handed down from one generation to the next. Playing and singing were a funda-mental part of family and community tradition. Although some owned wind-up Victrolas, radios were scarce and expensive, especially before electri-fication. It was not until the late 1920s that radios and phonographs became more commonplace.[2] Prior to these modern conveniences, people simply entertained themselves by creating their own music. It is thus no surprise that many early professional musicians had their roots in the mountains, farms, and mill towns.

Musicians in the textile South typically learned to play music at a very early age, guided by an older person in the family. Gray Troutman, a musi-cian during the early 1930s, in recollecting how he and his brother Fred learned how to play guitar, gives credit to his grandmother, who "showed us a C and G chord and taught us to play a few songs." Harvey Ellington, who grew up in the country, similarly remembers learning to play from his mother and father in the early 1920s:

> I learned them tunes Pa knew. Some of those tunes I play come from England over here, a lot of them, Granddaddy and all that . . . There was no radio. There was a few talking machines around, but we didn't have one.

Once people moved from the farms to the mill villages, those with musical talent found themselves in close proximity.[3] Harvey Ellington noted that in the country, there were few musicians close by. In the cotton mill village, in contrast, "there was a lot more people to pick from close together." "Whitey" Grant of the Briarhoppers, a popular radio group out of Gastonia, notes:

> Everybody tried to make the old-time music at the cotton mills . . . A lot of the boys that we knew, or heard of, after we came in formed bands and they would get together in the cotton mills and the first thing you know they would form bands . . . On Saturday or Sunday, when the mill wasn't running, they had a little band stand up there and draw a big crowd.

It was in the latter half of the 1920s that radio began to popularize these musicians and their music. By this time, many had honed their personal styles, influenced mostly by Appalachian mountain music, but by other styles as well. Music of the Piedmont, of rural blacks, of Mexican-Americans, and with Hawaiian roots all came together to influence the style of music generated within mill villages.[4] Even touches of chamber music could be heard in the tunes of some, such as Charlie Poole.[5] As the South industrialized, barriers that had once kept it isolated from the rest of the country were slowly coming down. Records and, later, the radio were influential in helping musicians meld together all of these styles to create some sounds unique to the place and time.

Vocal styles of Tin Pan Alley encouraged singers to adopt a somewhat smoother style than that of traditional mountain musicians. Barbershop quartets and shape-note gospel singing were also influential.[6] Some early recorded musicians sounded harsh by today's standards, in part in an effort to project in the era before microphones. With advances in microphones, however, musicians no longer needed to project as much as before and could incorporate more subtle nuances into their vocals.[7] The rougher sounds of Charlie Poole, for instance, were replaced by the smoother vocals of the Monroe Brothers.[8]

Subjects of songs and singing styles varied, of course, depending on the context of the performance, although the basic instrumentation remained the same. Fiddles, guitars, mandolins, and banjos predominated and were readily available through local craftspeople and catalog companies, such as Sears Roebuck and Montgomery Ward. Hawaiian guitars, also known as lap steels, were also popular.[9] Howard Dixon of the Dixon Brothers, originators of the song "Weave Room Blues," was featured on this instrument.

Aside from generational impacts and the role of mill-town concentration in forging and honing musical talent, mill-worker musicians were often needed for affairs where radio was less practical, especially dances. Such informal occasions provided opportunities for musical collaboration and the formation of partnerships. Indeed, musicians once separated by miles of hills and forests and who only got together a few times a year at festivals now had the advantage of living right next door to one another. "Whitey" Grant recalls the beginning of his lifelong musical partnership with Arvol Hogan, while working in a Gastonia mill:

> I hadn't been there but a couple of months. And my brother-in law was living with me then. He married my sister and was living in the same house with us. He and I was out on the back porch one day during the week, seems like it was on a Sunday. We were picking and singing and these two strange-looking guys came up around the back and just stood there. Finally they spoke. They said "Hey, there. How are y'all? We're Arvol and Andy Hogan." And I said, "I'm Roy Grant and this is Roy Rumfeldt, my brother-in-law." So, we talked and they asked us if we knew a certain song. We knew it and sang it for them. So, . . . Hogan said to me, "My brother works on the same shift your brother-in-law works on and you and I work on the same shift. I wonder if we couldn't get together over at my house or your house and see if we can sing?" And I said, well, I don't see why we couldn't. So, the next day or two, I went over to his house and took my guitar and we started fiddling around and singing.

"Whitey" and Hogan played together for the next sixty-six years, and lived in houses right next to each other for nearly fifty of those years. Obviously, ties made in mill villages ran deep. Lifelong partnerships, such as that of Homer "Pappy" Sherrill and Snuffy Jenkins who played together for fifty-two years, exemplified the dedication of these musicians to their friends and community more generally.[10] Furthermore, the myth of the family band was alive, if not revered. Musicians realized this early on, and even named their band so audiences would assume it was a family group, as was the case of the Martin Brothers.[11] Still, these connections were genuine and endured, as many from the era of burgeoning radio continue to refer to one another as "like a brother."[12] And, more than sixty years after their first performances on radio, many were still in contact with other performers of their era, or became excited when told that other musicians from this era are alive and well.[13] Family, friends, and commitment were, and remain, important in the lives of musicians who were raised in the southern mill villages of the 1930s.

Musicians and Millwork

Early southern radio musicians were strongly affected by their formative experiences in the textile mills and by their continuing association with friends and family who remained there. One could hardly help being touched by it in some way. "Whitey" and Hogan of the Briarhoppers began their playing careers while working in the mills in Gastonia.[14] The Tobacco Tags, who provided music to strikers in 1934, also formed in Gastonia.[15] Dorsey and Howard Dixon of Rockingham, known over the airwaves as the Dixon Brothers, never fully escaped the mills. Howard, in fact, eventually died on the job at a mill.[16] David McCarn, who recorded "Cotton Mill Colic" and "Serves Them Fine," was also at times a mill operative.[17]

Figure 10. "Whitey" Grant and Arvol Hogan during the early years of radio. Courtesy David Sichak and Hillbilly-Music.com.

Some remained mill workers their entire lives. Others went back and forth between life on the road and life in the mill. Those fortunate enough escaped mill work forever and played full-time. None, however, could completely escape their early work experiences, nor did they have the desire or need to escape their friends and relatives whose livelihoods revolved around the mills. This is perhaps why deprivation in mill life is present in many songs and stories told by the musicians. Dave McCarn, a native of Gastonia, North Carolina, wrote and recorded some of the most popular mill songs of the period and was blacklisted for his efforts. After having met McCarn in 1963, folk historian Archie Green (1961) wrote:

> After "Cotton Mill Colic" was released a Gastonia music store bought "1000" copies. It sold well because Gastonia was a mill town. McCarn stated of the sales, "Airy a one left in town." McCarn was never actually fired for composing or recording "Colic," but after his job ended "The guys told me that I was barred from the Victory Mill in South Gastonia . . ." Asked what friends thought of the Cotton Mill Colic series, McCarn says he was told by friends that he'd never get a job in any mill around *there* anymore, but that he didn't care if he did.[18]

Green (1963) also wrote that McCarn seemed nonplussed by his songs thirty years after their impact. Dave McCarn's days in the mills were over when Green found him. McCarn was working in a television repair shop at the time. His wife, however, still worked in a mill. Being a musician could nevertheless have its perks. Harvey Ellington noted that being a musician helped him get a job at the local mill before his days on the road:

> During the Depression, you couldn't buy a job. But I was very fortunate there. You know, if you played a little music, you was a "top man," you might as well call it. I've got to go into a few details to tell you how this came about. The straw boss of that mill, under the first boss, had a fine-looking wife, and she worked down there, and she was crazy about me. She was old enough for my mother. So through that girl, she got me a job in there through her husband. That was the onliest way I could get a job then. That's a fact. That's the way it was done then.[19]

Reasons for being a full-time musician, rather than a mill worker, varied. Harvey Ellington provided his rationale.

> You see, I had nobody but myself, and I was fenced in there. And I'd done a lot of playing around on the side, dances and all. Now you know, a man becomes ambitious; he's an adventurous creature. He likes to get out, and he don't like to stay closed in when he got nobody but himself. So I

could make just as good a living and meet more people . . . Which the living wasn't much to make, but I could make a little more money playing than I could in that textile mill, even at twelve dollars a week. And that inspired me to go off on the medicine show.

It is interesting that despite efforts to leave mill work and scratch out a living as a musician, many of these musicians remained attached to mill communities and their mill experiences—a fact that is reflected in the songs and music of some. Take, for instance, Charlie Poole and his North Carolina Ramblers. Poole and his band were able to play music full-time after landing a recording contract in 1925 and were extremely popular throughout the mill towns of the Southeast, playing popular tunes and songs that spoke to the lives of mill workers. In fact, the bulk of the music that mill workers listened to reflected not only mill work, but the whole existence of mill life.[20]

Interestingly, Poole shaped his own performing talents while a mill worker, where he developed a "habit of leaving a mill job and retiring to a bridge outside the factory, where he would pick his banjo and wave to fellow workers leaning out the window" (Grundy 1995, 1609). Poole found popularity first at local fiddlers' conventions and then through records.[21] He and his band cut numerous sides and toured extensively in the South. Playing locally and a few times a year at fiddlers' conventions was the route that most musicians took; however, there were always some, like Poole, who chose the life of a musician over the mill. One reason, of course, was the pay. A musician could make considerably more than a mill hand, and always had the hope of a recording contract and hit record. Playing music nevertheless came at the cost of significant travel. Poole and his band were known to travel throughout the southeast and into states on the western side of the Appalachians, such as Ohio.

Some musicians continued to work in the mills between regular paying music jobs. Homer "Pappy" Sherrill worked in a hosiery mill after tiring of life away from home. After a long-standing job at WPTF radio in Raleigh, North Carolina, he returned to Hickory, North Carolina, to work in a hosiery mill but soon grew tired of the work, which he characterized as simply "hard work." Afterwards, he understood and sympathized with those who remained in the mills. He returned to the life of a musician full-time, after hearing that some local radio personalities were playing at a nearby high school. When he showed up with his fiddle and played, they asked him to return to radio, and he did.[22]

Music thus provided many of these ex-mill workers with both a creative outlet and a means to support their families. Of course, playing locally could act as an aid to the family in more than simply cash benefits. J. D. McCormick, a musician and mill worker who eventually sold rights to some of his songs to John Denver, recalls other forms of payment when playing with Al Wall and others on the radio:

> We played on that Saturday Night Roundup. Back then, times was hard and we didn't get no money much but if we won, we'd get commodities, like flour and meal.

There were differences in terms of how far musicians were willing to travel for a performance. Some traveled throughout the South, eventually landing in Nashville as their home base. Others, such as Gray Troutman, remained in their local area, especially if they became regulars on a given radio show.

> Yeah, we went over to Winston-Salem every week. I don't even remember where the radio station—that's been, Lord, that was in 1934, '35, somewhere about that time. Somebody was talking to me about Charlie Monroe, Charlie and Bill Monroe, and I said, "Yeah, they started about the same time we did." [Laughs.] They were just starting and the Carlisle Brothers and all that bunch of outlaws over there in Nashville. [Laughs.] That was long before Chet Atkins. He, Chet Atkins, didn't come along till about the end of the '50s.

This reference to outlaws was said with humor, yet reflects some tension between those who decided to stay at home and play locally and those who chose to travel on a more ongoing basis. Although Gray Troutman refers to the Nashville musicians as "outlaws," the musicians from Nashville also had ideas about more local performers. In this regard, "Whitey" Grant, who performed in and around Charlotte, North Carolina, remembers being recruited by the Grand Ole Opry:

> The Grand Ole Opry called me and Hogan. Roy Acuff and Minnie Pearl were in town. Roy Acuff and Minnie Pearl set me down and said, "Don't get it in your head that we don't want you at WSM. We would love to have you." Minnie Pearl said, "Whitey, I know you. I know when it gets dark, you'll want to be home with your wife and kids." She said, "At WSM, you're going to have to be on the road twenty-six weeks out of the year. You're required to be at WSM twenty-six Saturdays and be on the road twenty-six Saturdays. And you wouldn't want to come home and have Polly tell them two girls [we just had two then] tell them two girls who this stranger was. You wouldn't go for that. I know you." So, we

didn't go. They called us twice. Acuff and her told us both times, don't go. So we didn't.

"Whitey" had something many of the Nashville musicians did not, stability. The experience and friendship of Acuff and Pearl led them to caution him about the rigors of the road. His respect for their judgment and love for his family led him to remain at WBT, where he and Hogan became local celebrities and traveled within a wide radius around Charlotte. Local travel to promote their radio stints nevertheless afforded them the opportunity to play with other local musicians. "Whitey" recalls:

> J. E. Mainer came to our house one night. . . well fact is, that was before Pap went down there. J. E. Mainer and the Crazy Mountaineers, now Snuffy was working with J. E. Mainer then. They came to our house and was playing over at Dallas and Hogan and myself was gonna work that night with 'em, as a guest appearance. We just had a ball that night and after the show was over J. E. wanted to take Wade Mainer, his brother Wade, and me and Hogan and go on the road, the four of us. And I said, we had too good a setup here and I didn't think we wanted to leave. He wanted Wade, me, and Hogan and J. E. Mainer to form a band.

Life on the road, even locally, was hard work. Traveling took its toll, as did the late nights. Even food could be a problem. Alton Delmore, a well-known musician of the time, noted that he and his band ate canned goods while traveling. They had heard stories of travelers dying from food poisoning and feared suffering the same fate.[23] Other problems included old cars. Musicians traveled on two-lane highways and often had trouble with flat tires. Homer "Pappy" Sherrill recalled that when he first moved to Asheville, North Carolina, to play on WWNC, the old car they traveled in "would barely pull the mountain." He and his bandmates rented a room together and made so little money that they sent their clothes home to Hickory, North Carolina, to be washed and pressed.

Travel itself could also be dangerous for the performers. Alton Delmore recalls riding down a mountain on the way to Nashville only to discover that his cars brakes were on fire. Some areas were treacherous, especially the Appalachian Mountains through which the Delmore brothers made many of their trips.[24] Other areas, however, such as the Piedmont areas to the east of the mountains, were more suited to travel from town to town than some areas of the country, like the southeastern coastal plain.

Even when musicians settled down at one radio station, they still undertook live shows in order to keep the bills paid. It was radio that provided a new platform for musicians and a new audience for their music. As J. E. Mainer, who played on radio at the time with his Crazy Mountaineers, suggested toward the end of his life, "I been in the music field for 50 years and has made more personal appearances throughout the south than anybody in the business . . . been on one hundred and ninety nine different radio stations."[25]

The highest concentration of textile mills were in the Piedmont. Al Wall, a noted bass player from Marion, North Carolina, known as "Slim" on the radio, recalls the convenience of the textile Piedmont as a home base for musicians. Wall suggests that Hickory, North Carolina, was once the home base for Lester Flat and Earl Scruggs for this very reason.[26] So, the Piedmont was a convenient base for musicians, had a number of radio stations to play within its radio belt, and was the home of a number of musicians, many of whom were former textile-mill workers trying to make a living as entertainers. Radio also provided a platform from which to advertise live performances across the southeast.

Musicians from the southern Piedmont textile villages traveled considerably to play local towns and often played on several radio stations. While some maintained a local base for years, others were not always in an area for the long term, having to change territory when they had worn out their popularity or jobs fell through.[27] Homer "Pappy" Sherrill recounts having moved from Hickory to Asheville to Knoxville to Charlotte to Raleigh and finally on to Columbia, South Carolina. The Monroe Brothers (Charlie and Bill) too were noted traveling musicians and played along with Sherrill on WPTF radio in Raleigh. From the Monroes' first show at WJKS in Gary, Indiana, in 1929, they played at venues as varied as "KFNF, Shenandoa, Iowa; WAAW, Omaha, Nebraska; WIS, Columbia, South Carolina; WBT, Charlotte, North Carolina; WFBC, Greenville, South Carolina; and WPTF, Raleigh, North Carolina" (Monroe 2000, 9). In the process of moving around from station to station, and playing at high schools and other arenas in the southeast, networks were created to the point where "Everyone knew everyone else."[28]

Variations and Musical Themes

Musicians from the textile mill villages often played upon local emotions and real-life experiences of mill work in their lyrics and musical selections. One of the most influential early musicians in this regard was Fiddlin' John Carson. His version of "Little Mary Phagan" was very popular with listeners of old-time country music. Although not specifically about mill work, this song demonstrated one of the problems facing southern workers, mistreatment by supervisors. Based on a real-life occurrence, where it seems the supervisor was wrongly accused, it provided a shocking example of the murder of a young factory worker by her supervisor. It was so popular that mill workers during the Gastonia strike of 1929 patterned strike songs after it.[29]

Initially, promoter Ralph Peer doubted the marketability of such music, but millions of southerners were looking for exactly the kind of music Carson played.[30] In fact, record producers became so aware of the public's taste for such music that they attempted to keep it "pure." Peer consequently traveled throughout the South to find similar talent. Mill-worker musicians, such as Dave McCarn, recorded songs like "Cotton Mill Colic" for Peer.[31] This music became known broadly as "hillbilly music," a derogatory term that implied "cultural inferiority."[32] This label haunted the music for decades, and some musicians tried desperately to overcome the stereotype of the degenerate country rube.[33]

Promoters nevertheless pitched hillbilly music to fit the stereotypes. Performers were often forced to wear overalls and straw hats to fit the image of a backward country bumpkin, despite the fact that many were technically accomplished and sophisticated in their singing and playing techniques. The image of the hillbilly persisted, however, driven by both promoters and demand. Many people who were turned off by the wild dances and music of the Roaring Twenties sought solace in the music of an earlier time. Hillbilly music supplied that need.

One of the most popular early groups, the Carter Family, sang mountain hymns and songs that extolled the virtues of conservative, southern Protestant heritage in an age of social change.[34] The clogging dances that often accompanied mountain music of rural whites tended to be fancy on the footwork but the hips were stationary, as opposed to their African-American counterparts.[35] This further reinforced the conservative quality that audiences wished to confer on the music. Musicians were caught in this contradiction and dealt with it in different ways.

Some early musicians, such as Jimmie Rodgers, resisted traditionality. The loss of his mother at an early age and his travels throughout the South were representative of the lives of many of the migrants who ended up working in the textile mills. His music was a combination of old-time country and blues, and was quite popular. Rodgers toured the southern Appalachians in a black-faced minstrel show and played briefly in a string band in Asheville, North Carolina.[36] J. D. McCormick remembers seeing Rodgers as a boy:

I saw him one time. He come through a little old village over here. There's a little village that he had a friend over there. And I was in the swimming hole down there and I heard him pickin' just like I'm a-doing here. And I said, "Boy, I hear a guitar up there." I just got out and we just had a little old pair of pants on. And I got out and I went up there and he was play-ing. He was doing just like I'm a-doing. Just sitting there playing. And he looked at me and (I can't describe how he looked) and said, "Boy, you like that, don't you?" and I said, "I sure do, man!" And those were the only words I got to speak to him.

Rodger's influence can be heard in McCormick's own songs "Hobo" and "Land of the Sky." After hearing J. D. singing "Land of the Sky," we asked him about his yodeling in the song. He said, "I caught that from old Jimmie Rodgers." Other musicians were also indebted to Rodgers and his blue-collar style, including Gene Autry and Hank Williams. Yet, Rodgers never played on the Grand Ole Opry. His image was not clean-cut, but rather that of the rambler.[37] His migrations were something mill hands could understand, because many had migrated from field to factory and felt trapped in the mill.

Musicians themselves were workers, performers, and at times crusaders. Charlie Poole was a musician who would rather play music than work in the textile mill. His music was extremely popular in the southern Piedmont. His song "Let Me Sleep in Your Barn Tonight Mister" was recorded by Vernon Dalhart who sold 75 million records in his lifetime.[38] The song was also the basis for "Won't You Let Me Sleep in Your Tent Tonight Beal?" penned by eleven-year-old Odel Corley during the 1929 textile strike in Gastonia, North Carolina.[39] From around 1918 to his death in 1931, Poole played with his band, the North Carolina Ramblers. Although he did not have a career in radio, he did perform on radio. Kinney Rorrer (1982, 45) notes:

[Roy] Harvey was definitely more attuned than Poole to what was selling. Every time a new fad gripped country music, Harvey tried it . . . When radio began to have an impact on country music, Roy pulled Charlie into several radio stations for shows, which he himself would MC. Poole was not a man who could be pulled where he didn't want to go, of course; it seems probable that he accepted these challenges willingly. However, by and large, Poole seemed much more interested in just rambling, playing and having a good time, and apparently left the managerial problems to Harvey.

Poole bucked common convention by resisting a return to the cotton mill even when he was in need of money. In his own way, he may have been engaging in protest against the industrialization of the South. Indeed, he sometimes played outside his local cotton mill to taunt supervisors while workers sat by the windows to listen.

Other musicians from textile towns did not play full-time like Poole. They made forays into the recording and radio business but remained mainly employed in the factories. The Dixon Brothers provide a good example. They worked in the mills of Rockingham, North Carolina, for nearly all their lives. Born in Darlington, South Carolina, Dorsey moved to East Rockingham in 1924 and was followed a year later by his brother, Howard. Dorsey got Howard a job tending a machine. When not working, the brothers played music in homes and provided informal entertainment for workers in their village. Dorsey noted that they played for people to help them "forget their cares and troubles for an hour or so, sometimes 2 or 3 hours."[40]

The Dixon Brothers' first performance at a local theater was met with compliments the next day at the textile mill. After seeing Jimmie Tarlton at a neighbor's house, they decided to take up his style of playing, which was based on a finger-picking guitar style rather than strumming. Dorsey would rise at 3 A.M. each morning to practice before his eleven-hour shift at the mill. Howard took up the lap steel guitar and by 1932 the brothers carved out a unique style. Their songs told of life in the mills and the hardships of the people who worked there.[41] Dorsey, an inspired musician, saw himself, to some degree, as a crusader, bringing the message of the working people to the world. In describing his songs, Dixon notes that "somehow, I wanted the people, people that God made and loved, to hear them . . . Somehow I felt like it would be a blessing to them . . . and I hope it was."[42] Consistent with his passion, even his fellow musicians saw Dixon as a preacher of sorts.[43]

The Dixons cut records and performed on WBT radio in Charlotte, singing the popular "Intoxicated Rat," "Wreck on the Highway," and "Weave Room Blues." The Dixons also recorded other songs about mill life, such as "Weaver's Life," "Factory Girl," "Spinning Room Blues," and "Hard Times in Here."[44]

Other musicians had different reasons for singing and writing songs. Many were concerned with righting social wrongs and used their gift of music for this purpose. Ella May Wiggins, the balladeer of the Gastonia Strike of 1929, provides a good example. Ella May's songs were written to bring workers together to fight the terrible conditions in the textile mills. She wrote her songs from the experience of personal hardship: four of her children died as a result of poverty.[45] The song "Mill Mother's Lament" perfectly sums up the tragedy of the mill mother who works hard all day and yet does not have the money to feed and clothe her children. Wiggins

Figure 11. The Dixon Brothers singing over the airwaves in Charlotte, North Carolina, 1934. Courtesy of John Edwards Memorial Collection, Southern Folklife Collection, University of North Carolina archives.

and those like her, who wrote and sang songs pertaining to mill life as activists rather than as professional performers, along with those such as Charlie Poole and the Dixon Brothers who made the leap to the professional musical ranks, help us understand the integral role of music to mill workers, its indigenous character, and ultimately its impact on community.

Charlie Poole's music and actions were certainly important in developing a cynicism among workers. Ella May's songs encouraged solidarity with workers during strike events in Gastonia. After her death, her songs remained popular and had the unintended result of influencing authors of protest songs in the 1950s and 1960s. The Dixons similarly had an impact on the collective identity of workers. Their recordings and broadcasts, along with those of such musicians as Dave McCarn and Wilmer Watts, came along at a unique historical moment, when they could be shared via records and played over the radio airwaves. Their songs of life in the mills reached many ears from the powerful WBT radio. During live "barn dance" broadcasts, some of these musicians would play together and share mill-related songs, some of which they wrote and some of which they picked up from mill workers themselves during their travels.[46]

Music, Musicians, and the Forging of Community

Music was part of everyday life for mill workers in the 1920s and 1930s. Songs went along with both work and leisure. Before the advent of the radio, the record industry supplied workers with musical variety and stars. It also began to discover that local audiences preferred local artists.[47] Old-time music, as early country music was often called, and its subsequent market were discovered early on by the big record companies. Subsidiaries such as Blue Bird released many old-time or "hillbilly" records. Musicians would travel to recording sessions in regional cities such as Charlotte or as far as New York City. From Fiddlin' John Carson to Charlie Poole, musicians sought fame and possibly fortune through records.[48] All this changed with the coming of the Depression.

In 1929, the stock market crash led to an economic downturn of staggering proportions, the Great Depression.[49] From the beginning of this depression till the start of World War II, the average unemployment rated hovered at around 18 percent. During this period, money was scarce and the public could no longer afford to buy records. Sales plummeted. Consequently, live music became a necessity for musicians who wanted to survive. As luck would have it, the radio provided a ready outlet for musicians to reach their listening public.

Radio also offered many of these musicians a larger paycheck. "Whitey" Grant remembers:

> Our greatest ambition was to play on WBT. All the personnel at WBT put on a bluegrass festival at the high school in Gastonia. And they called "Whitey" and Hogan at the radio station in Gastonia to see if we would work the indoor bluegrass festival. And I said sure. They said "Oh . . . we'll give you ten dollars apiece." The place was so full they were turning away people.

The local crowd rooted for "Whitey" and Hogan. Two weeks later, their supervisor in the mill said Charlie Crutchfield of WBT radio wanted to talk to them. They were making $9.20 a week in the mill. Crutchfield offered them $25 a week to work in radio.

J. W. Fincher's Crazy Waters Crystals' Saturday Night Jamboree, broadcast on WBT in Charlotte, and Fisher Hendley's Rhythm Aristocrats, broadcast out of WIS in Columbia, South Carolina, were two highly visible hubs of music opportunity and prestige. Both stations relied on local audience responses, including write-in requests, for particular songs. Although there was some tendency to balance more gritty-sounding songs with traditional and religious tunes, this was more a function of musicians' dependence on audiences than it was of radio station censorship. As we suggested in chapter 2, rather than being linked to traditional industries such as textiles, station owners tended to be universities and entrepreneurs. Performers were consequently afforded autonomy in what they played and sang.[50]

Mill workers looked forward to the live radio shows and the songs that were shared. Earlier, we noted that upwards of 70 percent of mill workers had radios in their homes. Where radio ownership was limited, neighborhood and community ritual developed around its usage and the music that was disseminated.[51] According to Peterson (1997, 7), "music played over the radio had an almost magical power for rural people growing up in the 1930s, drawing families together and at the same time opening isolated communities to the larger world beyond the county and even the state." This was particularly true when those whose music was broadcast came from the same mill towns as the listeners.

Playing live on the radio, however, did not always pay the bills. According to Alton Delmore, his stints with his brother on the Grand Ole Opry paid almost nothing. It was personal appearances that led to a paycheck.[52] Things were much the same for musicians in the southeast Piedmont. Some musicians adapted a strategy of keeping a strong local fan base during the week and augmenting this with broadcasts from neighboring towns on Saturday to expand their base.[53] Bands would drive long distances to play one show on the radio. Many would then take the time to play live shows in small rural towns along the way, only to drive into the early morning hours to get back to their home radio station and play another show.[54] "Whitey" Grant notes the exhaustion that followed, especially when trying to simultaneously raise a family:

> We lived within five miles of the radio station. We'd go in and do the radio program. Leave and go on a personal appearance. Come in that night anywhere from 12 to 3 o'clock A.M. Sleep till we got ready to get up. She [Polly] was there, bless her heart, would get the kids to school, and I could sleep. Get up, eat, take off and do the same thing over again.

Saturday nights were often reserved for these special, live events that musicians would play wherever and whenever they could. Indeed, the advent of local radio broadcasts "paved the way for some of the first hillbilly bands to earn their livings performing at a Spartanburg high school auditorium one night, at a Gastonia mill recreation center the next evening, and on a Charlotte radio station the following morning."[55]

Pratt (1990, 22) has argued that the creation and playing of popular music "serves potentially emancipatory functions if people *use* the setting in particular ways to generate and maintain enclaves of autonomy or free space." Such spaces were created during the Great Depression in the southeastern United States. Textile-mill villages were under the control of the mill owners, who often owned most of, if not the whole, town. However, there were spaces that mill owners did not control. Houses not owned by the mill, radios, and other venues where musicians played were not under the control of the mill owner. Musicians who felt a kinship with workers would often play for free, singing under streetlights or going from house to house playing their instruments for folks.[56] Gray Troutman notes that his band, the Ramblin' Cracker-Jacks, often played at people's houses around Statesville, North Carolina:

> Out here on the East Broad Street [there was a] big old house down off the road there. Big old house. We played places like that. Where they had big living rooms. Well, you get twenty-five or thirty people on the floor. Man, I've seen the pictures shaking on the wall. They'd move all the furniture out, had a few chairs around and most of the time when we get through the dancers would go in the other room and sit down. We set in one corner. Old man Henry Carter, we used to play out at his place . . . Out there close to where River Hill Road turns off. He lived back off down that road to the left, I mean right back down in there. All them people lived in big old houses and there was plenty of room to dance. They'd cut it up too. Old man Gus Summers called the dances most of the time and he never forgot—you could ask, somebody would ask for a certain pattern and he'd fall right into it. He didn't have to stop and think about it either. He just called it. But old man Carter, when he was dancing, they really danced, they didn't just shuffle around like they do now. They danced. And he'd jump up and click his heels together three times before he hit the floor again.

In the process of performing live on the radio, making recordings, and performing live in mill villages, a common culture was shared. Peterson (1997, 118) refers to these travels and live performances specifically as "barnstorming," something that "created a good deal of excitement when they [the musicians] first reached a town." Barnstorming allowed mill musicians to both draw from and contribute to the culture of mill life, and provided a ritualized, musical context within which the similarity of mill workers' experiences throughout the region became obvious. Radio broadcasts, in turn, allowed "those who missed the traveling musicians' performances to hear and enjoy the same music," thus fostering a strong sense of group

Figure 12. The Ramblin' Cracker-Jacks of Statesville, North Carolina. Courtesy Fred and Gray Troutman.

identity.[57] Musicians were, in essence, "traveling evangelists," in that they carried messages, oftentimes shared oppositional consciousness, and built personal relationships and commonality across mill towns of the late 1920s and early to mid-1930s.[58]

Conclusion

The founding of radio stations in the southeastern United States in the 1920s and 1930s, in concert with limited political restraints and an explicit recognition, if not sponsorship, of working-class cultural, artistic, and musical expression by the federal government, set the stage in the textile belt for the rise of local musicians with roots, experiences, and family in the mills. The concentration of mountain and farming populations, with a historical and an intergenerational legacy of music, ensured that mill towns would have within them significant local talent to fill the needs of local radio programmers—programmers who had an interest in fostering a large and local audience base.

Although there was significant variation in what was played at the time, most live broadcasts relied on fusions of southern music, typically referred to as "hillbilly." Such music included traditional Appalachian tunes, gospel, as well as lyrical themes that were consistent with the experiences and grievances of working-class people, including those in the mill. Indeed, as already noted, many of the musicians who rose to celebrity during the era had their own roots in mill work, felt a strong bond and connection with those still employed in mill work and living in mill villages, and thus wrote directly about and for these populations. Others who wrote songs never made the leap to professional musician status. They nevertheless expressed discontent through songs—songs that would often be picked up by traveling musicians and that would eventually be shared by mill workers across the region by the early to mid-1930s.

The importance of radio and its timing for the sharing of culture and mill-work experiences cannot be underestimated. Mill workers not only had access to radios but saw listening to it, and listening to music specifically, as their primary leisure-time activity. Community ties and celebration around radio were apparent and increased when local celebrity musicians, sometimes from their very ranks, would "barnstorm" a town for live appearances. In chapter 5 we describe how the music performed and disseminated by these musicians penetrated workers' everyday lives and sometimes, through the lyrical themes shared, challenged the legitimacy of mill-owner practices.

5

Music and the Mill Experience

Ta ra ra boom-de-ay-
ain't got a word to say,
they chiseled all my pay,
then took my job away.
Boom went the boom one day,
it made a noise that way.
I wish that I'd been wise,
next time I'll organize.
—Eula McGill

The emergence of songs and the richness of music in mill towns during the 1920s and 1930s—songs and music that spoke directly to the lives and experiences of Piedmont mill workers—should come as no surprise given the importance of such tradition in southern Appalachian mountain culture and the subsequent concentration of mountain folk in the new and growing mill towns of the southeast. Many of the musicians discussed in the prior chapter, who rose in celebrity with the advent of radio, indeed honed their already existent musical talents while engaged in mill work.

The importance of music as a galvanizing force, while partially attributable to radio musicians and live performances, was consistent with preexisting cultural tradition—tradition actuated by mill workers in their daily lives and then during protest. This tradition was sweeping and spoke to spiritual life, everyday life, and real grievances. Thus, unlike the assumption often embedded within social movement analyses that emergence of insurgency is dependent on the introduction of grievance frames and oppositional culture by a clear-cut social movement organization, we are suggesting that potential social movement actors may be just as likely to draw from their own histories and preexisting repertoires, particularly when little in the way of organizational resources, structures, and grievance frames is available.[1]

In this chapter, we discuss the role of music and song in shaping identity and consciousness among mill workers, and its reinforcement on the job, in leisure-time activities, and community celebration. Our analytic attention to mill-specific music and its lyrical themes, however, should not detract from the fact such songs constituted a relatively small portion of the music and tradition on which mill workers drew.[2] Indeed, much of the music mill workers listened to, requested, and even utilized during protest was traditional mountain folk tunes and even gospel music. This suggests that the impact of music was not purely cognitive, via lyrical themes, but rather also important because of its identity, emotional, and solidaristic impact—a fact highlighted in the analysis of the Gastonia and Marion strikes in chapter 6.[3]

Songs dealing specifically with mill work and mill life were nevertheless unique to the era and processes of collective mobilization on which we are focusing.[4] Such songs—written, sung, recorded, and/or played over the radio airwaves prior to 1935—were more than mere entertainment. Rather, they spoke directly to the personal and work lives of most southern mill workers and fostered clear in-group identity. Furthermore, many offered workers an explicit oppositional cultural interpretation of the problems they were facing and the causes of those problems. Intended or not, music and song represented a consciousness-raising tool—a tool that would be utilized prior to and then during the strikes that unfolded between 1929 and 1934.[5]

Music and Identity in Everyday Practice

Musical persistence and preference—preference specifically for the mountain music of the Appalachian South—became an important cultural symbol of group membership for many who migrated into mill towns from 1900 onward. The music itself, whether called by its listeners Appalachian, porch, or hillbilly, had its roots in the Scotch-Irish tradition, with some blending of African and European instruments and styles over time.[6] Lyrical themes were often religious, although many classic mountain tunes also dealt explicitly with troubled times, a hard work life, or sorrow and death.[7] Knowledge of certain tunes and songs, in fact, revealed one's origins in the mountains, at least relative to the more metropolitan locales of the South where elites pushed for musical entertainment consistent with high-brow, European, classical tastes.[8] For many migrants to the mills, knowledge of the old-time mountain music or the ability to play it provided an inroad to the mill community. As one mill worker recounts:

> I met more from the mountains of West Virginia, hillbillies that come down to live. And they were people of my own liking, my own choosing, because they weren't ashamed of hillbilly music . . . Every time we could find a good record, find a chance, we'd sing together. We didn't have no instruments of our own. But every time that we could come upon somebody picking hillbilly music, we would all stay and listen and make comments, and sometimes we would join in with them and sing.[9]

Knowledge and appreciation of one's roots nevertheless could come at a cost, especially when those roots were portrayed in popular media as backward, childish, or irresponsible, as they often were. We saw in the last chapter that initial efforts were made to broadcast classical music and to encourage tastes in that direction. Given stigmas associated with mountain people, many undoubtedly altered their musical tastes in response. Others, however, remained loyal to their cultural roots, in part because the music dealt explicitly with the realities of life.

> When I moved away from the mountains, people tried to disassociate themselves with the type of music that I loved, which was the mountain . . . Part of it they call it folk music, and some of it they call bluegrass, but it's all what was at one time called hillbilly music, changed a little bit. And I heard a lot of people throw off on it: it wasn't true music. True music was something that people overseas had studied up, and they brought it over here on paper. But now the young people, thank God . . . has come to realize that that's just as true music than that come over from other countries on paper. Now the other people, people that likes their blues and Bach, all of that, they might not like our music, but it's still music to us. So much of our music in the mountains had a story to it, a story that could always be told . . . tragic experiences . . .[10]

Indeed, many mill workers reveled in the mountain-music cultural tradition in which they were raised, and found it to be a form that was malleable to the conditions within which they now found themselves. Lyrics were, in fact, adaptable to already-existent traditional tunes, and mill workers found ways to weave their musical preference into their work lives and their leisure-time activities even beyond listening to records and radio. When possible, some would sing and play while actually on the job.

> We'd get our spinnin', get all our end up, and all our stuff done on the frame. We'd go out there and play. We'd carry little rocks in there and

we'd sit out there and play that . . . Then we'd have to jump up and run and catch up with our work, and go back and play a little more. They'd get together and sing in there . . . Get together some of them and sing.[11]

Another worker, referring to whether workers would get together and sing on breaks, recalls:

Oh yes, they would sometimes, yes. There was always somebody on the job that was, and they was going along pretty good. And they would; it was sort of a quartet thing. They love to get together and sing sometimes . . . the watchman, he'd come on. He used to sing tenor. The poor fellow's gone now, but they really did enjoy singing. And the mill would stop. Sometime at night, when they'd show up on the eleven o'clock shift, they'd get together and sing up there in the card room. All the time I'd be up there, taking down the hank and looking around, I'd hear them back there singing.[12]

Mill owners often took exception to singing on the job, however. This was particularly true when scientific management techniques were introduced to boost productivity. In such cases, singing on the job was a distraction and

Figure 13. A group of people making music outside a mill in Virginia. Courtesy Bettmann/Corbis.

an annoyance relative to producing output. Mill-owner responses also may have varied depending on the content of what was being sung. Some indeed saw the music with mill-work-specific themes and its consciousness-altering potential as a particular threat. For example, in Danville, Virginia, in 1930, local authorities and mill owners attempted to forbid workers from singing Dave McCarn's recently released "Cotton Mill Colic" within the mill village and while on the job.[13]

Beyond the shop floor, workers incorporated music into their off-hours, most notably on Saturday nights when they would have dances outside the confines and control of mill authorities.

> I used to go to dances at Henry Greer's; he was a real dancer. Henry Greer. We'd get up a gang, you know. Garvin Sellers, he was the manager of the ball team, and he'd get up a crowd of girls, and we'd go to that dance. Well, if Mr. Gwin said I could go, I'd go. And if he felt that I shouldn't go, he'd find out who was going. Well, he'd tell 'em, and that's be the last of it.[14]

Although dances would often be held in someone's house, some workers moved the activity outside the mill village itself. This was, in all likelihood, partially an effort to avoid the critical eye of mill owners, managers, and supervisors, many of whom also lived in the mill village.

> We'd go over there and sit on Saturday nights, and hang lanterns up in the trees, make it so we could have lighting. Have chicken stews and things, play and sing. Lord, there'd be every boy and girl in Bynum over there . . . Yeah, you'd hear 'em all over that place over there. We'd stay over there sometimes till nine, ten, eleven o'clock at night, playin' them guitars and things . . . They would get, they'd just play any kind of song, then they'd end 'em, maybe, they'd play some kind of crazy song and then they'd play a religious song.[15]

Unless some traveling radio band was in town and willing to play, mill workers provided their own music at these events. Often it was a family that played, with each member playing a different instrument.

> Used to have square dances. When I lived with my aunt, she had two girls about my age, and we'd go to square dances on Saturday night. This old lady and her husband, and they had a son and a daughter, and she played the banjo, and he picked, played the fiddle, and the boy played the bass fiddle and the daughter played the guitar, and they'd make music, and that's what they'd do on a Saturday night, go to them square dances.[16]

In other cases, the most talented musicians within the mill would form an ongoing group and would provide the entertainment. Some of them would be recognized as superior musicians with some legitimacy provided by periodic radio stints:

> The mill village used to have a band that'd get together, and they'd have it around the homes, or anywhere they'd let them have it. They'd draw a good crowd to like that, see . . . They'd have a dance or a supper, or something or other, and have the string music. We used to have some awful good guitar players around on the village. S. T. Dockins was one of them. He played on the radio. Well, there's just several of those boys.[17]

Music was thus integral to mill life, and was embedded within the cultural traditions of those who migrated to the southern mills during the 1920s and 1930s. While shared and spread on records, via the airwaves, and during live performances by traveling groups, mill workers actuated this cultural tradition in everyday practice, whether it was at work, during leisure-time activities, or as part of community celebrations.

Lyrical Themes, Identity, and Oppositional Consciousness

Equally important to the practice of music was its content, and the potential implications for collective action. In this regard, much of what mill workers and mill-worker musicians listened to, played, and sang was traditional mountain music, including old Appalachian folk songs (e.g., "Wildwood Flower," "Old Joe Clark," "Sally Goodin'") and traditional gospel tunes. Indeed, we know that such songs reflected the bulk of listener preferences and radio requests early on, and that such music was used during mill workers' strikes and when they were consequently arrested and incarcerated.[18] We also know, however, that songs specific to mill life and work became extremely popular in the late 1920s and early 1930s. Songs such as "Weave Room Blues" became staples for radio audiences in the Charlotte, North Carolina, and Greenville, South Carolina, areas. Other songs, such as "Cotton Mill Blues" and "Cotton Mill Colic," sold thousands of recorded copies upon their release, despite a cost that approximated half a day's wages, and would eventually receive radio airtime.[19] Mill workers sang these songs and others, including "Hard Times in Here" and "Factory Girl," while on the job given a beat that approximated that of looms slamming in the mill.

Often set to traditional mountain tunes, workers memorized the words to these songs, or altered them slightly to better fit their particular mill situation.[20] Finally, and perhaps most important, workers tapped into this body of work, penned by both ex-mill-worker musicians and mill workers themselves, during the strike upheavals that unfolded. Next, we examine the lyrical content of these songs with regard to the functions and interpretations they may have offered mill workers.[21]

Song and Interpretational Framing

Mill-specific songs during the late 1920s and early 1930s employed a collective sense of experience, using the words *we, us,* and *our,* and communicated anxieties specific to the experiences of most mill workers. These songs are clearly rich, with a multiplicity of concerns.[22] Recognizing the overlap in themes highlights their complexity.

Nineteen of the thirty-five songs considered (54.3 percent) denote material deprivations as the primary concern, while thirteen (37.1 percent) and eleven (31.4 percent) express concerns for physical and mental well-being and the family, respectively. Among those focusing on material deprivation, attention revolves around the low economic return for the amount of work put in. In four verses of "Let Them Wear Their Watches Fine," this grievance is coupled with a discussion of the social-status consequences of mill work:

> We work from week end to weekend,
> And never miss a day,
> And when that awful payday comes
> We draw our little pay.

> On pay day night we go back home
> And set down in a chair.
> The merchant knocks upon our door
> He's come to get his share.

> Those fancy folks that dress so fine
> And spend their money free,
> They don't have time for a factory hand
> That dresses like you and me.

> As we go walking down the street
> All dressed in lint and strings,
> They call us fools and factory trash,
> And other low-down things.

Among concerns for family well-being, children are often mentioned, something that undoubtedly evoked a broader concern and universal appeal among listeners. This concern is most obvious in some of the lyrics to a song aptly titled "Mill Mother's Lament":

And when we draw our money,
Our grocery bills to pay,
Not a cent to spend for clothing,
Not a cent to lay away.

And on that very evening
Our little son will say:
"I need some shoes, mother,
And so does sister May."

How it grieves the heart of a mother,
You every one must know;
But we can't buy for our children,
Our wages are too low.

Another song, "Cotton Mill Man," reflects the grieving heart of a mill
worker and his fear that his son may also end up working in the mill:

I watched my woman cry when our baby daughter
    died.
I couldn't make her understand why the doctor never
    came,
The lack of money was to blame.
I cussed the day that I became a cottonmill man.
Lord, don't let my son grow up to be a sweaty cotton-
    mill man.

It is notable that many of the thirty-five songs also specify the cause(s)
of the problems workers were facing—the work process and/or the negative
impact of human agents (i.e., bosses, managers, and/or scabs). Given our
interest in collective identity, group consciousness, and insurgency through
music, the distinction between cause and effect is important. If lyrics do
not address a cause, then consciousness relating to where grievances should
be aimed will remain unclear. This interpretational link between cause and
effect is crucial if social movement discourse and framing processes are to
be effective.[23] It is noteworthy that a cause is specified in more than three-
quarters of these songs. Twelve, or 34.3 percent, associate discontent with
the work process, while nearly three-quarters specify a human culprit.

Lyrics pointing to the work process fall into three principal categories:
general work conditions such as noise, speed, physical demands (six), the
length of the workday (five), and the introduction of scientific management
(one). One verse of "Weave Room Blues" provides a vivid image of the work
conditions mill workers faced:

> Slam out, break out, makeouts by the score,
> Cloth all rolled back and piled up on the floor.
> The bats are running into strings, they're hanging to
>   your shoes,
> I'm simply dying with them weave room blues.

Notably, however, much of the worker complaint is directed specifically at employers and managers rather than being seen as a consequence of mill work (twenty-six, or 74.3 percent). Complaints about the negative impact of human agents focus on paternalistic control or coercion by the owner (nine), wage exploitation by the owner (eight), and managerial control of the labor process (nine). Several scholars who study the labor process and the social and organizational aspects of work suggest that a focus on managers and owners, rather than on the labor process generally, may have stronger ramifications for group identity and consciousness.[24] Social movement scholars such as William A. Gamson (1995) and David A. Snow (2001) concur, suggesting that an injustice frame will be more effective at recruiting and mobilizing if the target is a concrete actor, preferably a person or corporation presented as malicious, selfish, or greedy. "The Big Fat Boss and the Worker"—a song penned by Ella May Wiggins, a mill worker and local organizer who was killed in an ambush during the Gastonia uprisings—conveys such specificity and resulting polarization by straightforwardly attributing worker problems to mill-owner exploitation. Two verses in particular stand out:

> The boss man hates the workers, the workers hates the
>   boss.
> The boss man rides in a big fine car and the workers
>   has to walk.
> The boss man sleeps on a big fine bed and dreams of
>   his silver and gold.
> The workers sleeps in an old straw bed and shivers
>   from the cold.

Some of this exploitation, as workers recognized, took the form of paternalistic practices, as related in the following two verses of "Cotton Mill Man":

> The company taught us all the rules on how to work
>   the spinning spools
> So the boss's son could drive a big black sedan.
> The company owned the houses and the company
>   owned the grammar school
> You'll never see an educated cottonmill man.

> They figure you don't need to learn anything but how
>   to earn
> The money that you paid upon demand
> To the general store they owned or else they'd take
>   away your home
> And give it to some other homeless cottonmill man.

Managers also are blamed for problems experienced by workers. In this verse from "Winnsboro Cotton Mill Blues," the cause of worker duress is clearly managerial oversight and greed:

> Old man Sargent sitting at the desk
> The damned old fool won't give us no rest.
> He'd take the nickels off a dead man's eyes
> To buy a Coca-Cola and a Eskimo pie.

Clearly, songs of mill-worker experience and discontent have a general appeal—an appeal that transcends the specifics of a particular mill town and that reverberates with the day-to-day realities of mill life in the South. Not only do these songs appeal to collective understanding and concerns relating to family subsistence, the well-being and future of children, and specific problems affecting workers, but they also provide a framework through which such concerns are interpreted in a causal fashion. This is crucial if the framing aspect of social movement culture is to invoke focused collective action.[25] Put simply, songs afforded workers a framework through which the similarity of their plight became increasingly obvious; they also shifted accountability away from the workers and toward the labor process and its beneficiaries.

Song and Efficacy

Music may be influential not only through its impact on collective experience and group identity, but also because it serves as a guiding force in addressing grievances.

About one-quarter of these songs (ten, or 28.6 percent) suggest no clear-cut solution, while seven (20 percent), suggest an individualistic escape, such as marriage, death, or moving back to the mountains, as do these lyrics from "Factory Girl":

> Yonder stands that spinning-room boss
> He looks so short and stout,
> I'm going to marry a country boy
> Before this year goes out.

(CHORUS)
Pity me all day, pity me I pray,
Pity me my darling, and take me far away.

I'll bid you factory girls farewell
Come see me if you can,
I'm gonna quit this factory work
And marry me a fine young man.

It is notable, however, that more than half (eighteen, or 51.4 percent) suggest a collective political solution (strike and union mobilization). Again, language is largely inclusive, referring to "we," "our," and "fellow workers." Some lyrics, such as these from "Here We Rest," attempt to maintain solidarity in the face of strikebreaking by scabs:

We are standing on guard
Both night and day,
We are doing our best
To keep scabs away.
We are twelve hundred strong
And the strike still is on,
And the scabs still are standing
But they won't scab for long.

Some lyrics appeal to the worker's broad sense of commitment to his or her fellow workers, as exemplified in this verse from "On a Summer Eve":

If we love our brothers as we all should do,
We'll join this union, help fight it through.
We all know the boss don't care if we live or die,
He'd rather see us hang on the gallows high.

Although songs of the mill experience by no means provide a monolithic message, interpretation, or solution, some tendencies within them are worth reiterating. First, many of these songs describe in quite detailed fashion the grievances and hardships of mill workers. Some of the hardship was personal and had to do with the work process and its physical and mental toll. Much of it also had to do with difficulties in providing for one's family and children. Blame is attributed throughout to the difficult nature of mill work and, perhaps more important, to greed and mistreatment by owners and mill supervisors. Finally, in terms of addressing the problems outlined, the majority of these songs lay out a collective solution pertaining to millworker mobilization.

Conclusion

Music was important for mill workers of the 1920s and 1930s. This importance was not merely owing to traveling musicians, the burgeoning recording industry, or the proliferation of radio stations through the South. Although these factors certainly helped disseminate and, in some sense, legitimate the music enjoyed by southern mill hands, mill music itself represented a contemporary expression of a preexistent Appalachian tradition, actuated within the constraints and circumstances in which southern mill workers now found themselves. It was, simply, indigenous in its origins rather than a newly created production of a labor union or social movement organization.[26]

The fact that many mill workers drew from their own preexisting repertoire is evidenced by their music's rich, intergenerational character and training, the setting of new lyrics to established tunes, and, most important, music's use in daily practice and ritual occasions. To be sure, much of the music mill workers listened to, played, and sang did not stray lyrically from its traditional form. It was nevertheless important in denoting identity and forging community through its ritualistic uses. The 1920s and 1930s saw its continuing use in this manner, but also the clear emergence of detailed lyrical themes dealing specifically with the mill work and mill-life experiences.[27] Whether rooted directly in tradition or altered lyrically, this music was, in its essence and use, ideology in concrete practice—practice that was, more often than not, community-based.[28]

Our analysis of patterns and lyrics has demonstrated the complex nature and substance of mill-worker songs. Many appealed to a collective understanding of job-specific problems, be they physical or emotional in nature, and an overarching concern for family and children. Moreover, many of these songs appealed to workers' sense of solidarity and social justice. Finally, they offered a valuable tool with which to recruit and/or maintain solidarity by specifying the concrete problems workers were facing and their causes.

The sharing of more insurgent themes within an existing cultural frame of reference, along with the dissemination of this music and more traditional tunes by traveling musicians and radio broadcasts, offered southern mill workers, perhaps for the first time, a sense of unity and solidarity that extended beyond the particulars of their own mill town. Given these facts, it should come as no surprise that music and song became an important tool in mill workers' protest repertoire once they engaged in strikes during the late 1920s and early 1930s—a topic to which we now turn.

6

Mill-Worker Consciousness, Music, and the Birth of Revolt

As the song rang out, the workers on the side lines began to draw nearer to our group. Their lips began to move; soon they were singing. Then we started to march again, two by two, two by two, the line growing longer and longer. The timid ones had been swayed by the militants; the revival spirit again gripped the crowd. From a window of one of the mills a worker shouted that the bosses had locked them in until quitting time but that they were coming out to join us. We answered with a cheer and sang louder, more sincerely than ever, "For the Union makes us strong" . . . *The strike was on.*

—Fred Beal

The year 1929 was a cornerstone in southern labor history, and a foreshadowing. Thousands of southern mill workers, often portrayed as lethargic or docile, walked off of their jobs in somewhat sporadic fashion, with little organizational resources, and in the face of powerful opposition from both mill owners and southern governors. The strikes themselves ended sometimes through very small concessions from owners, but, more often than not, through elite- and state-sponsored violence. Importantly, and despite the worker defeats that occurred, the 1929 strikes, particularly those in Gastonia and Marion, North Carolina, laid the groundwork, provided lessons, and aroused mill-worker consciousness throughout the region—a consciousness that would spread and intensify during the much larger General Textile Workers' Strike of 1934.

Prior to the Gastonia and Marion uprisings, a strike occurred in Elizabethton, Tennessee, and smaller strikes followed those in Gastonia and Marion. Yet, the strikes in these two North Carolina towns stand out as especially important. Within each emerged a clear repertoire of, and a solidaristic strategy that entailed, music and song. Gastonia, on the outskirts of Charlotte and its WBT radio, was fertile ground for the recruitment of musicians in the South. In fact, many of the musicians about whom we have already spoken came from Gastonia. It should thus come as no surprise that within this one town song was used as the cohesive force and battle cry for workers' rights.[1]

Marion, nestled in the remote mountains of western North Carolina, had a long-standing tradition of Appalachian culture and music. For this reason, many early radio musicians, such as Bill Monroe, "Pappy" Sherrill, and J. E. Mainer and his Mountaineers, would congregate outside the mill villages of Marion from time to time to play together, and share songs with the local residents.[2] On clear nights, Marion workers could pick up Charlotte's WBT radio over the airwaves or programming out of weaker stations in Asheville and Spindale, North Carolina.[3]

The traditional tunes and mill-related songs that became important to the strikers in Gastonia and Marion, it appears, may have been picked up, disseminated, and used by mill workers throughout the region.[4] At the very least, oppositional themes were highlighted and the use of music in workers' protests was established. Simply put, these earlier strikes activated an oppositional cultural blueprint that would further unfold in 1934.

Notable as well is the fact that workers in both locations began organizing prior to any systematic or formal involvement of unions.[5] Indeed, it was eventually workers themselves and their desire to organize and strike that brought the union in, rather than the reverse scenario where unions came in and tried to mobilize workers. Such incidents, which have occurred in other industries as well, challenge assumptions regarding the class-conscious character of American workers, or the lack thereof. Instead, an indigenous radicalism, along with related oppositional cultural repertoires, can and often do arise even in the most extreme and controlled situations, regardless of whether there is formal social movement organizational presence or resources. Although in both cases a union was eventually drawn in, it was only after workers' grievances and their desire to strike were established.

In the case of Gastonia, the organization that came in took the form of the Communist-led National Textile Workers Union (NTWU). In Marion, in contrast, workers recruited in the AFL's United Textile Workers (UTW). This divide in union presence was characteristic of most southern mill workers at the time. About a third who struck in 1929 had no formal union leadership, another third were associated with the NTWU, and the final third with the UTW.[6]

Despite this division in union affiliation, or the lack of affiliation, the 1929 strikes tended to unfold with workers taking the lead, and receiving little in the way of organizational support or resources from unions. Moreover, workers in Marion and Gastonia employed similar strategies and faced the same elite countermobilization and violence. These two towns consequently became the most visible southern mill towns in 1929, as seven mill workers and a sheriff were killed and the state militia was used to quell worker insurgency. The sociological relevance of these initial strikes lies in the fact that resistance unfolded in each despite considerable mill-owner power. Resistance was also internally driven within each rather than being forged by a union. Finally, both instances were rich in terms of oppositional cultural creation and use.

Music and the Development of Oppositional Culture in Two North Carolina Mill Towns

Marion and Gastonia were steeped in both textile work and music tradition. Marion had three large textile mills: East Marion, owned by the Baldwin family of Baltimore, Maryland, and two others, the Clinchfield and Cross mills. Gastonia's most visible Loray Mill, owned by Manville-Jencks of Rhode Island, was the largest mill in the South. Beyond the Loray Mill, Gastonia also had more than fifty smaller mills and the highest concentration of spindles of any county in the South.

Marion's location at the base of the Appalachian Mountains drew many workers from the hills. Some noted an independent streak especially among workers from the mountains, and attributed the radicalism that unfolded in Marion to these "mountain" populations.[7] In their move from the mountains, these workers also brought along their traditional music. Their songs addressed their everyday lives and Appalachian history. Now in Marion, their music was adapted to address their new reality of working in a textile mill and living in a mill village.

Along with workers, local musicians and those from the Charlotte area who were willing to make the trip typically congregated and played at Greasy Corners, the local hamburger grill adjacent to the East Marion Mill.[8] The Baucomb brothers of the Tobacco Tags radio and recording group, previous mill workers themselves, were from Marion. They later moved to Gastonia and traveled throughout the southeast with the burgeoning number of radio stations seeking live music. The Tobacco Tags even played at strike events.

The Monroe brothers likewise played in Marion, as did Jimmie Rodgers. Wade Mainer of the group J. E. Mainer and the Mountaineers noted that his brother, J. E., worked in the textile mills of Marion.[9]

Marion is on the main route between Hickory and Asheville and only eighty miles from Gastonia. It thus became a standard stop for musicians. Al Wall, who played with some of the earliest of southern radio figures, notes that Marion's location, jobs, and number of local musicians made it an ideal place for musicians to gather.[10] Along with worker grievances pertaining to paternalistic policies and the stretch-out, the deeply rooted Appalachian cultural tradition of many of those working in Marion and nearby towns, as well as the link to early, home-grown musicians, helped ensure that song would become a cohesive tool.

If Marion was geographically close to music and radio musicians, Gastonia was practically the core. Just outside of Charlotte, Gastonia was a hotbed of music and mountain migrants. With its high concentration of spindles, it also seemed to be a bastion of opportunity for job seekers. Recruiters for the mills often took advantage of this fact. Owners, however, quickly found out that with the implementation of the stretch-out their workers were not as compliant as they had hoped. Discontent was stirred, and it ran deep.

Many who migrated to Gastonia were steeped in traditional music and its thematic legacy of protest and the hard life, so song became the grievance outlet for many, and small musical groups within the Gastonia mill complex began to perform. These mill musicians of the 1920s were usually second-generation mill workers. Notable among them was Dave McCarn, who was born in Gaston County and worked in the mill as a young boy. In 1930, he wrote and recorded "Cotton Mill Colic," a song about the consequences of life in the mills. Malone (2002, 35) notes that "Performers who previously worked in the cotton mills, such as David McCarn and Howard and Dorsey Dixon, or who grew up in mill families, have in fact constituted the single largest body of occupational-derived performers in country music." The chorus to "Cotton Mill Colic" expresses McCarn's feelings about the cotton mill as a means to make a living:

> I'm a-gonna starve and everybody will
> You can't make a living in cotton mill.

The recording of "Cotton Mill Colic" sold out quickly in Gastonia and became popular throughout the textile belt. McCarn never took the pursuit of music as an occupation too seriously, although he did record a few songs with other Gastonia musicians called the Yellow Jackets.[11] He saw music largely as a diversion from the drudgery of mill work.

Other musicians came out of Gastonia and became famous within the region. "Whitey" Grant of the Briarhoppers was one such celebrity. He recollects the notoriety some of the music received and its reception in the village:

> Some good musicians come out of [mill towns] . . . I knew several of those [Tobacco Tags] . . . A lot of the boys that we knew, or heard of, after we came in formed bands and they would get together in the cotton mills and the first thing you know they would form bands . . . On Saturday or Sunday, when the mill wasn't running, they had a little band stand up there and draw a big crowd.

> Wilmer Watts and the Lonely Eagles of Gaston county recorded "Cotton Mill Blues" for Paramount. He "moved to Belmont in Gaston County seeking work after World War I. Watts spent his entire adult life in the mills, at times, a skilled loomfixer, but he left his mark as a spirited string-band musician rather than as a textile hand."[12]

Musicians like McCarn, Watts, and the members of the Tobacco Tags performed for mill-worker audiences, and often sang songs about life in the cotton mills. These songs did not praise the work, but rather pointed out its problems. Poor working conditions, the stretch-out, cotton dust, long hours, low pay, and unreasonable supervisors were key themes. Their songs resonated with other mill workers, partially because of these themes, but also because these musicians themselves were seen as mill workers, with credible claims, who often met workers face-to-face as they traveled.

The class-conscious character of the music appealed to mill worker's tastes, while at the same time speaking to their sense of discontent. Some from Marion and Gastonia, such as Watts, McCarn, and the Tobacco Tags, traveled throughout the region and had firsthand experiences as mill workers. Others, such as Ella May Wiggins and Sam Finley, had no professional experience as musicians but nevertheless sang songs of solidarity and resistance within their mill villages. In doing so, they became leaders to their fellow workers. An oppositional culture was no doubt already present in Gastonia and Marion, but the musicians who performed and created the new songs helped forge, if not legitimate, this protest repertoire, something that became important in the strikes and those that would follow in 1934.

The Gastonia Strike

Gastonia had the largest mill in the South, the Loray Mill, owned and operated by Manville-Jencks Corporation of Rhode Island. Many other nearby mills, including those in Bessemer City, were also involved in the strikes that unfolded in 1929. Conditions were much the same as those at other southern mills: twelve-hour shifts, five days a week, and half a day on Saturday. Paternalism prevailed, according to historian Thomas Tippett (1931, 68), who witnessed Gastonia firsthand in 1929:

> The company store and credit system kept most of the employees in debt to the mill. There were company boarding houses, company churches, and a company playground. The cotton mill dominated every phase of life in the village which it owned, body and soul.

The Manville-Jencks Corporation recruited the poorest people it could find for its Loray Mill. The hope was that lower wages could be paid, and that desperate workers would be the least likely to cause trouble.[13] Indeed, many were from elsewhere. Their families moved to Gaston County specifically to seek work. This recruitment from outside set up a situation whereby locals developed a clear sense of "us and them." Town folk, who often worked in service industries or held more supervisory jobs in the mills, saw the workers as "trash" or "lint heads," owing to the cotton dust that stuck in their hair. Many local farmers likewise saw those engaging in mill work as a lower order of worker and citizen, if not outright sellouts. Many of those working in Gastonia's mills felt torn about the move themselves, as many came from the blighted farms of the southern Piedmont.

The mill villages of Gastonia were much like Erving Goffman's total institution, with strict control in most facets of daily life, and where one might be expected to abide by the confines of a particular role (in this case, mill worker).[14] But, these mill workers were not like Goffman's mental patients. Despite significant constraint and control, they possessed a spirit of individualism that rivaled even that of the local middle class. Many had been small, yeoman farmers from the Piedmont and mountains, or their parents had been. The outsider's perspective on the mill worker as a docile and compliant laggard was a misconception—one that would soon fall by the wayside.

By the late 1920s, owners of the Loray Mill charged their managers with the task of increasing profits, even in the face of a downturned economy. The stretch-out system was consequently instituted, resulting in more work for some and no work for others; many workers were laid off. This policy also prevailed in other mills. Workers quickly came to resent the stretch-out system, with its oppressive supervisors, long hours, and low wages. The promise of a good life in the cotton mills had brought many of them from the hills and mountains adjacent to Gastonia. Yet, this promise remained unfulfilled. A disheartened and often angry workforce grew tired and began to organize and seek help. This led to social upheaval on a scale never before seen in this small southern town. As a precursor, fifty workers had already staged a wildcat strike a year earlier, in 1928.[15]

The bigger strike at the Loray Mill began on April 1, 1929. Workers went on strike over conditions in the mill and the villages that made their lives nearly unbearable at times. Although there was NTWU presence in the form of organizer Fred Beal, it was a local worker, Will Truet, who was "itching for action" and who organized workers initially for a meeting with Beal. Beal recounts mill workers' native radicalism:

> A capable fellow, this Will Truet; in one hour he somehow managed to notify all the membership of the day-shift about the meeting without going near the mill . . . I had spoken in a conversational manner, as one person to another, but the reply I received was more like a mass-meeting. The room turned into a bedlam of shouts and whoops. There were cries of "Strike Now! Strike Now! We've Suffered Enough!"[16]

NTWU involvement was moderate at best, and NTWU resources devoted to the unfolding Gastonia strike were minuscule given the size and importance of the campaign.[17] Beal himself notes these facts along with Gastonia workers' own desire for insurgent action in his recollections of what occurred. Efforts a decade earlier by the AFL-affiliated United Textile Workers in Gastonia focused more on negotiations with management than on strike action—a fact that workers remembered, and that lingered in their sense of betrayal and anger. Aside from their past experience with the UTW, the Gastonia workers did not really know what the differences were between the two unions. What they did know is that they wanted collective action and a walkout, and the NTWU and Fred Beal specifically assured them that their take on the situation, and their desire to strike, were legitimate.

Following the firing of several workers for attending an open meeting, workers began to congregate in the small union hall. Beal recollects what occurred:

> They got in the corner and sang hymns . . . They marched around the side of the hall singing whatever songs came to their minds. From experience I knew the tremendous value of singing the right songs on the picket line. These workers knew none of the union's strike songs. To overcome this, I typed a number of copies of Solidarity . . . Since the bosses had already fired a large number of workers, I asked the night workers, at the conclusion of my speech, for a strike vote. The vote was unanimous,

many putting up both hands. There was great enthusiasm, whoops and mountaineers' yells, the like of which I had never heard.[18]

During the first strike day, all was quiet and orderly, with approximately 1,800 of 2,200 workers taking part in the strike. Strike demands included better working conditions, no more piecework, a five-day work week, an eight-hour workday, repairs to company-owned houses, and recognition of the union.[19] The relatively peaceful beginning of the strike changed as interactions between the strikers and law enforcement became less cordial. Soon, the atmosphere was highly charged and leaders on both sides became more determined—the strikers to change the mills and the mill owners and law enforcement to enforce the status quo. The atmosphere in Gastonia would only intensify as time wore on, and as red-scare rhetoric was increasingly espoused by the *Gastonia Gazette*.

The *Gastonia Gazette* was instrumental in raising the pitch of the debate and creating a outside menace, fueled by red-scare fanaticism. Soon, all who struck were seen as being outside agitators, rather than locals who just wanted fair working conditions. That there was any NTWU presence only made the situation worse, as the paper charged that the strike was not about grievances felt by local workers, but rather reflected the manipulation of local workers by outside agitators and Communists. The paper's editorial page spewed forth foul accusations against anyone associated with the strike, and based its critique on ideologically slanted coverage presented in the Communist *Daily Worker*. Perhaps most well known in this regard were the *Gazette*'s editorials titled "A Deep Laid Scheme" and "Red Russianism Lifts Its Gory Hands Right Here in Gastonia."

Such editorials created public aggression toward strikers, caused workers to question their own national and religious loyalties, and had long-term consequences for southern attitudes toward organized labor.[20] The irony is that most workers were simply protesting unfair conditions rather than defending or fighting for a broader ideological stance,[21] a fact that Fred Beal was aware of and respected, but that nevertheless caused tension between him and Communist Party leaders.[22] Despite the red-scare strategy used by elites, letters poured into the Gastonia NTWU headquarters from nearby towns "begging" for someone to help organize their mills.[23] Within Gastonia, striking workers maintained solidarity through nightly meetings. The use of song, and the charismatic appeal of Ella May Wiggins, a worker, balladeer, and mother, undoubtedly helped in this regard and reinvigorated workers.[24]

They [nightly meetings] were interspersed with songs, reports from other strike areas, and tales of local incidents between strikers and the bossmen. No evening passed without getting a new song from our Ella May, the minstrel of our strike. She would stand somewhere in the corner, chewing tobacco or snuff and fumbling over notes. Suddenly someone would call for her to sing and other voices would take up the suggestion . . . The crowd would join in with an old refrain and Ella May would add verse after verse to her song. From these singers would drift into spirituals or hymns and many a "praise the Lord" would resound through the quiet night.[25]

Ella May penned approximately ten songs that would be used throughout the strike. Along with songs by Gastonia mill children such as Odell Corley and previous Gastonia workers turned musician such as Dave McCarn and Wilmer Watts, the songs by Wiggins resonated with mill workers' experiences.[26] Particularly impressive was the interplay of exploitation themes and concerns for one's children—something that resonated with most and that came from Wiggins's own experience of losing four of her children to pellagra.

Not only was song used on the picket line and in mass meetings, but it was also used among those who were arrested and taken to jail. Vera Buch Weisbord recalls sitting in a Gastonia jail cell one night with other female strikers:

> We sang a lot: "Solidarity Forever," the "Passaic Battle" hymn, the words of which we told them had been adapted by our union leader, Albert Weisbord, "The Red Flag," and some Wobbly songs. The strikers sang their own beautiful plaintive ballads, "Barbry Allen" and many more. It was time for unburdening a lot of grievances, personal histories and confessions, all very revelatory and important for Amy and myself. I wish I could remember all that was told, for we became much closer to the Loray strikers during that long night.[27]

Within one week of the strike's beginning, Governor Gardner, a North Carolina mill owner himself, sent in five companies of state militia. Skirmishes erupted between picketers and militiamen on a regular basis, as troops patrolled the streets and attempted to end all forms of picketing. Strikers responded by holding meetings and setting up a relief depot on the outskirts of the village. Local courts attempted to forbid this, and any union meetings, by issuing injunctions against any union activity whatsoever. State militia and local police enforced these injunctions through violence and mass arrests. According to Tippett's (1931, 87) eyewitness account:

> Their reaction to this unwarranted brutality is one of the most outstanding phases of the struggle. Their parades were broken up by force every

Figure 14. Two female strikers attempt to disarm National Guardsman sent to protect the Loray Mill. Courtesy Bettmann/Corbis.

day, and just as consistently the strikers would form again the following day to march, with full knowledge of what they were doing, into the clubs and rifles.

A local owner-sponsored mob, known as the "Committee of One-Hundred," tore down the union hall where supplies were kept. They smashed the building to bits and spread the supplies on the ground, covering them with chemicals. National Guardsmen sleeping a short distance away did nothing to stop the destruction but showed up later and arrested some of the strikers who were on hand.[28] The viciousness of this raid helped the strikers gain some sympathy from outsider organizations and newspapers in Greensboro and Raleigh, North Carolina. The American Civil Liberties Union was brought in to defend workers' right to organize and protest. Mill-owner power nevertheless went relatively unchallenged when, on May 6, eighty-five families were evicted from their mill housing. In response, evicted strikers formed a tent city outside of town. The land, described by Vera Buch Weisbord (1974) as "free land," was not owned by the company.

By June, hunger and desperation had arrived in the tent colony. Many began crossing the picket line to return to work, although these workers

Figure 15. The Howitzer Company of the 120th Infantry of the North Carolina National Guard, on duty on the grounds of the Loray Mill. Courtesy Bettmann/Corbis.

Figure 16. William Truitt and his family after eviction from their company-owned home by police deputies. Courtesy Bettmann/Corbis.

also periodically staged scab walkouts to disrupt production. On June 7, a mass march on the union ground was disrupted by the throwing of eggs and rocks. Later that evening, during a skirmish between a few striking workers at union headquarters and a few deputies, the chief of police, Aderholt, was shot and killed. Sixteen strikers and leaders, including Fred Beal, were arrested on charges of murder and conspiracy to murder. None were ever indicted for firing the shot that killed Aderholt, although all of them, thirteen men and three women, spent the summer in prison awaiting what would become a sensational and nationally viewed trial. Charges against nine were eventually dropped, and, despite a weak case, the other seven were found guilty and sentenced to five to twenty years of hard labor.[29]

Figure 17. Cover of the September 1929 issue of Labor Defender. *Courtesy Bettmann/Corbis.*

During the trial, the Committee of One-Hundred continued to terrorize the tent colony of striking mill workers, threatened, beat, and chased out of town any organizers, and threatened the lives of defense attorneys. The workers, in response, planned a massive rally on September 14 near the Loray Mill, which would include those from neighboring mill towns such as Bessemer City where conditions were described as even worse than those in Gastonia. An armed mob responded by blocking roads to Gastonia and targeted the truck carrying balladeer and mill mother Ella May Wiggins, who was subsequently shot and killed. A picture of her surviving five children was printed on the cover of the *Gastonia Gazette* the next morning. A mass funeral was held by striking workers in Bessemer City, at which her songs about the mill workers' plight, including "Toiling on Life's Pilgrim Pathway," "Chief Aderholt," "The Big Fat Boss and the Workers," and "Two Little Strikers," were sung. Perhaps the song that resonated most was "Mill Mother's Lament," sung by a fellow female striker standing next to her grave as others listened and sang along.[30]

Violence against strikers and organizers continued throughout the fall of 1929. The North Carolina supreme court upheld the convictions and sentences of the seven accused of killing chief Aderholt, while all of those put on trial for killing Ella May Wiggins were acquitted within two weeks. According to Tippet (1931, 108), the strike had been devastated and defeated by winter:

> There was no open activity of the National Textile Workers. The union had been driven completely underground. The huge Manville-Jencks mill was working its usual 12-hour shifts; the wages had been further reduced; the operatives were as undernourished and as miserable as before the strike. Ella May Wiggins was the only one at peace. The tent colony was no more; the old union hall remained. From an improvised flag pole nailed on its side the stars and stripes were flying in the breeze. The flag had been run up there by the Committee of 100 to indicate to the world that the Loray cotton mill and America had won.

The Marion Strike

Workers at the East Marion and Clinchfield mills were at their wit's end in the summer of 1929, much like their compatriots in mill towns like Gastonia and over the mountains in Elizabethton, Tennessee. Conditions at the mills and in the villages were poor. Both mills were controlled by outside owners from the North who cared little about the conditions, and whose presence in the mill village was a limited occurrence. This is in contrast to those working in the Cross Mill, a mill locally owned by the Cross family, who were perceived by workers as caring and as part of the mill workers' community.[31]

The conditions in Marion were some of the worst in the industry.[32] Author and journalist Sinclair Lewis was in Marion that summer and described the situation that workers faced, noting the dilapidated housing, poor nutrition, and an insurmountable cycle of debt to the company store. Sicknesses such as tuberculosis and pellagra were rampant.[33] Despite being much smaller than Gastonia, Marion grew as a focal point for the national press and media as nearly 25 percent of the city's population of eight thousand went on strike in the summer of 1929. Even more notable was the killing of six strikers by the local sheriff and his deputies.

As was the case in both Gastonia and Elizabethton, worker dissatisfaction and the stretch-out, rather than mere union presence, undergirded workers' desire to stage a walkout. In fact, Marion workers went out of their way to find an organizer who would help them plan the strike they desired. Radio and newspaper reports of what was occurring in both Elizabethton and Gastonia offered some sense to mill operatives in Marion that they could change their situation. Three operatives made their way over the mountains to Elizabethton seeking advice and help.

> They just kept tightening down on people. And Roy Price, and Lee and another fellow, Ashton, talked to a man over there at the labor camper. And he couldn't help us much, but he told us where to go to find this union organizer, Fred Hoffman. There was a strike at that time in Elizabethton, Tenn. We went over there to find out what to do, and he come back with us, and started to organize. Well, they took in anybody that wanted to join.[34]

Unlike those striking in Gastonia, Marion workers recruited into their town Alfred Hoffman, an organizer of the AFL's United Textile Workers, who warned workers about affiliating or associating with Communists as the Gastonia strikers had done.[35] Despite the difference in union presence, however, workers' desired strategy of walking out, their strike demands, and the elite countermobilization they experienced were strikingly similar.[36]

By mid-June, enough workers at the Clinchfield and East Marion plants had signed with the union and began to hold open meetings. Because a larger segment of the East Marion Mill was organized (nearly three-quarters versus about 20 percent at Clinchfield), initial attention and resources were devoted to the East Marion Mill. The two mill villages nevertheless shared information and took part in meetings and rallies throughout.[37] The re-

sponse of R. W. Baldwin, a Baltimore lawyer and owner of the East Marion
Mill, was swift. He called a meeting of all of his employees in which he
made a speech with not so thinly veiled threats. Red Hall, a worker at the
East Marion Mill, recalls:

> Well, Mr. Baldwin, he wanted to make a speech to all the mill. We
> knew he was gonna do it that day. And he shut the mill down. And they
> brought two big horses up there, and put boards on it. He was a short
> feller, a lawyer, like I said, a Baltimore lawyer. And they set him up on
> that. And people was standing in the mill grass and sitting in the mill
> grass. I got me a seat down on the bank, where I could hear it, every bit
> of it. He wouldn't speak till he sent and got Hoffman [UTW organizer].
> He [Hoffman] was staying at the hotel. So, some of them, they brought
> him over there. And he [Hoffman] was standing up beside him [Baldwin]
> before he spoke. He [Baldwin] got to speaking and he told what all the
> company had done. He said, "We pay as good a wage as we can. We hope
> to pay more and we can sometime." But he said, "Things is tough right
> now." He said, "We built this building out here for people to use, a place
> for your kids to play, gotta place for them to go to church and school."
> Well, he made a good speech. But, then he said, "Why do you want to
> give this son of a bitch [Hoffman] your money?"

Baldwin's reaction to the union meetings was to hire company spies to create
a list of those involved, and to fire them immediately. Sam Finley remembers
the moment when he was told to leave the mill:

> When I come into work that evening, the supervisor met me at the
> door and had my pay. And he handed it to me. And I said: "What's this
> for?" "Oh," he says, "you know what it's for." "No," I said, "but I'd like
> to know." I says, "Is my work satisfactory?" "Absolutely perfect; there's
> nothing wrong with it." "Well," I says, "What did I do?" He says, "It's for
> joining that union and getting uppity too." I said: "Well, I admit to join-
> ing the union." I said: "But I have not been trying to get uppity." "Well,"
> I says, "I've got nothing else to do now but . . . " "Oh, don't do that." I
> said, "Well, you've left me nothing else to do."

Union meetings continued nightly as more and more workers were
laid off at the East Marion plant. In a futile effort to remedy the situation,
mill workers attempted to meet with Baldwin, but were simply ridiculed.
Such events precipitated the July 21 walkout by the East Marion workers,
despite the direction and efforts of national AFL president McMahon and

local organizer Hoffman to prevent the strike. Indeed, aside from Hoffman's presence, the AFL office of the United Textile Workers provided little, if any, support to the Marion strikers.[38]

Strikers in East Marion nevertheless drew strength and solidarity from both religion and song, much as their counterparts in Gastonia had done. The generation of a cohesive, oppositional culture expressed through song first became apparent at their nightly meetings:

> The people themselves were expressing the sensation of industrial freedom for the first time in their lives. Hymns from their churches were sung at the strike meetings, and were later transcribed into the songs of the strike. Religious emotions too were transferred into the labor struggle. A striker would rise to speak, and in his zeal for the brotherhood of unionism he used the very terms of a church revival meeting.[39]

The picket lines that formed around the mill gates were likewise situations where song was used to express unity and solidarity and, like Ella May in Gastonia, local leaders and balladeers such as Sam Finley emerged.

> Every evening, they'd meet down there at the mill and this old flat-bedded truck. They'd put some chairs up on it. Old Sam Finley, he'd get a guitar and he come up to our house and stop and sing. They'd sing some of them songs they made up. They'd say "Old Dory Wood" (that was Mrs. Wood, she was such a good woman), said "Old Dory Wood, she'd join us if she could. Old Mr. Yellowdog, take him away." And they talk about Jim Law and the boss Cautheron. They'd sing, "Old Man Loftin, he drinks his capedine, but we won't let him sit on the picket line. He just a yellow dog, take him away."[40]

Others sang for striking workers but, according to Red Hall, preferred not to be quite so visible to mill managers and owners.

> Now, they made a song about the stretch-out system. Seem like them Hall boys come out with it. Jay, Hugh, and Jerry and his other brother, they was together. They got them to singing up here at the café one night. We was up there. They said, "How about singing that song?" They said, "Well, shut the door." They couldn't let nobody hear it. They was . . . they worked at the mill. They talked about the old stretching out. They said, "the elevator, it won't stretch."

Although free space in which to assert grievances was harder to find in Marion than Gastonia, workers nevertheless found safe locations in which to do so. They also shared songs at Greasy Corners, the local hamburger joint, with traveling radio musicians, according to Al Wall, an early radio entertainer.[41] Perhaps this is why Marion strikers, along with singing their own ballads, sang more popular mill tunes such as "Factory Girl," "Cotton Mill Girl," and "Hard Times in Here."[42]

Historian Thomas Tippett (1931, 292) recalls that it was not only the balladeers that sang, but all workers on the picket line:

> Everyone who participated in the early part of the Marion strike will remember those days—the picket lines at night with their camp-fires burning; the women and men stationed there chanting re-written Negro spirituals across the darkness to inspire faith and courage; the mass meetings oftentimes in a downpour of rain, and the strikers singing.

In the early days of the strike, workers from the East Marion Mill would stage parades between their mill village and that of the Clinchfield Mill, with "thousands of singing workers in line."[43] Although Clinchfield supervisor Hart did not initially taunt or fire his union employees the way Baldwin did in East Marion, he began to lay off union employees by late July and, sensing a walkout, locked the doors to the plant. When he tried to reopen the plant on August 19, employees of the Clinchfield Mill staged a picket and joined the strikers of East Marion. While the AFL largely turned a cold shoulder to the strikers,[44] the strikers did receive some limited support from other organizations, such as Brookwood Labor College, the Federal Council of Churches, the Quakers, and the Young Women's Christian Association. Most pressing was food, for which strikers predominantly relied on sympathetic farmers on the outskirts of town.[45] Mill owners, in response, sought court injunctions against strikers and spurred the governor to send in the National Guard, which he did.

Strikers responded to the repressive presence of National Guardsmen, and efforts to halt their picketing, by trying to keep those crossing the picket line from sleeping. They did so by throwing dynamite on lawns and driving through the mill villages late into the night, singing and shouting from the back of trucks.[46] Eventually, the National Guard set up in the East Marion village, essentially suppressing all strike activity in what amounted to control by force and martial law. Officially, the strike was called off on September 11, when a settlement was reached. The settlement entailed a "gentlemen's agreement" to reemploy striking workers, except for twelve whom Baldwin did not want back, and a reduction from sixty-five to fifty-five hours a week (with a corresponding reduction in pay). Hoffman of the

UTW left Marion that evening and left John Peel, a UTW organizer, to handle the aftermath. National Guard troops were likewise removed and Baldwin returned to Baltimore.[47]

Almost immediately following the agreement, Hart of the Clinchfield Mill and Hunt, superintendent of the East Marion Mill, disregarded the terms of the agreement or simply added names to their blacklist of people they would refuse to employ. More than a hundred strikers at the East Marion plant were refused reemployment. With Peel at a national UTW meeting in South Carolina and more union workers being denied work, Baldwin returned to Marion, met several times with the local sheriff, and stationed several deputies around the East Marion Mill. A spontaneous strike occurred in the middle of the night, when a weaver was reprimanded for union activity. Workers left the plant, marched through the village, and left some stationed outside to let the morning shift know another strike was on. The sheriff, in response, deputized and armed several mill supervisors.

By morning, workers were picketing the mill entrance against the sheriff's orders, while operatives for the morning shift refused to cross the picket line. What occurred next has been debated widely, although it appears that Sheriff Adkins released tear gas near the face of a sixty-five-year-old striker, who began to grapple with the sheriff. Deputies opened fire on the crowd, injuring twenty-five seriously and killing six, just two weeks after the murder of Ella May Wiggins in Gastonia.[48] Evictions from company-owned housing followed shortly thereafter.

National news reporters rushed to Marion from Gastonia. Union forces swore out warrants for the mill superintendent, the sheriff, and his fifteen deputies. During the trial, deputies claimed that they shot back in self-defense, although no gun was found among the workers and all of those killed were shot in the back. Not one mill official or deputy was hurt. At the first hearing, all were released, with the exception of seven deputies, who were later found not guilty. In a mass funeral on October 4, the slain workers were buried without the presence or participation of local ministers.[49]

Following the shooting of workers and the funerals that followed, union activity came to a standstill. Petitions to get the governor to undertake a special investigation fell on deaf ears. The union essentially divested itself from organizing more workers. Those who had participated in the strike had no protection whatsoever from the massive blacklist that was generated and that continued to be used against the children and grandchildren of the Marion strikers as late as the 1990s.[50] This is not to suggest that the insurgent spirit of Marion strikers was quelled, but rather that the union itself lost interest and hope. The mill community in Marion was certainly

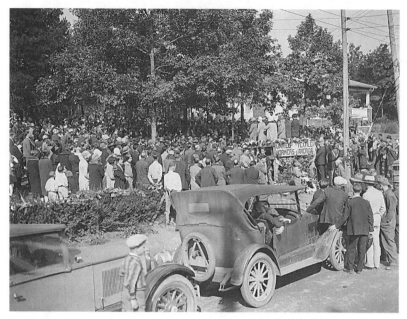

Figure 18. Community funeral for slain Marion strikers. Courtesy Bettmann/Corbis.

torn and in pain,[51] although many, according to Tippett (1931, 166–67), understood why they had to stand up against the mill barons and did not regret expressing themselves collectively.

> Never once did we hear a word of regret or bitterness because of their struggle. And we would talk of other things to remove the specter of their plight. But the strike always crept in. We might be swimming or rowing boats—way out into the lake under a cool moon. From another boat or on the shore some ex-striker would send across the water the opening bar of one of the old strike songs, it would be picked up by others in the water—and soon the old strike meetings, the old parades, the whole spirit of their lost struggle would animate the lake and live again. In their souls the Marion strikers still retain hope.

Conclusion

Despite the defeats in Gastonia and Marion, the two strikes hold theoretical relevance for those interested in strike action and insurgency, while also providing practical implications for those wishing to understand the union organization and strike activity that would occur in the South into the early

1930s. Indeed, many of the dynamics that played out in Gastonia and Marion in 1929, including the native radicalism of workers, the creation of their own oppositional cultural practices, limited union involvement and support, and the manipulation and use of state coercive apparatuses by local elites, would play out on a much grander scale in the years to come.

The desire of workers to take action was internally driven rather than being forged by a particular union. In Gastonia, workers were practically organized and most assuredly had discussed the possibility of a walkout before NTWU organizer Fred Beal even arrived. In Marion, workers similarly discussed the possibility among themselves and then sought the formal organizational advice of the United Textile Workers. These facts run counter to certain assumptions about American workers. Such assumptions include the view that unions radicalize workers and convince them to walk out. Another is that American workers, and particularly those from the South, are conservative, if not incapable of expressing, through words or action, their class character and interests. Marion and Gastonia workers, living in the relatively oppressive and controlled confines of the southern mill village, saw, for a moment in history, the possibility of collective revolt, even if that revolt was merely of the reformatory variety. The two quite ideologically distinct unions that were drawn into the fray generally followed the workers' lead, although, in the case of Marion, actually attempted to quell workers' desire to walk out. That southern workers were or are conservative, or that they somehow disliked or distrusted northern unions, is not supported by the evidence and firsthand accounts.

The radicalism that unfolded in each case was, interestingly enough, forged and expressed through preexisting cultural practices, most notably music and singing—practices that reach far back into Appalachian mountain culture, leisure-time activities, and political-economic expression. Some of this was spurred on by very early traveling mill musicians, such as Charlie Poole, and later by others such as Dave McCarn, the Tobacco Tags, and Wilmer Watts. By 1929, many of these musicians, beyond traveling for personal appearances, began to find a new outlet through records and the earliest radio stations at the time, which were just beginning to discover and disseminate "hillbilly" music. The interim period, between the 1929 strikes and the massive 1934 strike, would witness many more station foundings in the textile belt and more radio airtime being taken by ex-mill musicians, who would share and play traditional and mill-specific songs over the southern airwaves.

Music was part of everyday cultural practice and identity building among mill workers. This translated into grievance sharing while on the job and, as the cases of Gastonia and Marion demonstrate, into oppositional expression at mass meetings, while on the picket line, and even during periods of defeat and death. That a balladeer and mill mother would become the martyr and symbol of the Gastonia struggle, and that another singer and union leader would be specifically targeted by Marion deputies,[52] speaks not only to the centrality of song and the charismatic and emotional power of singers, but also to mill owners' awareness of those posing the greatest threat to their interests. The centrality of song would only intensify later, as more ex-mill musicians cut records and received airtime, and songs forged in these earlier struggles, including one called "The Marion Massacre," would become popular across mill communities.

Although one might expect that the violence occurring in Marion and Gastonia, and the media publicity surrounding it, would sway workers in the region from undertaking such action themselves, historical accounts suggest that this was not the case. Rather, the two campaigns and the grievances and demands that were shared, if anything, invoked further mill-worker identity and consciousness. For example, a strike broke out in Danville less than a year later, and that same year, other workers in Marion, Gastonia, and many other mill towns approached UTW organizers to start an organizing drive. The union however, having suffered defeats in Marion and Elizabethton and running low on resources, essentially turned the workers away.

> A committee from there came for a second time to request an organizer. A group had signed up and applied for a charter. The United Textile Workers, fearing a strike, did not send one. Thus various opportunities for useful union activity were allowed to slip by largely because of the lack of a union policy and leadership.[53]

That the courts, the state militia, local deputies, and mill-sponsored mobs suppressed the strikes speaks quite clearly to the strength of southern mill owners. The governor of North Carolina, a mill owner himself, not only provided national guardsmen for the defense of the mills and their property, but chose not to intervene or forge any form of investigation of what occurred. His rationale had to do with the power of mill owners statewide[54]—a power that would remain intact and that would be drawn upon again during the 1934 strike.[55]

Although this southern elite power dynamic did not change in the aftermath of the 1929 strikes, the election of Franklin D. Roosevelt, and his use of radio in the interim period of 1933 and 1934, did seemingly alter the leverage of mill workers throughout the entire textile region. His radio fireside chats, which workers looked forward to hearing, gave them the sense that federal power and authority were now on their side. Many workers, increasingly connected through radio, political broadcasts, and a common music, now looked beyond the confines of their one mill village toward a broader southern community of textile workers and their friend in the White House. As one observer of the 1929 strikes forecast:

> A new labor renaissance is at hand. The American Federation of Labor can take it or leave it alone, but down underneath the southern unrest is a germ with a will to live that neither mobs nor massacres nor prisons can extinguish.[56]

In 1934, the spirit of the 1929 strikers would indeed be rekindled, and on a magnificent scale.

7

The General Textile Strike of 1934

I can't understand why my dad didn't tell me. He could talk about the war and talk about people being blown to bits but he couldn't talk about his neighbors being killed. And it's like somebody trying to hide a dirty secret about their family, like they're ashamed of what happened to their families. They ought to be proud of 'em, they stood up when other people wouldn't.
—Kathy Lamb

The solidarity and strikes of 1929, and the violence that occurred, were not ignored by mill workers across the region, nor were they forgotten. Despite the use of National Guardsmen and the violence that erupted, as well as the persistent blacklisting of those that struck, southern mill-worker oppositional consciousness and solidarity only escalated into the 1930s. The emergence of a broader-based solidarity and its impact on the massive 1934 strike, as we argue in this chapter, had more to do with the burgeoning of radio in the interim years, and the expression of both oppositional consciousness and political opportunity over the airwaves, than with active support or organizing by unions. Indeed, the Communist-led NTWU was all but chased out of the South with the Gastonia defeat. And, although the AFL's United Textile Workers eventually represented the hundreds of thousands of southern workers, it was southern workers' native radicalism that would lead to the walkout, force UTW involvement, and promote intra- and intercommunity solidarity through two notable strike innovations: "flying squadrons" and "dancing pickets."[1]

We begin this chapter by discussing the interim years, the mounting of workers' grievances, and the dissemination of oppositional consciousness. Especially important was the increasing popularity and spread of radio between 1929 and 1934. With more station foundings in the southern textile belt, increasing numbers escaped cotton-mill work to become professional musicians, and found an audience among southern listeners—listeners who would periodically request oppositional mill music. These musicians, as noted earlier, maintained personal contact with those in the mill and linked otherwise dispersed villages by undertaking live performances. This began much earlier, of course, but became especially true between 1932 and 1934 as music presented as "hillbilly" explicitly made its way onto the southern airwaves and found a large and vocal southern mill hand audience. What was an indigenous oppositional consciousness in 1929, often expressed and fostered through music in a particular mill town or during a certain strike, now traversed the confines of a singular mill village.

As important as native consciousness and cultural expression was the rise in power and the election of Franklin Roosevelt in the interim years. Roosevelt began his radio fireside chats in 1933, which communicated to southern workers that a national political force was now on their side. Beyond workers' view that they had the right to collectively organize, workers now believed that the federal government, and Roosevelt in particular, would provide a buffer against local elites and mill owners' use of state political apparatuses (state militia and state courts) against strikers as they did in 1929. Consequently, mill workers' sense of possibility escalated relative to the earlier waves of protest and now extended throughout the textile belt.

The Dissemination of Oppositional Consciousness and Political Opportunity: 1929–34

Strike activity between 1929 and 1934 was sporadic. The tragedies of Gastonia and Marion played heavy on the minds and hearts of southern mill hands. Yet, discontent remained intact and, if anything, intensified. Workers in villages outside of Burlington and in Hickory, North Carolina, for instance, staged periodic walkouts without any union presence.[2] Others, throughout South Carolina and North Carolina, attempted to rekindle the spirit and organization of the Gastonia and Marion strikers, but to little avail. A strike in Danville, Virginia, in 1930 was short-lived, but strikers nevertheless shared some of the same grievances expressed in other mill towns. As noted in chapter 6, the song "Cotton Mill Colic" became very popular among Danville workers.[3] This is notable given that the song's author, Dave McCarn, was an ex-mill hand not from Danville, but from

Gastonia. The song's popularity in Gastonia, Danville, and the rest of the region was a testimony to its broad-based appeal and the spread of music concerning the plight of mill workers. In certain cases, authorities actually moved to prevent workers from singing it.[4] Other musicians similarly recorded and performed songs pertaining to the mill experience and struggle. One group, the Martin Brothers, noted for their live radio barn-dance appearances, quickly recorded and performed the song "The Marion Massacre" in 1930—a song that chronicled the killing of workers by deputies during that strike.

The period between 1929 and 1934 was especially important for generating an audience through recordings, radio appearances, and live performances. "Pappy" Sherrill was playing with the Monroe Brothers, among others, at WPTF radio in Raleigh before moving to play on a Danville station. He recalled another group of textile workers turned radio and recording group, the Tobacco Tags, playing at strike events around Danville at this time. The Baucomb brothers, the two founding members of the group, were born in Marion and then moved to Gastonia as adults to work in the cotton mills. They grew up in the southern mill village and spent much of their adult lives working in the mills or playing for textile mill workers.[5]

By the beginning of 1934, the hillbilly music craze was in full swing. Barn dances were all the rage and musicians played old-time music to please their primarily mill-worker audiences. The popularity of this music intensified the musicians' travels and gave them the opportunity to reach more people. WBT radio in Charlotte, North Carolina, was the hub of the southern Piedmont. The station realized the potential of music that appealed to the mill hands and began featuring such music more and more. In the fall of 1934, about a month before the general strike, Crazy Water Crystals' Barn Dance went on the air with host Fisher Hendley. One of the most popular acts on WBT and other North Carolina stations was the Dixon Brothers, whose "Weave Room Blues" spoke to the difficulty mill workers faced trying to make ends meet. The song was so popular that Hendley also recorded a version of the song, and then broadcast it often when he moved from Charlotte to Columbia, South Carolina, to host his own show on WIS radio.

These musicians acted as cultural conduits, both directly and indirectly, between mill villages in the southern Piedmont. This only intensified over time with more stations, recording contracts, and opportunities to perform live between radio stints. These musicians functioned, for all intents and purposes, as "traveling evangelists," given their role in social movement linkages and spatial diffusion, by carrying messages, by spreading ideology, and by building personal relationships across the network.[6] Although this was no means the only way commonality and community were shared, it is certainly the case that these performers understood and sympathized with the plight of the mill worker. "Pappy" Sherrill, for instance, recalling his own escape from mill life, recollected how he continually "felt sorry" for the folks working in the mills.[7]

Mill-related music and its often oppositional character traversed the constraints associated with paternalism and the confines of a solitary mill village in the early to mid-1930s. The music was an innovation and extension of preexisting Appalachian cultural practice and tradition. It was realized in day-to-day life and leisure-time activities, and became all the more apparent during moments of resistance and mobilization. This was obvious in earlier strikes, such as those in Gastonia, Marion, and Danville. By the early 1930s, however, the modern medium of radio directly and indirectly allowed mill-oriented music, including music that was clearly oppositional in character, to be disseminated more widely than ever before.

The spread of radio and the fostering of musicians' networks were just two of the changes occurring with implications for mill-worker mobilization. The new medium of radio was also changing the way politicians and others in power reached the people, with implications for mill workers' sense of political opportunity and efficacy. Franklin Delano Roosevelt's fireside chats were extremely popular and spoke to the needs of his constituents, including the hardworking but poor mill hands of the South. The rise of Roosevelt to national prominence, his chats, and his popularity and support by southern mill hands occurred between 1929 and 1934.

Soon after FDR's inauguration in 1933, he began a hundred-day burst of legislative reform. By June 1933, he signed the National Industrial Recovery Act (NIRA). This bill gave mill workers the right to push for decent hours and working conditions through collective bargaining, while section 7a afforded a minimum wage, a forty-hour workweek, and the prohibition of child labor. The radio strengthened his voice on these matters and afforded him popular and political leverage to push through the changes. Consequently, he was revered in the southern cotton mill villages like no other.[8] Although his actions may have served a catalytic function in the massive strike of 1934, by most accounts this was not Roosevelt's hope or intention. Perhaps Roosevelt, like the unions and the mill owners, underestimated the southern mill worker. According to William Leuchtenburg:

> Essentially a "patron" of labor, Roosevelt had far more interest in developing social legislation to help the workers than in seeing those gains secured through unions.[9]

The impact of Roosevelt's radio speeches and New Deal legislation on southern mill workers nevertheless cannot be underestimated. Workers of the South listened to him intently, as witnessed by investigator Martha Gellhorn, held him in the highest regard, and were confident that he believed in their right to collectively organize if treated unjustly. These feelings were confirmed by the implementation of New Deal policies, which boosted mill workers' emotions as their lives, at least initially, took a turn for the better. As one recounts:

> In '33 is when Roosevelt was elected and that's when things—well, they was on the bottom then. Most everything was closed down. But they come out with this NIRA and Roosevelt, when he was elected, they started up mills and people started getting jobs. The wage scale and everything gradually started going up then.[10]

Mill-owner response to the legislation, in the face of a desire for greater profits, was swift and simple: intensification of the stretch-out that had begun earlier. Workers, feeling that they now had some leverage in the form of a president, not to mention an important avenue of social, political, and economic complaint, wrote and complained to Roosevelt and his administration directly.

> The Pacolet Mills Mfg. Co. is violating the code by speeding up. The spinning dep't has been speeded up two (2) times and are working people to death . . . They keep stretching out on a small scale in different parts of the mill affecting a few hands at a time.[11]

Beyond trying to make Roosevelt aware of the stretch-out, workers went out of their way to report specific violations of the NIRA and the textile code. Such violations included, in the workers' view, elite sanctioning of those who attempted to organize into unions. Mill hands, such as Mae Wise, now believed they had the right to do so via Roosevelt's words and legislation:

> The GM won't recogn. the collective bargaining . . . I joined the union when the NIRA was made law and I was discharged 12 days after the 8 hr. day went into effect.

The fact that Roosevelt received thousands of such letters reflects worker optimism that the federal government would intervene on their behalf and that their complaints and desire to collectively organize were not only legitimate, but legal. This fact distinguishes the 1934 strike period from the earlier 1929 strike events. Workers themselves were aware of this difference and counted on this new federal leverage. According to one:

Organizing in the textile mills didn't really start with section 7a; it had started earlier than that in places like Elizabethton, Marion, and Gastonia, North Carolina. But, all their attempts over there were futile, and no wonder they were. The bosses were against 'em, we had no protection whatever, but when we got section 7a, then we had protection and we felt we had the right to organize. And along with those rights, we were given dignity, well, we considered it dignity when we were no longer called "cotton mill hands" and "lint heads," we're textile workers.[12]

The dignity about which this worker speaks, the recognition of southern textile workers by a president, and an interpretation that offered mill workers the right (and protection) to collectively organize would ultimately spur the massive worker response in 1934 to owner abuses, political and paternalistic control, and the stretch-out they now faced. Their response, although guided somewhat by the United Textile Workers, had its own indigenous origins.

The insurgency that unfolded was, nevertheless, complicated by prior experiences with unions, fear of job loss, variations in managerial style, mill-owner power, and geographic separation. Indeed, attention to such matters provides some explanatory leverage when it comes to why many workers had misgivings about strike action and why some individual workers and mill communities did not participate in the 1934 strike. The suggestion we offer, most broadly, is that factors conducive to social movement participation and formation, such as information flow, consciousness and grievances, perceptions of opportunity, and even the availability of resources, may be mitigated in certain instances by workers' cost calculations as well as their more day-to-day interactions and experiences within their particular mill village.

Worker Organization, Radio, and the Strike of 1934

Many southern mill hands felt a kinship with local radio musicians, the president, and other mill workers across the region by 1934. The horrible legacy of violence of 1929 was not forgotten, but a president's backing gave them an outlet of complaint against unfair treatment by mill owners. Moreover, the new medium of radio gave cotton-mill workers a larger sense of place and community than they had ever experienced. Indeed, it was *their* music that was popular and renowned throughout the region. Even the president listened to this music, both at the White House and as he vacationed in the mountains of Georgia.

These factors helped to spur hundreds of thousands of exploited and paternalistically controlled southern workers to push for, and then mount, the General Textile Strike of 1934, the largest strike in U.S. history up to that time. Nearly half a million workers went on strike.[13] Although the strike was national in character, and included big and highly publicized strikes in Lowell, Massachusetts, and Patterson, New Jersey, the majority of strikers were in the South as textile production was now concentrated there.

The road to the strike was a long one. Although it was not necessarily inevitable, key events occurred along the way that helped foster a social fabric conducive to unrest. Thomas Tippett noted that in the late 1920s and early 1930s, unions failed southern workers by not taking advantage of the indigenous discontent and workers' own drive to organize.[14] Following the 1929 strikes, southern workers would often search for union support and organization in vain. This was only exacerbated by the 1929 defeats as unions, including the AFL, virtually gave up on southern mill organizing and instead devoted resources to coal mining. Indigenous radicalism and unorganized insurgency inevitably emerged again, however, ultimately provoking UTW involvement.

Significant wildcat strikes began to occur in 1933. The Horse Creek Valley between Aiken, South Carolina, and Augusta, Georgia, provides an example.[15] Paul Fuller, a labor organizer from Brookwood Labor College and a Methodist Episcopal minister, took to the airwaves in Augusta to speak to workers.[16] By integrating Christian and patriotic discourse, he was able to counter the kind of red-scare rhetoric experienced by the Gastonia strikers. Fuller thereby helped to ensure both significant worker participation and popular support. Workers in Augusta were eventually able to reach agreements with their employers for a time.[17]

Strike activity intensified in early 1934. On February 12 a strike broke out at K. S. Tanners Stonecutter Mills in Spindale, North Carolina, near Asheville. Five months later, on July 14, a strike occurred in Guntersville, Alabama, and wildcat strikes soon rolled across the state involving twenty thousand workers. Southern workers, like their peers in the North who were already experiencing considerable strike activity, were clearly restless and would be willing to take matters into their own hands.[18] They wanted to organize, and often took it upon themselves to do so even without a union presence.

> Well, we figured that we could organize like some of the unions in the North and become strong enough to sustain our positions, and, uh, we could get a reasonable agreement with the companies on, on everything. When we first started organizing, we met over the company store in what was at the time also a theater. And, finally, the company gave us orders not to use their hall. So we built a hall over on a hill not too far from the

village. Hmm, well it felt good thinking that we gonna have a place now, we thought it'd be there forever.[19]

Such internal organizing activity and the willingness of mill hands in places like Alabama to engage in wildcat strikes forced the hand of the UTW. Since the incidents and defeats in places like Marion and Elizabethton, UTW leadership was tentative and skittish about southern workers and their desire to strike. According to historian George Calvin Waldrep (2000, 59):

> At Cowpens as in other countless mills, workers were on the verge of taking matters into their own hands in mid-1934, leaving the UTW with a difficult choice. The union could call a general strike—as it nearly did in June—and ride the crest of worker discontent to wherever it might lead, realizing the immense risk such a course of action would entail. Or the UTW could remain still and watch, for a third time, as its southern membership melted away. It was an unpalatable dilemma, but, from an organizational standpoint, one with a single solution: The union would have to go on strike with its members or else be repudiated entirely in the South.

Southern representatives met with other UTW delegates in New York City in August 1934. The southern workers were the most radical in calling for a strike.[20] They gave speeches telling others of their deplorable working conditions. The letter-writing campaign to the National Textile Labor Relations Board (also know as the Bruere Board, named after its chairman) was seen as a farce by southern workers, who expressed dwindling confidence that the federal and state boards would actually follow up on complaints. Instead, the board was seen as merely a tool of the mill owners. The board sent back form letters to the workers telling them their grievances were noted, and the board usually sided with the owners.[21] It is thus no surprise that southern workers felt compelled to collectively act, especially because working conditions had actually worsened for many.

The delegates to the UTW convention followed the lead of their southern membership and agreed to strike on September 1, 1934. Francis Gorman, the vice president of the UTW, was elected to lead the strike, in part because of UTW president Thomas F. McMahon's reluctance to react to the previous sporadic strikes in Alabama in 1933. Gorman's first effort aimed at getting the support of FDR. These efforts, however, were in vain. Roosevelt remained out of the negotiations at the request of his advisers. The Bruere Board quickly became an ineffectual body, and the problem of the potential strike was handed to the National Labor Relations Board (NLRB). George

Sloan, head of the Cotton Textile Institute (CTI), representing the mill owners, refused to talk to the NLRB or Gorman in spite of their requests. Mill owners were reasonably confident, given the low rate of unionization, that workers would not actually strike. Southern cotton-mill workers nevertheless began to organize their own locals with little, if any, UTW resources. According to Eula McGill, the organization of workers was "pretty well left up to the rank and filers."[22]

To the extent that radio mattered, it did so informally, through oppositional music and cultural content that linked communities, through consciousness raised through Roosevelt's addresses, and most directly through organizing broadcasts aimed at mill workers. Workers had already heard of the strikes in the region and other parts of the country. Now, Gorman along with others took to the airways. Gorman addressed mill workers a dozen times on NBC-affiliated stations and spun stories of massive union organization throughout the southeast, despite the reality that UTW presence was weak. Although many mill communities had already begun organizing themselves, others, who were on the fence, were now persuaded by what they heard. In referring to the organization of workers that was unfolding, one worker recalls:

> I didn't belong to the union. I wasn't for it nor against it, see. Until one time I heard a man speaking on the radio and he said, "Suppose you go into the mill tomorrow to do your job, and they's to tell you they didn't need you anymore? Who'd you turn to?" So I got to thinking about that. The next morning I asked one of the members for a card, and I signed that card, I went in.[23]

Despite what appeared to be a groundswell of support among southern mill workers, it remained unclear just how many would strike. Mill owners doubted many would walk off, UTW leadership remained uncertain, and mill workers themselves had no clear sense of whether the enthusiasm felt was particular to their one mill village or the entire region.

> And when the strike took place, overnight, overnight it, it was, uh . . . , a rush like a migration of people who suddenly had seen a new idea or a new light, and out they came. It amazed everybody.[24]

As workers garnered news from radio broadcasts and newspapers on the morning of September 3, their excitement escalated. This was owing, in part, to the realization that other mill workers across the region were, in fact, similar in wanting the action. Lucille Thornburgh recalls both her surprise and her enthusiasm:

At the beginning of the strike we didn't know how widespread it was going to be, and were really elated when we found out, you know, well, this is going on everywhere, everybody else is thinking just like we are.

Within a week, newspapers reported approximately four hundred thousand workers on strike. We have seen that there was a rise in stations during this period and their geographic proximity to the textile belt, as well as the significant ownership and listening patterns among mill workers. But to what extent was radio related to the strikes that unfolded? Figure 19 is a map of strike events across southern mill towns in 1934. It shows a significant concentration of strikes throughout the textile and radio belts discussed in chapter 2.

In fact, chi-squared and logistic regression analyses reveal that strikes were much more likely to occur in 1934 in mill towns that had their own radio station. Because transmissions extended beyond the limits of a particular city (twenty to forty miles, on average), the impact of having a radio station proximate to the city—that is, not in the city, but in the county or in an adjoining county—albeit weaker, is likewise significant.[25] It is clear that many southern mill workers lived and worked within the concentric rings of radio transmission. In conjunction with anecdotal and interview accounts of listening patterns and what was actually broadcast, this lends

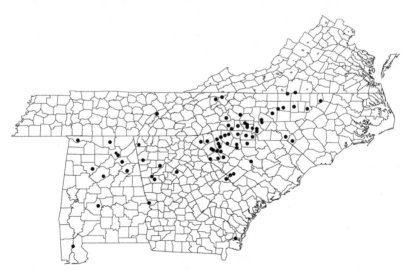

Figure 19. Dispersion of textile strike activity across the U.S. South, 1934. Sources: Hall et al. (1987), Nolan and Jones (1976), Salmond (1995), Simon (1998), Yellen (1936).

some support to the assertion that radio indeed helped foster the insurgency among workers.

The General Textile Strike of 1934 was the result of owner exploitation, unanswered worker grievances, and unmet government promises. Its extent was undoubtedly bolstered by the cultural and informational linking of mill workers in prior years, and now, through direct broadcasts of organizers such as Gorman. The use of radio would not end there, however. It would be used during the initial stages of the strike to mobilize and encourage more mill workers to walk off, and was the clear conduit for tactical sharing between leaders and rank-and-file strikers.

Mobilization, Oppositional Repertoires, and Community Cohesion and Tension

For southern mill workers, the National Recovery Administration eagle represented the freedom to organize and the backing of the federal government. Mill workers' raised expectations were much like those of African Americans after World War II. They expected, and were told, they would get a fair shake with federal backing, but they did not. The resulting sense of betrayal and discontent was evident in the strike action itself, as well as in the practice of indigenously bred protest repertoires.

Figure 20. Strikers participate in massive Labor Day rally and parade on the streets of Gastonia, North Carolina, 1934. Courtesy Bettmann/Corbis.

Workers utilized parades down main city streets to show their serious-ness at the initial stages, and made sure to utilize symbols of patriotism to en-sure that outsiders would not interpret their action as radical or Communist-oriented. Also, much like the 1929 cases of Gastonia and Marion, they made use of their own songs, created during earlier waves of protest, shared and spread by musicians and radio, and sometimes altered to describe the spe-cific situation or personalities in their own mill town.[26] The use of song as a protest tool was apparent during parades and on picket lines, helping to galvanize workers and foster solidarity within a given community.

> On that picket line, well, we did, we did everything good and right and bad [laughs] and, uh, everything like that but we didn't let 'em know we were worried, because we danced and well, sang . . .[27]

Reworked renditions of old songs, with a recognized melody, were popular, the new lyrics telling of the problems in the mill villages.[28] Spiritu-als were another musical outlet, since many mill workers legitimated their participation in religious terms, as the Christian thing to do.[29] Aside from using these songs during meetings and parades, an innovation appeared on the picket line called the "dancing picket." Rather than merely standing and picketing, strikers would dance to various songs in order to simultaneously express their solidarity and block the mill entrance. And, periodically, it was radio musicians, ex-mill workers themselves, who would travel to the mill town to provide music for the strikers. According to Al Wall, an early radio musician from Marion, North Carolina, it was during this time that "Country and folk groups were constantly on the move, supporting their fellow man in his strife with the cotton mill."[30] Music and dancing bol-stered strikers' sense of community and helped them deal with the tedium and fear they felt while on the picket lines. It also helped to counter any possibility that state militia or local deputies might construe mill-worker actions as threatening.

Strike and picket-line participation by women was notably high. Al-though one might conclude that this was because women and girls were paid less on average than their male counterparts, evidence suggests that other issues were more pressing. Women, it appears, were disproportion-ately victims of the stretch-out, and the layoffs that followed. And job security was an issue of particular concern for women, especially because taking time off for pregnancy or childbirth might mean being replaced at the mill. Like their compatriot Ella May Wiggins, who was killed five years earlier, women's grievances and strike participation were articulated more often as in the interest of their children and families.[31] Outsiders and

Figure 21. Musicians play for dancing strikers, blocking the entrance of the Clark Thread Mill near Austell, Georgia, 1934. Courtesy Walter P. Reuther Library, Wayne State University.

nonparticipants, in contrast, would view women's protest involvement in a negative light, as unwomanly and inappropriate.[32]

The fact that many mills struck, and that support for the strike and participation by mill workers was so high, should not obscure the reality that some mill communities did not take part at all in the strike. Even in mill communities where strikes occurred, some chose to cross the picket line. The reasons for nonparticipation are complex, and worth noting. Outside portrayals—portrayals that continue to characterize theoretical explanations of low unionization in the South—suggested that southern mill hands may have been too conservative, antiunion, or apathetic to mount any serious, collective action campaign. We disagree, and instead concur with in-depth historical explanations that delineate why some communities and workers did not participate. These explanations revolve not around a conservative psychology of mill workers, but rather the ways in which mill-owner power and expressions of that power directly and indirectly impacted workers' expression of discontent within the context of the 1934 strike.[33]

As noted in chapter 1, many mill villages were relatively isolated, in a geographic sense, and functioned in a paternalistic manner. Paternalistic

Figure 22. Strikers picketing the Cannon Textile Mill in Concord, North Carolina, jeer at nonstrikers as they arrive for work. Courtesy Bettmann/ Corbis.

practices were implemented to reduce labor mobility and afford owners some control over their workforce. Yet, workers' interpretations of this control varied significantly depending on how and if paternalistic sanctions (e.g., eviction) were utilized in the past, especially relative to union activity. With regard to sanctions, many mill workers, particularly those who were older and had small children to feed, were quite aware of earlier efforts of the UTW to organize southern mill hands in 1919 and 1920, and the evictions and blacklistings that ensued after the UTW pulled out. Those who recalled such sanctions, and the virtual disappearance of the union, despite understanding that workers had to do something, often stood back in fear of losing their jobs and housing in the face of an encroaching winter. Rather than conservatism or pure aversion to unionism, rational fear, informed by history, was the primary obstacle. As one worker recounted:

> But the old hands that'd been there all their lives, they wouldn't even talk about it, they weren't signing nothing. They didn't, they was afraid they'd lose their job, that was it. And they'd never worked nowhere else, and they didn't think they could get a job nowhere else. I really felt the same way.[34]

Workers' attitudes, grievances, and how they were expressed also varied depending on how owners and supervisors conducted themselves, and whether these owners and supervisors were integrated into the daily work routines and community lives of mill villages. Some workers, particularly those in more isolated villages, felt a sense of loyalty to their solitary mill village and its owners and supervisors.[35] This makes sense because paternalism in an isolated village would be more likely to foster a mill-specific identity, something bolstered by a history of employment, kinship, and lack of mobility in and out of the village. Owners and supervisors in such villages tended to be local people, with knowledge of kinship relations, social mores, and what, in the view of their workers, reflected appropriate supervisory behavior. Recollections of good, kind managers and owners weighed heavily in mill workers' decision making:

> They got the union over here at Pittsboro at the hosiery mill. And they made good money when we weren't making nothing. But everybody thought a lot of John London and Mr. London, the old hands did. I will never forget when Miss Lula Smith got to become sixty-five, she'd been there ever since she's just a little girl . . . When she retired, they give her fifty dollars . . . that's what he give her, just tickled her to death.[36]

Five years earlier, in Marion, one of the three larger mills, the Cross Mill, did not strike for this very reason. Workers at that mill saw Mr. Cross as a good neighbor, who treated workers with respect, and who knew and concerned himself with the well-being of each worker's family.[37] Some managers and owners in 1934 acted similarly in the eyes of their workers. Consequently, if workers at these mills had grievances, they were more likely to interpret them as a local issue that could be negotiated with their supervisor. The huge Burlington Mills of North Carolina hired a supervisory manager, J. C. Cowan, for this very reason. From western North Carolina, Cowan knew mill-worker culture. As such, he was able to push workers to work harder and faster, but in a way that did not violate their sense of dignity.[38] This is not to suggest that workers in such a situation would not engage in resistance. They did. However, their resistance took on a more informal, day-to-day character. Unlike the strike activity spanning mill villages now, workers in mills with a village-specific identity and sense of community with supervisors and owners found ways to negotiate the terms of the manager–worker relationship at their local mill.[39]

Despite fear, loyalty bred through both paternalistic isolation and trust, and severe sanctions such as firings, evictions, and blacklistings that unfolded once the strikes began, many mill communities did strike while others rode the fence on whether to walk out. Many communities not committing to the strike initially were, however, emboldened to take action and participate relatively early on because of an important, second strike innovation—the flying squadrons. The squadrons themselves were groups of mill hands who would travel in cars or trucks through the countryside to a mill that was still running.

Chanting, shouting, and singing mill songs, the squadrons, sometimes composed of fifty or more cars, would enter a village and either urge their fellow workers to walk out or run into the mill themselves and shut off the machinery.[40] They also reinforced pickets at smaller mills and "provided workers at wavering mills with precious moments of space and time in which to organize."[41] The importance of this tactic lay not only in its ability to empower workers through sheer numbers, through the sharing of cultural tradition, and by intimidating mill owners by creating an air of mass revolution, but also in its inter-mill character. For the first time, through the flying squadrons, the consciousness and identity of many southern mill workers, rather than being tied to a specific mill town, took on a regional and intercommunity character—a fact that posed perhaps the most serious threat to mill owner hegemony to date.[42]

Just how the squadrons came into existence and were implemented as a tactic is unclear, although it appears that they initially emerged from the workers themselves. Joe Jacobs recalls:

> They started coming out of it [the mills] so fast you couldn't keep up with it. So we sat down and started thinking, well, why don't we get a group of people together and go, have them go from one mill to another, "flying squadrons," and help bring 'em out of the plant. When they brought 'em out, sign 'em up and we'll get a flying squadron in this area, and that we can cover a lot more than the handful of organizers.[43]

UTW vice president Gorman, informed of what was occurring and somewhat surprised at southern mill workers' enthusiasm, jumped on the opportunity and, according to historian Jacquelyn Hall and her colleagues (1987, 329),

> took his cue from the rising generation of Millhands. He went on the radio, gaining hours of air time at no expense. He encouraged "flying squadrons" of cars and trucks to speed through the countryside—and they did, closing mills so rapidly that "tabulators almost lost check."

The flying squadrons met a quick state response within the first week of the strike. Mill owners spurred southern governors to employ National Guardsmen not only to protect mills and those crossing the picket line, but, in several cases, to intercept, arrest, and incarcerate flying-squadron participants. In the case of Georgia, martial law was declared and flying-squadron participants in Newnan were caught on the roadways, arrested, and put in

Figure 23. Mill workers gather and observe the National Guard's camp outside a mill in Charlotte, North Carolina. A few moments after this picture was taken, an altercation with guardsmen resulted in the bayoneting of two mill hands. Courtesy Bettmann/Corbis.

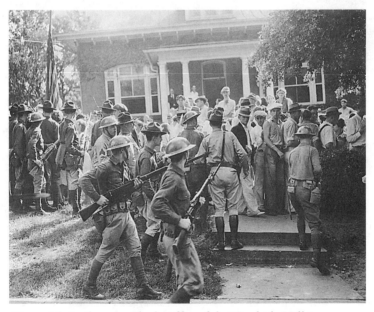

Figure 24. Strikers outside the office of the Woodside Mill in Greenville, South Carolina, give way to the bayonets of National Guardsmen. Courtesy Bettmann/Corbis.

an internment camp. Once rounded up, they were placed behind barbed wire, and forced to wear the uniforms once used for German prisoners during World War I. In other cases, National Guardsmen, with machine guns, rifles, and bayonets, simply created an intimidating presence on the picket line, often tussling with strikers. In several instances, picket-line altercations ended in bayonet stabbings, serious injury, and eventual death.

More dangerous than the presence of the National Guard were situations of escalating intensity, with no guard presence, wherein armed local police and deputized mill workers defended the mill against strikers. In the most notorious case, occurring in Honea Path, South Carolina, police and armed mill workers, fearing the presence of the flying squadron, shot strikers in the back as they fled. Six workers died and several were seriously injured. The extent that mill communities were now linked, and that mill workers saw their community in broader terms, is evidenced by the funeral for the slain strikers, attended by ten thousand mill workers from the region. As at Marion and Gastonia, workers sang at the burials.[44]

Figure 25. Flying squadron of mill workers captured by the Georgia National Guard in Newnan, Georgia, to be sent to an internment camp at Fort McPherson, near Atlanta. Courtesy Bettmann/Corbis.

Figure 26. Women textile workers imprisoned for strike activity by Georgia National Guard. Courtesy Bettmann/Corbis.

Figure 27. Funeral for Ernest Riley in Mount Holly, North Carolina. Riley, a mill worker, was killed by a National Guardsman's bayonet in Belmont. More than ten thousand mill hands from the region attended the funeral mass. Courtesy Bettmann/Corbis.

The impact of this incident, and its effect on striker confidence and tension across and within communities, was immense. Sol Stetin recalls the mood of workers:

> Well, it created fear in the hearts of the workers, no question about that. They were afraid, they were afraid of their jobs, they were afraid of their livelihood, they were afraid for their children. And the federal government stood by and, and permitted this to go on. That was a terrible image of our country, to have something like this.[45]

With the escalating tension, the deaths of several strikers, and internment of squadron participants in Georgia, the UTW leadership began to question the use of flying squadrons, perhaps out of concern for worker well-being. However, UTW leaders also lacked adequate control over the locally led squadrons and feared that further internment of squadron participants or more striker deaths would be perceived of nationally and regionally as evidence of UTW defeat. Whatever the rationale, the UTW's southern vice president, John Peel, issued an order one week into the strike that flying-squadron activity be halted—a decision that had demoralizing consequences for striking southern workers, and that effectively fragmented the regional (as opposed to mill-specific) nature of their struggle.[46]

Into the second week of the strike, and following the UTW decision to prohibit flying squadrons, union resources began to dwindle and many workers began to cross the picket line. Those who remained on strike were forced to rely on the support and food of local farmers, and began to seriously question what the union leadership and federal government were going to do. What they were hoping for, according to Waldrep, was a general right to organize and reemployment without discrimination.[47]

Roosevelt proposed the Winant Settlement, along with an appeal to southern mill hands. The settlement proposed reemployment of the strikers, replacement of the Bruere Board with the Textile Labor Relations Board, and an investigation of the stretch-out. Three weeks into the strike, on September 24, the UTW leadership accepted the proposal and the strike was officially ended. Unfortunately for striking workers, there was no procedure in place for carrying out the Winant Settlement. Thus, while the national UTW leadership claimed total victory, many southern mill workers returned to work that Monday morning only to realize that they had no jobs and that southern mill owners were, in fact, victorious. Moreover, mill communities were now torn, and would remain so for generations.

The Aftermath and Conclusion

The General Textile Strike of 1934—a strike on a scale never before seen in the South, and never seen since—lasted only three weeks. Southern workers provoked UTW involvement and, despite little power and resources compared to mill owners, mounted the beginnings of a mass disruption of the existing order. Unlike earlier organizing campaigns in the South, many mill workers, although by no means all, for the first time interpreted their grievances and saw their plight in a broader context. This was owing, in large part, to the burgeoning industry and medium of radio. Radio culturally and politically linked these workers to one another as never before, and was more directly commandeered for informational and tactical diffusion during the strike itself.

Radio bolstered new strategies of resistance and the use of preexisting cultural forms of expression. Tactics such as singing and dancing enlivened worker solidarity and reinvigorated picket lines throughout the course of the strike. Although not necessarily new relative to previous strikes, hillbilly music, including music pertaining to mill life and that was sometimes oppositional in nature, was more widely distributed across the region in 1934. It offered tired, poor, discontented mill hands a common culture and language that cut across the boundaries of space. Dancing pickets extended the use of music within the context of protest. Beyond the immediate goal of blocking mill entrances, dancing pickets provided a ritualized, collective expression of empowerment and community celebration in the face of struggle.

Flying squadrons similarly provided important functions. Most obviously, they boosted confidence through sheer numbers, reinforced the battle lines, and sent a signal to mill owners throughout the region. More important, however, squadrons of mill hands reflected and reinforced intercommunity solidarity over regional issues—a fact that clearly distinguishes the strike of 1934 as unique compared to earlier mill-specific strikes, and that underscores the importance of this historical moment in U.S. and regional labor history.

That the strike itself failed, and that workers suffered sanctions in the aftermath, speaks to the power and resolve of mill owners and the determination of southern legislatures and governors to keep unions out of the region. Immediately following the Winant agreement, many who participated not only found themselves without a job, but discovered that they were blacklisted from mill employment more generally. Marion "Peanut" Brown recalls workers showing back up at the mill for work:

When they start hiring them back, they come up, they come up to the office desk, you know, and you'd give 'em the name, they'd look on the list, if he was on the list it was "Good-bye Charlie," see? They wouldn't, wouldn't hire you back. They had on there whatever you'd done. All the things you'd said.

Some strikers were taken back only on condition that they sign an agreement never to mention or join the union again. Others refused. Consequently, according to Laura Beard, they suffered immediate eviction and unemployment:

They went around to all those with a, a letter. That if we would, uh, sign that letter that we would never mention the word union ever again in the plant, that they could work. And all we that did not sign it are the ones that didn't have a job . . . They laid off the ones that didn't sign the paper, the ones that was in the plant houses they threw them out on the sidewalk, clothes and all . . . One particular family I'll never forget, they had a little invalid boy twelve years old, they had four little girl—little children, they set them in the rain, with that baby on the cot, and watched him die. That's right. You can go up and down that street there in the cotton mill village and all over town and find them, people on the sidewalks, on the streets and on the shelters, because they had no place to go, and no job.

The consequences of the strike impacted not only striking workers, but entire mill communities, which were now fractured along lines of striker and nonstriker. Hard feelings and memories of what occurred would persist for generations.[48] To the extent that antiunion sentiment emerged afterwards, it was only in relation to the violence and fracturing of community that resulted, rather than from workers' perceptions that unions are inherently bad or corrupt. What was good about the traditional, paternalistic mill village of the South—community, caring, and strong identity—had been unraveled, leading to discomfort and division between friends and kin.

In a thing like that, you know, you're stunned. You know how you'd feel if something had happened that . . . If somebody that you . . . Like her. How would you feel? It makes a bad feeling that you can't hardly explain, because its sad. And a lot of those people was very close, you know. A small place like that, you know about everybody.[49]

Lack of worker protections following the strike, and the relative silence of the UTW leadership, only exacerbated a return to the status quo. These factors also had the effect of muting oppositional tendencies and insurgent excitement that, only weeks earlier, had flooded through mill communities via flying squadrons and that had spread across the airwaves of southern radio. With the UTW's decision to end the squadrons, the struggle of southern workers reverted back to a local fight, something workers could not win. Just why the UTW bureaucratic leadership put a halt to the flying squadrons—an innovation that created excitement and mounting inter-mill enthusiasm and sense of community—continues to be speculative. What is not speculative, however, is that the decision drained the lifeblood of the massive mobilization and all but guaranteed worker defeat.[50]

The federal government had little power to intervene once the strike was over. Mill owners were free to act in their own interests, and certainly continued to do so at the expense of mill workers. As for the South more generally, it remained poor, and largely nonunion. Within ten years, the CIO, a union new to the southern field, would itself attempt to organize southern mill workers in what would be called "Operation Dixie." The table, however, had been set and "Operation Dixie" was largely defeated.[51] Mill-owner power was firmly entrenched. For their part, southern mill workers were still recovering from the not so distant violence and blacklistings of 1934. Businessmen and legislators went further in defining and ensuring a future nonunion South, helping push through the Taft-Hartley Act (1947), which banned the closed shop and allowed southern states to instigate "right-to-work" laws.[52] Southern workers' desire for collective organization and action, although not extinguished, was largely suppressed and would remain so for the remainder of the twentieth century.

Conclusion

They saw the union as a means of improving their lives in the mill where they made their living. And when the strike came along, they responded to it because they wanted a voice. And for a while, it was their voice. Some stayed with their philosophy of how they could improve themselves and others tried to blank it out.

—Joe Jacobs

Textile-worker mobilization in the U.S. South between 1929 and 1934 remains, to date, one of the biggest collective actions by working people. What is particularly astounding is that this mobilization seems to have occurred against all odds. Paternalistic control and the possibility of severe sanctions were the reality in most mill workers' lives, workers had little resources or political power on which to draw, and the formal organizational presence of a union, to the extent it was ever existent, was typically so only after worker radicalism was formulated. Workers drew from their own cultural tools, music in particular, in establishing and reinforcing an oppositional consciousness expressed in their daily lives, on picket lines, at strike meetings, and as they took part in flying squadrons in 1934. This consciousness and workers' own political efficacy at the time were constructed and then shared, directly and indirectly, through the new medium of radio.

In this Conclusion, we revisit the factors that drove southern mill hands to strike, tensions relating to paternalism that ushered in worker action in some communities but not others, and the role that locally molded oppositional culture and radio played. Short- and long-term consequences for mill workers, and for the South more generally, are also discussed. These foci, we suggest, are important in explaining the historical case, but are also informative with regard to sociological understanding of the labor process and resistance, working-class oppositional culture and music, political opportunity and aggrieved groups, and the role of media in social movement diffusion. The integration of these theoretical concerns with a historically embedded understanding of social action is essential to sociological models of collective struggle and conceptions of human agency and possibility.

Southern Textile-Worker Mobilization, 1929–34

Textile-worker mobilization in the late 1920s and early 1930s might seem an especially unusual occurrence. It certainly was for many mill owners, middle-class professionals, and southern politicians. Although some academics had predicted the unrest, others saw it as unlikely.[1] Nevertheless, a conflation of factors, not the least of which were paternalistic coercion, poverty, and the stretch-out, converged to a point wherein workers felt little option but to collectively organize and strike.

Particularly problematic for southern mill hands were poverty, long work hours, the well-being of their children, and illness. As expressed in a variety of songs, such as "Mill Mother's Lament," "Weave Room Blues," and "Cotton Mill Colic," mill workers felt at times as though they were literally fighting for their lives and the lives and futures of their children. Consequently, they resisted informally, and on an ongoing basis, by helping one another on the shop floor or simply moving on to another, possibly better, mill, if the opportunity arose.[2] Quitting, however, particularly when one had a family to feed, was only effective under loose labor market conditions. As unemployment rose, leaving became less of an option. To make matters worse, employers further stretched out the process of production in the face of New Deal legislation intended to make mill hands' lives and jobs more bearable.

The stretch-out, as indicated in the interview and correspondence material presented, was problematic in terms of its physical and psychological consequences. Moreover, the stretch-out process and the related appearance of efficiency experts represented a very real affront to worker dignity and pride. Many mill workers recalled enjoying the creative aspects of their work, but felt a sense of betrayal and mistrust by ownership and management when their work speed and efficiency were called into question.[3]

The structure of paternalism and paternalistic practices, evident in many mill villages at the time, created contradictory feelings about whether and how issues of exploitation could be addressed. On the one hand, the traditional mill village forged a specific identity and sense of community, usually through mill-sponsored programs such as baseball, sewing and quilting clubs, and churches. Consequently, workers in a given village often thought of themselves as "like a family."[4] To undertake insurgent action in such a context was paramount to taking part in the fracturing of community. Beyond the actual coercive power of paternalism and paternalistic sanctions and their depressant effects on worker activism, then, there was also a very real social cost having to do with the disruption of one's own community, often composed of kin, friends, and acquaintances. Many southern mill hands and mill villages—out of fear, distrust of unions, or the simple desire for community stability—did not strike. Others ultimately decided that walking out was worth the social and more tangible employment and monetary costs.

One of the key differences between villages that struck and those that did not had to do with the integration of owners and supervisors into the mill community and the general treatment of employees on the shop floor. Indeed, especially in cases where owners and supervisors were integrated into the village, strike action was less likely. Such supervisors were often viewed by workers as being part of the community themselves, with concerns for the well-being of their workers. In contrast, where supervisors and owners were somehow distant or isolated from the culture, concerns, and history of the workers they employed, mill hands were more likely to interpret the "community" benefits of paternalism more as a tool of manipulation and social control.

Regardless of variations that existed across mill communities and among workers themselves, significant strike action unfolded in 1929 and then on a much more pronounced scale in 1934. The historical evidence suggests that, rather than being driven by union presence, the insurgency that unfolded was propelled by a native radicalism, forged on the shop floor within mill communities themselves, expressed and bolstered by preexisting cultural repertoires. From the mountains and farms, workers brought to the mill village a distinct musical taste and style. The particular form of music that emerged was activated as an important celebratory and emotional tool, and knowledge of it was indicative of insider/outsider status. Many mill-specific songs that were oppositional in character also emerged during this era. These songs were shared and disseminated by early mill musicians and became important in the protest repertoires of strikers in Marion and Gastonia, North Carolina, in 1929. They were shared even more broadly across the region between

1929 and 1934, with the advent of radio, records, broadcasts, and live performances that catered to southern mill-town audiences. Perceptions of political opportunity and efficacy were spurred at roughly the same time with the broadcasts of a president and labor organizers. Such facts converged by 1934, fostering a sense of community and collective action potential that, for the first time, extended beyond the confines of any one mill town.

That mill workers' own radicalism was influential in 1934 is evidenced by the fact that mill hands across the region sought unions, rather than vice versa, and that they were willing to engage in walkouts with or without union representation. They did so on a large scale in Alabama and, to a lesser extent, in other southern states before the general strike. It was also southern workers who eventually pressured the UTW to back the strike. The UTW agreed to take part in a somewhat lukewarm manner, and with little in the way of actual resource commitment. Four hundred thousand southern workers walked off their jobs en masse in September, singing their own songs and implementing their own innovation, the dancing picket. Furthermore, and with UTW broadcasts coming usually after the fact, southern workers engaged in flying squadrons—a tactic that explicitly linked mill communities and that turned the struggle of southern mill hands into a regional and industry-wide fight. Mill workers' sense of political opportunity was heightened upon hearing Roosevelt's radio addresses, and was witnessed by their direct letter communications with the president's office prior to, during, and after the mobilization.

Despite the sheer magnitude of the strike, striking southern workers lost their struggle—a defeat that had immediate effects as well as long-term consequences for labor relations in the South. Mill-owner political power at local and state levels enabled them to control picket lines, intercept and incarcerate flying squadrons, and use violence against the strikers. Within the first week of the strike, the UTW leadership curbed the use of flying squadrons. In doing so, strike battles were relegated back to particular mill towns. This had devastating consequences for workers themselves, who saw little federal protection happening. They also began to wonder about their campaign, which, just one week earlier, had been a regional struggle that had mill owners seriously concerned, if not frightened. Some mill workers understandably began to return to work. Claiming victory, the UTW agreed to end the three-week strike with a promise of reemployment for striking workers and an investigation of the stretch-out. Protections and provisions for carrying out the agreement, however, did not exist.

In the short term, workers felt fearful; state- and elite-supported violence left many fighting for their lives, jobs, and futures. The deaths of mill workers in such places like Gastonia, Marion, and Honea Path left an ever-present possibility that it could happen to anyone, anywhere. Many were evicted, and many were blacklisted. Scars were apparent in mill communities themselves, with divisions between those who struck and those who did not. Such scars and community splits, according to one surviving mill worker from this era with whom we spoke, persisted for extended periods and continue to exist to this day for the children and grandchildren of those who struck.[5] Another worker recalls the pain:

> Everything in the South is handed down. It's like tradition . . . And the pain's been passed to them, and their children, and their children's children.[6]

Although some southern mill workers were radicalized by the experience and expressed pride in having stood up, many more were left with feelings of solitude, bitterness, and loss. It was, simply, an experience they did not want to revisit, and one that was not strictly tied to antiunionism. Many workers continued to see the usefulness and need for worker organization, but given their historical experiences and memories of divided communities, mill-owner power in the South, and defeat at the hands of militia, police, and the courts, they saw the probability of success as small compared to industries like steel, coal mining, automobile manufacturing, and trucking. One worker expressed such mixed feelings as follows:

> I've never worked under a union, and I don't think I ever would if I lived to be two hundred, from what I seen back in the thirties. But I know that in the better places, like these car factories and things, it helps the working people out. And they've tried to get in a lot of hospitals, and in a big hospital it might be right. But in a small place it don't work, because it just makes enemies among friends, is all it'll amount to in a little place.[7]

As a consequence of what had occurred, the docile and compliant workers the mill owners were once expecting had now become more of a reality. For many, fear replaced militancy, and this would dampen efforts to organize southern workers in the years to come. To be sure, union activity continued sporadically, beginning again in 1939 with Operation Dixie, led by the CIO's Textile Workers Union of America (TWUA).[8] Operation Dixie, however, never garnered the momentum of the 1934 strike, and the unionization of southern textile hands would remain a fleeting hope for the remainder of the twentieth century. The case we have discussed nevertheless provides useful sociological insights, to which we now turn.

Labor Process, Worker Resistance, and Unions

The contradictory feelings of southern mill hands in the 1920s and 1930s and the fact that some mill workers struck and others did not can inform our understanding of the labor process more broadly and its impact on worker attitudes and action. The structural context within which southern mill workers resisted was quite constrained, with mill-owner power travers-ing work, family, and community life. Under such controlled circumstances, and with poverty and debt prevalent, one should expect resistance strategies to emerge. At the same time, however, the paternalism exercised in the southern mill village also had benefits for workers, not the least of which was a sense of commonality, identity, and community. One can envision how such cohesion might provide social control for community members, including those contemplating radical action. It is equally plausible that community identity may provide the footing for solid, broad-based mobi-lization against an employer. Just which scenario unfolded, we believe, was patterned by social relations within the mill village and on the shop floor.

In more isolated mill villages, where owners and supervisors lived within the village and understood employee culture and workers' norms for what constituted legitimate managerial oversight, strikes were less likely. An out-side view might interpret this pattern as managerial domination over workers not only structurally, but socially as well. Such a characterization, however, would be insensitive to the actual interpersonal dynamics of manager–worker relations as they are played out on the shop floor. Interview materials pre-sented in this book, which include workers' own recollections, suggest that supervisor knowledge of workers' cultural and normative expectations al-lowed supervisors to effectively push production, but without overstepping the boundaries of fairness—as defined by workers themselves. Furthermore, some of the workers recalled that managers, aside from being fair, cared about their mill hands and their families, and would often help out when a family fell on hard times.[9] Whether it represented manipulation or not, the fact that supervisors understood workers' sensitivities, treated workers with respect, and showed interest in workers not just as employees but as friends, kin, and members of the same community afforded many mill hands re-spect, which counterbalanced, to some extent, problems such as poverty, long work hours, and poor work conditions.

That social relations on the shop floor can be just as meaningful to workers as structural aspects of production is not a new insight. Researchers such a Vallas (1987) and Hodson (1999, 2001) have noted the centrality of workplace social relations. Worker interpretations of fairness and what constitutes a good workplace, although certainly affected by the structural organization of work, will be shaped by treatment on the shop floor:

> Mismanagement, abuse, and supervisory fiat are principal contributors to worker resistance and are equally corrosive of worker citizenship. Mismanagement, abuse, and supervisory fiat also increase infighting among workers and undermine the foundations for solidarity and mutual assistance. Across a wide range of workplaces, employees are interested in taking pride in their work and gaining meaning from it. Mismanagement and abuse, however, rob them of this opportunity. (Hodson 2001, 260)

This is not to suggest, of course, that all mill workers or villages that did not actively engage in strike action were completely content with their lives in the mill and with their supervisors. Far from it. Inaction, probably more often than not, was a function of sanctions against potential insurgents, historical recollections of previous unionization attempts, and fear of losing one's job, home, and community.

Many mill workers, despite such constraints, did ultimately walk off the job. Although reasons for doing so varied significantly, poor wages, long work hours, and debt fostered through company credit and housing were among the principal grievances. The stretch-out especially appears to have been an insult to workers' sense of autonomy and dignity. Indeed, several recounted with disdain the efficiency expert looking over their shoulders, stopwatch and clipboard in hand. Although the gender division of labor did not play much of a part in fostering discontent, other issues did become salient to women in the mill. Among these were sexual harassment on the job and, even more pronounced, difficulties in parenting and ensuring the well-being of children in the face of low wages and long work shifts. Such grievances radicalized many mill hands even without an organized union presence.

That many southern mill workers began to radically interpret their situation, and that the insurgency that unfolded was forged by these workers themselves, speaks to our theoretical understanding of class consciousness among American and southern workers. It also speaks to the interplay of worker radicalism and labor unions. It is clear from historical evidence that during the era described, southern workers did, in fact, formulate a reformatory class consciousness—a fact that runs counter to models or theoretical speculations that portray southern workers as averse to collective action, or psychologically and politically conservative. Such depictions, sometimes accepted by researchers and sometimes adopted by labor unions themselves, have led to an ignoring of the South.[10] This is unfortunate and misleading. Kimeldorf's (1999) analysis of striking longshoremen and restaurant and hotel workers in the 1920s and 1930s likewise provides a notable exception, as well as an important alternative to such depictions of the American worker. A more cogent representation, we believe, is one in which class-based consciousness and action are seen as activated at particular historical junctures, driven by a confluence of structural, political, and cultural factors.[11] That it may not be explicit or apparent, as has been largely the case since the 1934 strike, does not imply that it does not exist or that worker conservatism rules the day.[12] Rather, as our case suggests, collective identity and action potential may be being suppressed by structural factors, a realization of history, or outright fear and sanctions.

Southern mill-worker consciousness and insurgency unfolded prior to union involvement. This fact turns the commonly accepted perception that unions formulate grievances or create a critical consciousness among workers on its head. Rather than unions forging radicalism among fragmented or detached workers, the cases of both Marion and Gastonia in 1929 suggest, more or less, the reverse. Radicalized workers, with an already-established sense of collective identity and efficacy, sought union organization on their own. By 1934, workers effectively organized their own locals, called wildcat strikes, and forced UTW involvement. Workers' own preexisting culture played a role throughout the course of these mobilizations. The Communist National Textile Workers Union, it appears, was more effective at explicitly encouraging the incorporation of workers' cultural strategies into the protest repertoire, whereas the UTW often attempted to curb action and keep workers' native radicalism in check. The case of Marion was informative and, perhaps, a foreshadowing of the role that the UTW would play later in 1934. In this earlier campaign, workers sought union representation and, often against the wishes of the union, walked off the job. Perhaps most telling is the fact that UTW leadership could not even be found in Marion when the second walkout and massacre of strikers took place. The UTW, in the face of this defeat, withdrew its remaining resources and turned away those from nearby villages that wanted a union.

The spread of radio in the interim years of 1929–34 offered one of the greatest potentials for broad-based textile industry organization as mill communities were now culturally linked, via traveling musicians who provided a shared identity. Furthermore, Roosevelt imparted confidence that workers had rights, including the right to collectively protest. Under such circumstances, it is notable that the UTW did not initiate a unionization drive in the South as it did in other industries and regions, at least until southern workers' own insurgent spirit forced the issue.

The fact that organizational presence seems not to have been paramount to

the formation of identity and the unfolding of collective action, suggests—
at least in this case—that processes central to social movement formation
may be quite distinct from those relevant to understanding movement
persistence or success. More specifically, it appears that clear-cut grievances, identity building, perceptions of opportunity, and some mechanism
of diffusion may bolster the likelihood of, if not create, a social movement
even without formal social movement organizational presence. Resources,
typically conceived of as being derived from formal organizational presence,
may not be entirely necessary at the early stages of social movement formation. Organizational presence, and the coordination and resources it affords,
nevertheless will prove essential to movement persistence and success over
time. These points perhaps explain why southern workers were able to
mount such a significant campaign, but were unable to sustain it.

Working-Class Oppositional Culture and Music

Beyond issues of class consciousness, worker radicalism, and unions, the case
of southern textile workers highlights the richness and strength of working-
class oppositional culture, and the role of music in particular. Music was
clearly important in the lives of southern mill hands, and provided a link to
their cultural and historical origins as well as to their broader sense of community. The cultural practice of musical expression was activated in workers'
daily lives, in their leisure-time activities, and even on the shop floor.

The use of traditional mountain and gospel music provided a preexisting cultural frame, rooted in ritual and expressed in collective celebration.
Such music, adapted to mill hands' new surroundings, increasingly took on
an explicitly critical character, with lyrics delineating grievances, identity,
and the capacity and call to action. Its use was evidenced within mill communities prior to strike activity, at strike meetings, on picket lines, during
dancing pickets, and among flying-squadron participants in 1934. Some of
this music, adapted from traditional Appalachian folk tunes, was created by
mill workers themselves such as Ella May Wiggins and Sam Finley during
the heat of their early struggles. By 1934, more traditional music and more
oppositional adaptations were being written and disseminated by ex-mill
workers turned musicians who recorded such songs, sometimes sang them
over the airwaves, and performed them live as they "barnstormed" mill towns
between radio stints.

Much of this music we described in chapter 5 provided a ritualized context in which to collectively express grievances. Indeed, workers sang and
played the music of their musician counterparts and met traveling ex-mill-
worker musicians with enthusiasm.[13] The more oppositional lyrics proved

important to social movement culture and mill workers' own repertoire. Specifically, most utilized the plural *we, us, our,* and *fellow workers,* thereby delineating identity and insider/outsider status. In their vivid depictions of mill life and worker grievances, they also provided an interpretation of cause and effect. Nearly all specified a human culprit (owners, supervisors, and police), and presented that culprit as malicious, greedy, and corrupt. Finally, the preponderance of these songs, and especially those that emerged just prior to and during the strikes, expressed a collective solution to the problems southern mill hands were experiencing. For social movement scholars such as Taylor and Whittier (1995), W. Gamson (1995), and Snow (2001), these three dimensions—identity, interpretational framing, and collective efficacy—are essential if social movement culture is to both resonate and play a part in collective mobilization.

Although our focus on music is consistent with theorizing on collective identity and social movement culture more broadly, it is notable that little systematic attention in the literature has been devoted to examining the role of music as an element of the social movement repertoire—one that provides a basis not only through which collective identity may be realized, but also in which an interpretational frame of cause and effect is offered to the listener. The targeting of balladeers during strike events, and the suppression of these songs after the defeat of the 1934 general strike, clearly speaks to music's centrality, importance, and power. Indeed, songs of textile life, complaining of the problems of the mill villages, quickly became taboo in many villages and remained so for years. The song "The Marion Massacre" by the Martin Brothers was not allowed to be played on the radio as late as the 1960s in Marion, North Carolina.[14] Others, like "Cotton Mill Man," were considered "too provocative" to be played on many radio stations in southern mill towns.[15]

Many ex-mill-worker musicians, particularly those who wrote oppositional music, fell by the wayside after 1934, were forced to return to mill work, and never could quite understand why they no longer received radio airtime or recording contracts.[16] Some would revisit this music later, and balladeers such as Ella May Wiggins became icons in the movement for workers' rights.[17] Pete Seeger would later record a series of oppositional mill songs,[18] and some have suggested that the mill music of the 1920s and 1930s had an influence on the protest songs of the 1960s.[19]

One might question whether the importance of music, and the centrality we accord it, is limited to textile workers or to one particular era of worker unrest. We do not believe so. In fact, during our data collection, we came across a significant amount of material highlighting the importance of music for a variety of historical struggles pertaining to class, race, and gender, and across a number of industries and geographic locations. It seems that many movements have had a well-developed repertoire of songs, utilized both before and during active, collective protest. Workplace and strike issues, for instance, have received notable attention and commentary in songs pertaining to the coal-mining industry, among others, and the importance of music is clearly a part of the African-American experience, from slave gospels, to blues lyrics, to contemporary societal critiques embedded within rap music.[20] Song likewise seems to have been central to the repertoires of other working-class movements—including striking longshoremen, lumbermen, steelworkers, and automobile workers—and for as long as we can tell.[21] What is lacking, despite archival collections and some historical accounts, are systematic analyses and substantive, sociological interpretations of these lyrics, if and when they are important, and how they are often tied to both stratification processes and efforts to remedy inequality.

It it is not merely oppositional lyrics, and the possible effects of lyrical content on cognition and understanding, that are influential. Certainly lyrics may be meaningful, but shared music and its activation on a community level may be meaningful in and of itself. Indeed, it was often traditional mountain or gospel tunes that southern mill workers reveled in, that delineated insider status, and that were used in the heat of protest and during workers' incarceration. Music in and of itself, without clearly defined oppositional lyrics, can be an act of identity expression, interpersonal connection, and community acknowledgment and celebration.

Much like worker consciousness and action, oppositional cultural frames and practices may not be apparent at all times. Rather, as suggested by Denisoff (1972) and Fantasia (1988), oppositional cultural repertoires are activated at particular historical junctures, and often when struggle becomes apparent. Often this activation is triggered and expressed by subordinated groups in response to battles over dignity and worth. When such battles are not apparent or explicitly being fought, oppositional culture or the possibility of oppositional cultural creation from preexisting practices and histories remains just below the surface.

That the literature on social movements has downplayed the possibility that even "old" social movements have rich cultural repertoires and identity dynamics is unfortunate. Perhaps part of the problem is that data and evidence of oppositional cultural processes, practices, and creations within "old" social movements are more difficult to come by given the historical nature of the case. Our case and the data on which our analyses are based nevertheless suggest that oppositional cultural-identity dynamics, interpretational framing, and collective efficacy were important for southern textile workers.

Political Opportunity and Mobilization

Political opportunity theory, as discussed at the beginning of this book, has been useful in specifying the importance of leverage and its historically contingent nature. What is often missing, however, is an explication of the mechanism(s) through which potential movement participants' perceptions of opportunity may be altered. Media, whether in an earlier historical era or the present day, is important in this process.[22] Radio stations in the South, the information that was disseminated over the airwaves, and the informal networks that it helped foster offered a mechanism through which mill workers' understanding of political opportunity was altered.

Mill workers perceived an opening in the political structure that was conducive to the seeking of workplace changes. Roosevelt, in his fireside chats, assured workers of their federal protections. Within this context, they believed they had the legal and federal right to lawfully organize. The NRA and the NIRA bolstered their confidence that indeed a new era of workers' rights was at hand. Combined with Roosevelt's support of working-class cultural programs and music, southern mill workers felt as though they had both a powerful ally and the protection of the federal government.

Although what was disseminated by radio fostered hope and enthusiasm, and indeed lent legitimacy to strike action, the hope that southern mill hands had and the opportunity they perceived proved largely hollow. The federal government sought negotiations with mill workers through the Bruere Board, which was controlled by the mill owners and their allies. FDR, though in sympathy with the workers and their plight, lacked the political power to battle mill owners. Had striking mill workers waited, it is conceivable that they might have had stronger legislation and protections on which to draw. As it turned out, however, the implementation of the textile code (section 7a) ultimately lay in the hands of southern states, whose governors and legislators were more apt to protect mill interests. Although Roosevelt and UTW leaders attempted to negotiate with owners through the collective bargaining facilities of the Bruere Board, mill owners had no desire, and the federal government little power, to force them to the table. Without the federal protection or strength they had hoped for and assumed, workers were vulnerable. Red-scare rhetoric, appeals to paternalism, and promises of a better future were used by the textile owners. When these did not work, threats of violence and use of sanctions were more convincing.

As important as Roosevelt's initial support and speeches were in fostering a sense of opportunity, a distinction must be made between actual and perceived political opportunity. This distinction is particularly important when the analytic focus is on movement success and those forces that persuade or dissuade social movement participation.[23] Where there is a disjuncture between the two, as in the case of southern textile mobilization, insurgency may indeed unfold, but its potential success will likely be curtailed by countermobilization. In the case of southern mill workers, perceptions of political opportunity were altered via radio. What emerged was a belief that the president was on their side, that they had federal justification for their actions, and that the federal government would intervene when the pivotal moment came. Little effective intervention, however, actually occurred.

Media, Radio, and Social Movement Diffusion

Our focus on media technology partially bridges social movement perspectives, such as political opportunity or collective identity theory, by addressing the question of how processes relevant to social movement formation are manifested across space. In our view, the melding of identity, political opportunity, and oppositional culture foci with an understanding of diffusional processes and media's role offers researchers the most useful set of theoretical tools for understanding the complex and dynamic character of historical, contemporary, and future movement formation across space.[24]

In the case of southern textile workers, the new medium of radio reinforced a common culture, a critical interpretation of the world in which workers lived, and a forging of community. It reflected and provided, for all intents and purposes, a common thread. For southern mill workers, preexisting cultural forms and emerging oppositional formulations were directly and indirectly diffused across communities through this new, relatively autonomous medium. What was broadcast, whether intended or not, altered mill workers' perceptions of political opportunity and legitimated to the broader public their own culture, including, for a time, even oppositional elements of that culture. Indirectly, radio in the South also created new occupational space for, and a network of, traveling musicians. Many of these musicians were ex-mill hands, who spread information and similarity of experience in towns throughout the region.

The radio as a cultural and political conduit became especially potent in the years just before, and then during, the 1934 strike. Radio at the time was characterized by little political oversight and control, heterogeneous ownership patterns, a desire of programmers to appeal to their local audiences, and the realization by early political and cultural celebrities that this new medium could effectively touch forgotten populations. This autonomy, however, would not last much beyond the 1934 strikes. Corporate control and political oversight became more prevalent when teeth were given to the Communications Act of 1934. This legislation eventually led to the near saturation of local radio broadcasts by national network programming.

Corporate interests won out, owing both to bureaucratic changes in law and to the ever-increasing role of sales revenue for local and national radio. Autonomy of local stations was politically curbed by the Federal Communications Commission in the mid- to late 1930s when smaller owners and universities, advocating radio in the "public interest" and greater flexibility in what was aired, lost out to "commercial interests." More stringent guidelines for broadcasts that could be interpreted as "political" or "propaganda" were set in place, and radio operators who violated new policy ran the risk of losing their operating licenses.[25] The relative success of the recording industry and its linkage to the largest of the corporate broadcast networks also nationalized music played over the airwaves, leaving little room and little market for music explicitly dealing with worker grievances and the concerns of local populations.[26] Thus, while the decline in local radio station autonomy was partially a function of institutional bureaucratic tendencies, it should also be seen as a political process—one whose trajectory leaned toward, although was not completely determined by, corporate-political hegemony.

Along with providing insight into the impact of radio early on, and how our case holds sociological implications for understanding the labor process and resistance, oppositional culture, and the impact of political opportunity on protest, the analysis of southern textile mill-worker mobilization and the role of radio presented in this book also contribute to the growing body of research on media, communication technology, and community.[27] Although much of this work focuses on media and communication technology in the contemporary era, specifically television and the Internet, many themes are parallel. Do media and new communication technologies enhance the degree of social integration? Do they result in collective identity, and might such collective identity facilitate group action? What tends to be missing in this literature, however, is the historical context in which new information mediums unfold, and the consequences for social groupings. As Calhoun (1998, 375) argues, "we need to set our discussions of electronic media in a bit deeper historical context—not just of technology but of the spatial organization of power and movements challenging that power."

Our analysis highlights the power of radio to transform consciousness and to partially instigate challenges to existing structures of inequality. However, we also acknowledge its limits—lessons that may be, more or less, applicable to understanding the potential influence of television or the Internet on collective action. These newer technologies unquestionably enhance collective experience through the maintenance of dispersed networks, through the encouragement of "sociospatial" enclaves, and by facilitating group activities.[28] Similar to the historical situation of radio, however, the influence of newer media and communication technologies on these social processes and collective mobilization may vary, depending on the level of political autonomy and the degree to which information transmitted appeals to the unique experiences of individuals and specific social groupings.[29]

These issues of limited autonomy and overly generalized appeal apply most straightforwardly to television and suggest a limited potential impact on collective experience and the unfolding of collective action. The Internet, on the other hand, seems to be different. It is a medium of multidirectional information flow, and it exists in a multinational context. As such, it affords its users both autonomy from political controls and specificity of group interest, at least at the present time. As such, it will likely have stronger consequences for group-specific identities and the coordination of collective action. As was the case with textile workers and radio in the 1920s and 1930s, however, such relations should be seen as tenuous at best, because they require "connection maintenance"—something that is extraordinarily difficult to nurture and preserve for a significant length of time, and on such a wide geographic and sociopolitical scale.[30] Moreover, if the Internet follows the pattern exhibited by radio, its potential impact may very well be curbed by rules and regulations, particularly if its use runs counter to dominant ideological positions and stratification structures.

Conclusion

The sociological approach we have taken in this book to understanding labor insurgency, and southern textile-worker mobilization specifically, is one rooted in the goals of both general explanation and historical and cultural specificity. Broad, general theories of collective action, such as collective identity theory, political opportunity theory, and perspectives on social movement culture and diffusional processes, are clearly useful for understanding how and why subordinate groups generally manage to mount collective protest, even in the face of substantial constraint and hardship. Such frameworks and their utility, however, must ultimately be grounded and evaluated within the context of historical contingencies, macro- and microprocesses, and the complexities, continuities, and even contradictions in human action. Such grounding has been our intention throughout this book.

Although the goals of generality, on the one hand, and specificity, on the other, are ostensibly at odds, this tension in the sociological enterprise is, in our view, not only useful but necessary. Indeed, the grounding of general expectations and understandings of process within the intricacies of context, change, and nuances, as we have done in our analysis of southern mill workers, allows for a more accurate and complex depiction of human rationality and action. Human beings and social groups, as in the case of southern mill hands, are well aware of the constraints in their lives, the probability of changing their situation, and the costs and possible benefits that action might entail. As we have shown, cultural forces and interactional dynamics play a role as well, conditioning perceptions of possibility and ultimately influencing the decision to act or not to act.

Southern textile workers of the 1920s and 1930s mounted a formidable challenge to the southern mill complex, just when employers, politicians, and even labor union organizers thought it unlikely or even inconceivable. The founding of radio stations within the region directly and indirectly linked mill communities, and altered many workers' conceptions of place, community, and collective opportunity. The realities of mill life and altered conceptions of that life were disseminated and expressed through workers' own cultural repertoires prior to and during the mobilization. Interactional processes on the shop floor, within mill communities, and between workers and national actors (the federal government and labor unions), however, conditioned workers' evaluations, their sense of efficacy, and, ultimately, their decision as to whether to take part in the strikes. Despite the complexity, the Gastonia and Marion strikes in 1929 and then the broader-based collective action in 1934 offer a window into a unique historical moment and an unambiguous expression of working-class possibility. Although strikers were eventually defeated, their struggle provides unique insight into the complex, creative, and dynamic character of individual and collective behavior.

Notes

Introduction

1. Hall et al. (1987); Yellen (1936).
2. Griffith (1988); Hall et al. (1987); McLaurin (1971).
3. Hodges (1986); Tippett (1931).
4. Saposs (1930, 924–25).
5. Sherrill (2001a); Hall (2001).
6. Beal (1937).
7. Roscigno and Danaher (2001).
8. Transcribed interview with W. W. Williams (1995).
9. See, for instance, Piven and Cloward (1977).
10. See, for instance, Melucci (1985).
11. Cornfield and Leners (1989).
12. See Roscigno and Kimble (1995) and Tomaskovic-Devey and Roscigno (1996).
13. In these regards, see especially Anderson (2000), Brown and Boswell (1995), Hodson (1999, 2001), Kimeldorf (1999), and Vallas (1987).
14. For elaboration, see Epstein (1990), W. Gamson (1992a), J. Gamson (1995), Melucci (1985), and Taylor and Whittier (1992).
15. Morris (1984); Nagel (1994); Stotik, Shriver, and Cable (1994); Mathews (1982); Meyer and Whittier (1994); Taylor and Whittier (1992); Fantasia (1988); Hodson, Ziegler, and Bump (1987).
16. For instance, see Brown and Boswell (1995) and Kimeldorf (1999).
17. Giddens (1982, 157).

18. On the topic of ideological challenge specifically, see Della Fave (1980, 1986) and Oliver and Johnston (1999).

19. Gamson and Meyer (1992); Jenkins (1985); Jenkins and Perrow (1977); McAdam (1982); Pichardo (1995); Tilly (1976).

20. Lachmann (1990); Tomaskovic-Devey and Roscigno (1996).

21. See also Brown and Boswell (1995), Brueggeman and Boswell (1998), Roscigno and Kimble (1995), and Wood (1986).

22. Leiter, Schulman, and Zingraff (1991); McLaurin (1971).

23. Oliver and Johnston (1999); Meyer and Staggenborg (1996).

24. For a good example, see Rupp and Taylor (2003).

25. See, for instance, Oliver (1989), Olzak (1992), Rogers (1995), and Soule and Zylan (1997).

26. Fantasia (1988); Morris (1984); Oberschall (1989); Myers (2000); Strang and Meyer (1993).

27. W. Gamson (1995); Kahan (1999); Oberschall (1989); Spilerman (1970).

28. On this point, see McAdam (1982), Kurzman (1996), and Tarrow (1988).

29. Brown (1998); Hall et al. (1987); Kahan (1999).

30. Flacks (1999); W. Gamson (1992b); Goffman (1981); Lichterman (1999); Mills (1939, 1940); Eyerman and Jamison (1998).

31. Mills (1940, 913).

32. For example, Melucci (1985); Taylor and Whittier (1992).

33. See also Flacks (1999), Kizer (1983), and McLaurin and Peterson (1992).

34. See especially Pratt (1990) and Flacks (1999).

35. Malone (1979).

36. See, for instance, Piven and Cloward (1977) and McCarthy and Zald (1977).

37. See also Roscigno and Hodson (2004).

38. Redding (1992).

39. It is also the case that both populist uprisings and labor organizing in the South occurred in geographic locations relatively distant from textile production, and that in both, the major obstacle and/or accomplishment had to do with racial divides in the workforce. Many southern mills in the 1920s and 1930s were located in areas of quite limited African-American population concentration and, where there was a sizeable African-American population, few were employed in mills or were segregated into the lowest-rung jobs (e.g., scrubbers and sweepers). African Americans were also moving to the North in record numbers (Uhlenberg 1973; Scott 1969). These facts make the mobilization of mill hands somewhat analytically distinct.

40. For a critique of literature suggesting a conservative tendency among U.S. workers, see especially Kimeldorf (1999).

41. Although some scholars have suggested that creative cultural repertoires that tap into identities are more characteristic of "new" as opposed to "old" social movements, our analyses suggest that this is not the case. The importance of music to southern textile-worker mobilization, as something that carried the necessary and influential components of social movement culture, demonstrates that even "old" movements required and included rich cultural content. Although few analyses of social movements systematically explore the functions and importance of music the way we do here, we believe this focus and the systematic approach we bring to it can inform and be used to analyze movement formation and cohesion among most, if not all, aggrieved groups, across time and place.

1. The World of the Southern Cotton Mill

1. Yellen (1936); Mitchell and Mitchell (1968).

2. Hall et al. (1987).

3. Transcribed interview with Sam Finley (1975).

4. Transcribed interview with George R. Elmore (1976).

5. Transcribed interview with Opal McMichael (1995).

6. Transcribed interview with Albert N. Sanders (1980).

7. Green (1993) provides a fascinating look at the evolution and dissemination of a cotton mill song across time.

8. Hall et al. (1987).

9. Transcribed interview with Opal McMichael (1995).

10. Vera Buch Weisbord (1974) notes that while Ella May Wiggins was in favor of organizing African Americans, George Pershing, another Young Communist League organizer, was not. A union organizer in the film, The *Uprising of '34* (1995) says that his union would give blacks a charter to organize themselves but they were not allowed in the white union. Simon (1998) observes that race relations in South Carolina were notably better during the strikes but, once mill workers achieved the ability to purchase creature comforts, such as cars and refrigerators, they were less likely to lean toward integration.

11. Transcribed interview with Icy Norman (1979).

12. Transcribed interview with Abner Darden Asbury Jr. (1976).

13. Transcribed interview with Albert N. Sanders (1980).

14. Cornfield and Leners (1989); Griffith (1988); Leiter, Schulman, and Zingraff (1991); McLaurin (1971); Pope (1942).

15. Transcribed interview with Mack Fretwell Duncan (1979).

16. Transcribed interview with Father Kloster (1995).

17. Quoted in Haessly (1987, 14).

18. In this regard, see Rorrer (1982).

19. See Grundy (1991).

20. Transcribed interview with Louise Jones (1976).

21. Transcribed interview with Eula McGill (1995).

22. Transcribed interview with Grady Kilgro (1995).

23. See Byerly (1986) and Miller (1980) for more on lives of mill mothers.

24. Transcribed interview with Jessie Lee Carter (1980).

25. *Uprising of '34* (1995).

26. National Organization for Women (1979, 4).

27. Transcribed interview with Grover Hardin (1980).

28. Tribe and Morris (1975).

29. Letter correspondence from J. E. Mainer to Archie Green (1965).

30. Transcribed interview with Eva B. Hopkins (1980).

31. Transcribed interview with Grover Hardin (1980).

32. Transcribed interview with Ernest E. Chapman (1979).

33. Transcribed interview with Lloyd Davidson (1979).

34. Letter correspondence from P. M. Mooney to FDR (1934).

35. Transcribed interview with Lloyd Davidson (1979).

36. Interview with Carl Martin (2001).

37. Transcribed interview with Sam Finley (1975).

2. Radio in the Textile South

1. Initially, radios were small crystal sets with few signals to pick up. Later, Lee De Forest's audio vacuum tube, described by Barfield (1996) as the most important technological discovery of the twentieth century, would become the key to the success, adoption, and dissemination of radio and then TV. Yet, technology was in some ways a lesser influence on the development and acceptance of radio in the United States, and particularly in the South, than early station ownership patterns, listening patterns of audiences, government regulation, and battles over what constituted the public good.

2. Lazersfeld (1971).

3. Douglas (1987, 15).

4. Douglas (1987); Hilliard and Keith (1992). For additional history of radio, see Barnouw (1966).

5. The business of radio was a long-shot investment of modernizer elites relative to more traditional elites, vested in agriculture, textiles, and lumbering, and who had deep ties to local newspapers. New technologies were strongly linked: the automobile and radio walked hand in hand. It is thus no surprise that Democratic President Franklin Delano Roosevelt later used the radio to circumvent largely conservative local newspapers. We draw the modernizer and traditionalist distinction from Luebke (1990), who links elite interest and political action to the industrial base on which they depend.

6. Federal Radio Commission (1929).

7. Hall et al. (1987).

8. Kittross (1977).

9. Hogan (1971 [1930]). For further discussion of radio frequency, see Codel (1971).

10. On this point, see Grundy (1991). Often, on clear nights, Southerners could pick up stations transmitted from a number of East Coast stations. Local stations, however, transmitted more clearly and consistently, and also drew more attention from mill workers because local station operators catered to local interests in their programming choices. Especially important in this regard was the programming of hillbilly music during specified times, particularly in the morning and on Saturday nights.

11. Hampton (1935).

12. Interview with Homer "Pappy" Sherrill (2000).

13. Bittner (1982); Garofalo (1997).

14. Summers (1958).

15. Quoted in Barfield (1996, 16).

16. Quoted in ibid., 8.

17. See Luebke (1998); Simon (1998).

18. Quoted in Barfield (1996, 7).

19. Grundy (1991).

20. Barfield (1996, 15).

21. See Barfield (1996) and Barnouw (1966).

22. Grundy (1991).

23. Malone (1979, 71).

24. Grundy (1991).

25. Interview with Roy "Whitey" Grant and Polly Grant (2001).

26. Grundy (1991).

27. *Clark's Directory of Southern Textile Mills* (1929).

28. Malone (1985); Grundy (1991).

29. Grundy (1991).

3. The People's President

1. Indeed, few, if any, analyses of historical movements that we are aware of pose the question of media impact on the perceptions of potential social movement actors. Rather, the mechanism of diffusion typically focuses on social movement leaders "spreading the word" through formal and informal networks. One exception might be the focus on the perceptions and legitimacy of the southern civil rights movement, as communicated across the television airwaves. Even this focus, however, is not dealing explicitly with political opportunity and perceptions among

social movement actors, but rather with the impact of media presentation on the attitudes on the more general public.

2. McChesney (1999). For further discussion of FDR's fireside chats, see Chester (1969).

3. Craig (2000).

4. Roosevelt (1933).

5. Ibid.

6. Hall et al. (1987, 292).

7. Sussman (1963).

8. Hall et al. (1987); Hodges (1986); Wood (1986); Irons (2000); Hayes (2001).

9. Transcribed interview with Solomon Barkin (1995).

10. Transcribed interview with Lucille Thornburgh (1995).

11. Transcribed interview with Mr. Nealy (1995).

12. McElvaine (1983); Sussman (1963).

13. Transcribed interview with Lucille Thornburgh (1995).

14. Hall et al. (1987).

15. Transcribed interview with Eula McGill (1995).

16. Tullos (1989).

17. Wood (1986).

18. Letter from W. E. McCoy to Hugh S. Johnson (1934).

19. Anonymous letter from transcripts of *The Uprising of '34* (1995).

20. Bindas (1995).

21. Levine (1988).

22. Bindas (1995).

23. Filene (2000).

24. Ibid.

25. In this regard, see Kurzman (1996).

26. We suspect that the popularity of FDR, and the perceived opportunity among workers generated though his programs and speeches, also helps explain more general labor unrest throughout the country during this period. Although it may be the case that southern mill workers' perceptions were shaped by labor struggles in other regions, we found little evidence in archived interviews, our own interviews, or historical materials to suggest that strikes in the Northeast or the West Coast, for instance, fundamentally altered southern workers' desire or inclination to strike.

4. The Musicians

1. See Gurlach's (1999) discussion of "traveling evangelists" and the role they may play in social movement linkages and spatial diffusion, by carrying messages, spreading ideology, and building personal relationships across the network.

2. Barfield (1996).

3. Green (1993).

4. Malone (1993).

5. Green (1993).

6. Transcribed interview with Harvey Ellington (1979).

7. See Malone (1985) and Wolfe (1977).

8. Yet, even Poole was influenced by Tin Pan Alley, as evidenced by his song "Budded Rose," which has that characteristic sound. After viewing the movie *The Jazz Singer* starring Al Jolson, Poole was even said to have mimicked Jolson's style. For further discussion, see Rorrer (1982).

9. Malone (1985).

10. Sherrill (2001b), interviewed backstage at a Cypress Gardens concert near Monck's Corner, South Carolina.

11. Peterson (1997).

12. Interview with Roy "Whitey" Grant and Polly Grant (2001).

13. Interviews with Alvin Wall (2001), Homer "Pappy" Sherrill (2001a, 2001b), Wade Mainer (2000), Roy "Whitey" Grant and Polly Grant (2001), and J. D. McCormick (2001).

14. Interview with Roy "Whitey" Grant and Polly Grant (2001).

15. Tribe (1983).

16. Morris (1987).

17. Malone (1985). Also see Koon (1975).

18. Green (1961).

19. Transcribed interview with Harvey Ellington (1979).

20. Hall et al. (1987).

21. Rorrer (1982).

22. Interview with Homer "Pappy" Sherrill (2001a). See Aherns (1970) for further information on Homer "Pappy" Sherrill.

23. Delmore (1995).

24. Ibid.

25. Mainer (1965). See also Tribe and Morris (1975).

26. Interview with Alvin Wall (2001).

27. Delmore (1995).

28. Interview with Alvin Wall (2001).

29. Lynch (2001).

30. Malone (1979).

31. Greenway (1953).

32. Malone (1979, 62).

33. Grundy (1991).

34. Malone (1979).

35. Lomax (1993).

36. Malone (1979).

37. Garofalo (1997, 44).

38. Ibid.; Rorrer (1982).

39. Lynch (2001).

40. Dixon (1962) letter correspondence with Archie Green.

41. Green (1963).

42. Dixon (1948). In Green (1966), Dixon does not see himself as a champion for other mill workers, but this seems to contradict his overall view of himself, as portrayed in a letter to Green in 1962. Regardless of how Dixon characterized himself, the popularity of his "Weave Room Blues," and its coverage by other artists, attests to its potential impact. Those we interviewed also remembered the song, albeit sometimes after we sang it for them.

43. Sherrill (2001a).

44. Grundy (1995); Roscigno and Danaher (2001).

45. For firsthand accounts of conditions, see Haessly (1987) and Miller (1980).

46. Green (1963) and Malone (1985) write on radio musicians of the mill period, such as the Dixons. See also Paris (1973) on the Dixon Brothers. Haessly (1987) comments on the legacy of Ella May's music.

47. Russell (1970).

48. Rorrer (1982); Wiggins (1987).

49. Hodges (1986).

50. Grundy (1995). For more on Charlotte music, see Holt (1985).

51. Hall et al. (1987).

52. Delmore (1995).

53. Interview with Alvin Wall (2001).

54. Interviews with Homer "Pappy" Sherrill (2000), Roy "Whitey" Grant and Polly Grant (2001), and J. D. McCormick (2001).

55. Tullos (1989, 2).

56. Transcribed interview with Harvey Ellington (1979).

57. Hall et al. (1987, 261).

58. Gurlach (1999).

5. Music and the Mill Experience

1. At the very least, and even if a social movement organization such as a labor union is present, potential movement actors will be inclined to adopt those frames to the extent that they are consistent with lived experiences and familiar cultural cues.

2. For another in-depth discussion of this music, and its creation by mill workers and recording artists, see DeNatale and Hinson (1993). Although these authors make the case that it is important to distinguish between music generated by record-

ing artists and that generated by workers during protest, we see such distinctions as somewhat arbitrary and problematic given that the two populations shared both lived experiences and music itself.

3. As we show later, music was used during strikes to promote solidarity, both within the context of a given village and across villages through its use on "dancing pickets" and "flying squadrons." Sometimes traditional mountain tunes were also used by strikers on picket lines and in jail cells. Although lyrical themes pertaining to inequality, mill work, and exploitation were especially poignant, given potentially simultaneous effects on emotion, cognition, and interpretation, the act of singing and/or dancing together to shared melodies is in and of itself an important act of community celebration and social cohesion (see Flacks 1999; Roscigno, Danaher, and Summers-Effler 2002; and Summers-Effler 2001).

4. Some might argue that such songs were, in fact, not as important to, or influential on, mill workers as historians have speculated. This conclusion is likely based on Southern Oral History interview material, within which few workers ever recall specific song titles. We believe that such a conclusion would be greatly overstated. Workers were interviewed nearly forty years after the strikes and forty years after the mill-specific music about which we are speaking ebbed. In our own interviews, we too found that workers, and even musicians themselves, from that era could not recall the specific titles of these songs, but did recognize (with enthusiasm) these songs, as well as their lyrics, upon hearing the actual song played.

5. One might make the argument that understanding the songwriter's intention should be a central concern to us in this book. We disagree. The fundamental question is whether workers heard this music, adapted this music, and activated it during the course of their work lives and protest activities. Certainly, social-psychological questions pertaining to reception and cognition may be relevant as well, but they are tangential to our more basic sociological concern with cultural diffusional dynamics, media technology, and collective action.

6. Scholars of music and the South have delineated, in finer detail, the specific strains or traditions that compose this body of music. We nevertheless use the terms *hillbilly, mountain, Appalachian,* and *porch* somewhat interchangeably, precisely because the listening audiences at the time as well as the musicians did so.

7. McNeil (1993).

8. Grundy (1995).

9. Transcribed interview with Roy Ham (1977).

10. Ibid.

11. Transcribed interview with Alice P. Evitt (1979).

12. Transcribed interview with Vernon Durham (1979).

13. Rorrer (1982).

14. Transcribed interview with Naomi Sizemore Trammel (1980).

15. Transcribed interview with Vernon Durham (1979).

16. Transcribed interview with Mozelle Riddle (1979).

17. Transcribed interview with Grover Hardin (1980).

18. Weisbord (1974).

19. Green (1961).

20. Greenway (1953); Malone (1985); Lynch (2001).

21. Of course, the songs discussed in the next section reflect recorded music, music that was played over the airwaves, and music solely sung by workers. Although one might argue that there are key differences between type, and thus that each should be treated separately, we see the lines between type as being somewhat blurred. For instance, some worker songs were adaptations of recorded songs, and some recorded songs and songs that received radio airtime were, in fact, utilized by workers during protest.

22. Initially we broke these songs down by whether they were clearly intended to be strike songs or not (Roscigno and Danaher 2001). Upon further analysis of particular strikes and the songs that were sung, however, we found that the boundaries of song usage were not so clear-cut. For instance, songs like Dave McCarn's "Cotton Mill Colic," which has no clear collective mobilization intent, were used prior to and then during strikes. Consequently, we examine all thirty-five songs simultaneously and attempt to define general patterns in the interpretations and potential remedies they offer.

23. W. Gamson (1995); Snow and Benford (1992); Taylor and Whittier (1995).

24. Billings (1990); Della Fave (1980); Vallas (1987).

25. W. Gamson (1995); Snow and Benford (1992); Snow et al. (1986); Taylor and Whittier (1995); Mattern (1998).

26. For a detailed theoretical discussion of subcultural or oppositional cultural emergence, relative to preexisting cultural forms, see Kleinman and Fine (1979) and Mansbridge and Morris (2001).

27. Malone (1985); Greenway (1953).

28. For a detailed and informative discussion of ideology, and how it gets manifested in concrete social practices and community ritual, see Fine and Sandstrom (1993) and Summers-Effler (2001).

6. Mill-Worker Consciousness, Music, and the Birth of Revolt

1. Huber (1998).

2. Interviews with Red Hall (2001), Homer "Pappy" Sherrill (2001b), and Alvin Wall (2001).

3. Interview with J. D. McCormick (2001).

4. See Huber (1998). There is evidence that songs out of Gastonia, such as "Cotton Mill Colic," were sung in other parts of South, such as Danville, Virginia, both in leisure time and during strikes (Rorrer 1982; Tippett 1931).

5. Transcribed interview with Sam Finley (1975); see also Beal (1937), Lewis (1929), Tippett (1931).

6. Saposs (1933).

7. Tippett (1931).

8. Interview with Alvin Wall (2001).

9. Interview with Wade Mainer (2000).

10. Interview with Alvin Wall (2001).

11. Paris (1970).

12. Roy "Whitey" Grant and Polly Grant (2001).

13. Weisbord (1974).

14. Goffman (1961).

15. Salmond (1995).

16. Beal (1937, 123).

17. Some have suggested that Communist leadership, resources, and influence were more pronounced in Gastonia than we are suggesting. Our reading of the historical evidence, however, including Fred Beal's own recollections, suggests that this was not the case. Although several Communist organizers and union bureaucrats periodically appeared in Gastonia, this was more a function of the union's effort to convince Beal to push the party's ideological stance on workers—something he resisted, for obvious reasons. Beal similarly notes that the resources afforded to him and the workers of Gastonia by the union were very limited. We strongly suspect that the view that Communist union influence was great is being driven largely by analyses that disproportionately draw from newspaper accounts at the time that were responsible for, if not strategic in, fostering red-scare rhetoric.

18. Beal (1937, 132–33).

19. Tippett (1931, 80).

20. For southern attitudes toward organized labor and the impact of red-scare rhetoric, see Billings (1990), Nolan and Jones (1976), Salmond (1995), and Simon (1998).

21. Salmond (1995).

22. This tension is evident in Beal's own account, in which he discusses the party's efforts to have him address the race issue, and his recognition that bringing up race was beyond the immediate concerns of these workers and not powerfully relevant, given the small number of blacks employed in the Gastonia mills. To the disapproval of higher-ranking union officials, Beal held back in pushing broader ideological themes, given what he saw as an immediate and more proximate reformatory stance of the majority of Loray Mill workers. He also worked hard to make sure that Young Communist League organizer George Pershing did not to scare the strikers by calling for a Communist uprising during his visit to Gastonia (Salmond 1995).

23. Beal (1937, 148).

24. Haessly (1987).

25. Beal (1937, 159).

26. See Lynch (2001) for an in-depth discussion of these songs.

27. Weisbord (1974, 9).

28. Weisbord (1974); Beal (1937); Salmond (1995); Tippett (1931); Williams and Williams (1984).

29. Several of these workers escaped to the Soviet Union with Beal, only to die of sickness, return to the United States to face their prison sentences, or live in hiding in the United States for the rest of their lives (Beal 1937).

30. Beal (1937); Tippett (1931); National Organization for Women (1979); Weisbord (1974).

31. Interview with J. D. McCormick (2001); interview with Carl Martin (2001).

32. See Daniel (2001).

33. Lewis (1929).

34. Transcribed interview with Sam Finley (1975).

35. Ibid.

36. Tippett (1931).

37. Ibid.

38. Yellen (1936); Tippett (1931); Lewis (1929).

39. Tippett (1931, 120–21).

40. Interview with Red Hall (2001).

41. Interview with Alvin Wall (2001).

42. Interview with Red Hall (2001).

43. Tippett (1931, 119).

44. Tippett (1931); Yellen (1936).

45. Interview with Sam Finley (1975).

46. Interview with Red Hall (2001).

47. Tippett (1931).

48. Some accounts suggest that deputies had been drinking all night in preparation for the shootings, and that there was, in fact, a "hit list" of which organizers to shoot. See interview with Sam Finley (1975).

49. Tippett (1931).

50. Interview with Carl Martin (2001).

51. Interview with Red Hall (2001), and transcribed interview with Sam Finley (1975).

52. Transcribed interview with Sam Finley (1975).

53. Tippett (1931, 164).

54. Tippett (1931).

55. The 1929 strike in Elizabethton, which, like Marion, occurred with UTW representation, also was ended with state militia presence and violence.

56. Tippett (1931, 294).

7. The General Textile Strike of 1934

1. It appears that the "flying squadron" was initially used by Minneapolis Teamsters in early 1934. In this regard, see especially Preis (1964). All available interview material on southern textile workers, however, seems to suggest little connection to or awareness of the Minneapolis strikers and the use of squadrons. Rather, and much like Preis's discussion of the squadron or "cruising picket squad" of Minneapolis coming from the rank and filers, our evidence suggests that southern workers themselves (rather than their union representatives, if any) came up with the idea of helping shut down neighboring mills.

2. See Wright (1994).

3. Rorrer (1982); Tippett (1931).

4. Rorrer (1982).

5. Interview with Homer "Pappy" Sherrill (2001a).

6. Gurlach (1999).

7. Interview with Homer "Pappy" Sherrill (2000).

8. Gellhorn (1934).

9. William Leutchtenburg, quoted in Hodges (1986, 46).

10. Transcribed interview with Lloyd Davidson (1979).

11. Letter correspondence from James and Kirby to FDR (1933).

12. Transcribed interview with Lucille Thornburgh (1995).

13. Hall et al. (1987) set the number at more than four hundred thousand workers. See also Preis (1964, 36).

14. Tippett (1931).

15. Simon (1998).

16. Fuller (1931).

17. Hodges (1986).

18. See also Waldrep's (2000) discussion of worker protest activity in Spartanburg, South Carolina, the summer before the general strike. For broader discussion of the strike, see Marshall (1967) and Brecher (1997).

19. Transcribed interview with Lloyd Kirby (1995).

20. Transcribed interview with Joe Jacobs (1995).

21. Hodges (1986).

22. Transcribed interview with Eula McGill (1995).

23. Transcribed interview with Grover Hardin (1980).

24. Transcribed interview with Joe Jacobs (1995).

25. The conclusions are derived from chi-squared tests of statistical significance

(see Roscigno and Danaher 2001), as well as from logistic regression estimates of the likelihood of strike activity relative to radio station foundings, with controls for state and textile mill concentration. Although not presented here, these findings are available from the authors upon request.

26. For instance, the lyrics to an earlier mill-worker protest song such as "Winnsboro Cotton Mill Blues" or "Hard Times in Here" could be easily changed in a manner to insert a specific mill name or a particular manager or supervisor's name. Interview material suggests that this was the case in many southern mill towns.

27. Transcribed interview with Laura Beard (1995).

28. The practice of generating new labor songs using recycled melodies, including hymns, is not necessarily new. South African house servants during apartheid, for instance, constructed more radical verses to traditional folk melodies. The Industrial Workers of the World (IWW), in its Little Red Songbook, similarly set new labor-oriented lyrics to established and more well known melodies.

29. Tippet (1931).

30. Letter correspondence from Alvin Wall to William F. Danaher (2000b).

31. Transcribed interview with Esther Jenks (1977).

32. Simon (1998).

33. In this regards, see especially Waldrep (2000), Wright (1994), Hall, Korstad, and Leloudis (1986), and Wingerd (1996).

34. Transcribed interview with Mozzelle Riddle (1979).

35. Transcribed interview with Lucille Thornburgh (1995). See also Wingerd (1996), Wright (1994).

36. Transcribed interview with Mozzelle Riddle (1979).

37. Interview with J. D. McCormick (2001).

38. See Wright (1994).

39. Transcribed interview with Abner Darden Asbury Jr. (1976).

40. Hall et al. (1987); Hodges (1986); Simon (1998). Also interview with Homer "Pappy" Sherrill (2000).

41. Waldrep (2000, 96).

42. See Waldrep (2000).

43. Transcribed interview with Joe Jacobs (1995).

44. See video footage from ABC News (1999).

45. Transcribed interview with Sol Stetin (1995).

46. For a good discussion of the flying squadron, its demise, and its consequences for the strike of 1934 more generally, see Waldrep (2000).

47. See ibid., 97.

48. Interview with Red Hall (2001).

49. Transcribed interview with Lillie Morris Price (1975).

50. See especially Waldrep (2000) on this point. Preis's (1964) recounting of

Roosevelt's role in the calling off of the strike seems to suggest that Roosevelt merely promised a follow-up survey of mill-work conditions. Our understanding, however, is that negotiations for the strike's end also included reemployment of striking workers. In this regard, Roosevelt may have made promises, but had no institutional infrastructure in place to ensure that such policy was carried out. Consequently, employer power remained firmly intact and workers were both not reemployed and in many cases blacklisted.

51. Hall, Korstad, and Leloudis (1986).

52. See Griffith (1988), Minchin (1997), Roscigno and Kimble (1995), Wood (1996).

Conclusion

1. For a discussion of conceptualizations of mill workers and their treatment by academics and others, see Zeiger (1997).

2. Transcribed interview with Eula Durham (1979).

3. Transcribed interview with Sam Finley (1975).

4. Hall et al. (1987).

5. Transcribed interview with Red Hall (2001).

6. Transcribed interview with Kathy Lamb (1995).

7. Transcribed interview with Mary Ruth Auton (1976).

8. See Griffith (1988) and Minchin (1997).

9. Interview with J. D. McCormick (2001).

10. On this point, see Cornfield and Leners (1989).

11. See Anderson (2000) for a more recent look at unionization in Kannapolis, North Carolina.

12. Kimeldorf (1999) makes a similar argument in his historical analysis of collective action among longshoremen and restaurant and service workers in the Northeast during the same general time period.

13. See Roscigno, Danaher, and Summers-Effler (2002).

14. Malone (1985).

15. Peterson (1992).

16. Letter correspondence of Dorsey Dixon to Archie Green (1962).

17. Filene (2000); Larkin (1929).

18. Seeger (1992).

19. See Denisoff (1972) and Peterson (1992). See also Greenway (1953).

20. See Danaher and Blackwelder (1993).

21. See, for instance, Greenway (1953), Lomax, Guthrie, and Seeger (1967), and Pratt (1990).

22. See Calhoun (1998), Kahan (1999), Myers (2000), Brown (1998), and Gamson and Wolfsfeld (1993).

23. See McAdam (1982), Kurzman (1996), and Tarrow (1998)

24. In these regard, see especially W. Gamson (1995), Gamson (1998), Gamson and Wolfsfeld (1993), Taylor (1996), and Myers (2000).

25. Federal Radio Commission (1929); McChesney (1993).

26. Cantril and Allport (1971); Dowd (2003); Malone (1979).

27. Calhoun (1998); Cerulo and Ruane (1998); Purcell (1997).

28. Calhoun (1998); Cerulo and Ruane (1998).

29. Gamson, Croteau, Hoynes, and Sasson (1992).

30. Cerulo and Ruane (1998).

Bibliography

ABC News. 1999. *The Century: Nothing to Fear* (video). Narrated by Peter Jennings. New Hudson, Mich.: ABC News.

Aherns, Pat J. 1970. *A History of the Musical Careers of Dewitt "Snuffy" Jenkins, Banjoist and Homer "Pappy" Sherrill, Fiddler.* Columbia, S.C.: Wentworth Corporation.

Anderson, Cynthia. 2000. *The Social Consequences of Economic Restructuring in the Textile Industry.* New York: Garland.

Barfield, Ray E. 1996. *Listening to Radio, 1920–1950.* Westport, Conn.: Praeger.

Barkan, Steven E. 1984. "Legal Control of the Southern Civil Rights Movement." *American Sociological Review* 49: 552–65.

Barnouw, Erik. 1966. *A Tower of Babel: A History of Broadcasting in the United States.* Vol. 1. New York: Oxford University Press.

Beal, Fred Erwin. 1937. *Proletarian Journey: New England, Gastonia, Moscow.* New York: Hillman-Curl.

Billings, Dwight B. 1990. "Religion as Opposition: A Gramscian Analysis." *American Journal of Sociology* 96: 1–31.

Bindas, Kenneth J. 1995. *All of This Music Belongs to the Nation: The WPA's Federal Music Project and American Society.* Knoxville: University of Tennessee Press.

Bittner, John. R. 1982. *Broadcast Law and Regulation.* Englewood Cliffs, N.J.: Prentice Hall.

Blau, Peter. 1977. *Inequality and Heterogeneity: A Primitive Theory of Social Structure.* New York: Free Press.

Brecher, Jeremy. 1997. *Strike!* Boston: South End Press.

Brown, Cliff, and Terry Boswell. 1995. "Strikebreaking Solidarity: The Great Steel Strike of 1919." *American Journal of Sociology* 100: 1479–1519.

Brown, Robert J. 1998. *Manipulating the Ether: The Power of Broadcast Radio in Thirties America.* Jefferson, N.C.: McFarland and Company.

Brueggeman, John, and Terry Boswell. 1998. "Realizing Solidarity: Sources of Interracial Unionism during the Great Depression." *Work and Occupations* 25: 436–82.

Byerly, Victoria Morris. 1986. *Hard Times Cotton Mill Girls: Personal Histories of Womanhood and Poverty in the South.* Ithaca, N.Y.: ILR Press.

Calhoun, Craig. 1998. "Community without Propinquity Revisited: Communications Technology and the Transformation of the Urban Public Sphere." *Sociological Inquiry* 68: 373–97.

Cantril, Hadley, and Gordon W. Allport. 1971 [1935]. *The Psychology of Radio.* New York: Arno.

Cerulo, Karen A., and Janet M. Ruane. 1998. "Coming Together: New Taxonomies for the Analysis of Social Relations." *Sociological Inquiry* 68: 398–425.

Chester, Edward W. 1969. *Radio, Television, and American Politics.* New York: Sheed and Ward.

Clark's Directory of Southern Textile Mills. 1929. 41st ed. Charlotte, N.C.: Clark Publishing Company.

Codel, Martin, ed. 1971. *Radio and Its Future.* New York: Arno Press.

Cornfield, Dan, and Mark V. Leners. 1989. "Unionization in the Rural South: Regional Patterns of Industrialization and the Process of Union Organizing." *Research in Rural Sociology and Development* 4: 137–52.

Craig, Douglas B. 2000. *Fireside Politics: Radio and Political Culture in the United States, 1920–1940.* Baltimore: Johns Hopkins University Press.

Dahrendorf, Ralf. 1959. *Class and Class Conflict in Industrial Society.* Stanford, Calif.: Stanford University Press.

Danaher, William F., and Stephen P. Blackwelder. 1993. "Afro-American Music as Social Criticism: A Comparison of Blues and Rap." *Popular Music and Society* 17(4): 1–12.

Daniel, Clete. 2001. *Culture of Misfortune: An Interpretive History of Textile Unionism in the United States.* Ithaca, N.Y.: Cornell University Press.

Della Fave, L. Richard. 1980. "The Meek Shall Not Inherit the Earth." *American Sociological Review* 45: 955–71.

———. 1986. "Toward an Explication of the Legitimation Process." *Social Forces* 65: 476–500.

Delmore, Alton. 1995. *Truth Is Stranger Than Publicity.* Nashville, Tenn.: Country Music Federation Press.

DeNatale, Doug, and Glenn Hinson. 1993. "The Southern Textile Song Tradition Reconsidered." In Archie Green, ed., *Songs about Work: Essays in Occupational Culture for Richard A. Reuss,* 77–107. Bloomington: Indiana University Press.

Denisoff, R. Serge. 1971. *Great Day Coming: Folk Music and the American Left.* Urbana: University of Illinois Press.

———. 1972. *Sing a Song of Social Significance.* Bowling Green, Ohio: Bowling Green University Popular Press.

Dixon, Dorsey. 1998. *Babies in the Mill.* Oakland, Calif.: HighTone Records/ HMG.

Douglas, George H. 1987. *The Early Days of Radio Broadcasting.* Jefferson, N.C.: McFarland and Company.

Dowd, Timothy J. 1992. "The Musical Structure and Social Context of Number One Songs, 1955–1988." In R. Wuthnow, ed., *Vocabularies of Public Life: Empirical Essays in Symbolic Structure,* 130–57. London: Routledge.

———. 2003. "Structural Power and the Construction of Markets: The Case of Rhythm and Blues." *Comparative Social Research* 21: 145–99.

Epstein, Barbara. 1990. "Rethinking Social Movement Theory." *Socialist Review* 20: 35–66.

Eyerman, Ron, and Andrew Jamison. 1998. *Music and Social Movements: Mobilizing Traditions in the Twentieth Century.* Cambridge: Cambridge University Press.

Fantasia, Rick. 1988. *Cultures of Solidarity: Consciousness, Action, and Contemporary American Workers.* Berkeley: University of California Press.

Federal Radio Commission. 1929. *Third Annual Report of the Federal Radio Commission to the Congress of the United States Covering the Period from October 1, 1928, to November 1, 1929.* Washington, D.C.: U.S. Government Printing Office.

Filene, Benjamin. 2000. *Romancing the Folk: Public Memory and American Roots Music.* Chapel Hill: University of North Carolina Press.

Fine, Gary Alan, and Kent Sandstrom. 1993. "Ideology in Action: A Pragmatic Approach to a Contested Concept." *Sociological Theory* 11: 21–38.

Flacks, Richard. 1999. "Culture and Social Movements: Exploring the Power of Song." Paper presented at the Annual Meetings of the American Sociological Association, Chicago, August.

Fuller, Paul. 1931. "Workers Education in Augusta, Ga., and the Horse Creek Valley, S.C." *Textile Worker* 19: 11–13.

Gamson, Joshua. 1995. "Must Identity Movements Self-Destruct? A Queer Dilemma." *Social Problems* 42: 390–407.

———. 1998. *Freaks Talk Back: Tabloid Talk Shows and Sexual Nonconformity.* Chicago: University of Chicago Press.

Gamson, William A. 1992a. "The Social Psychology of Collective Action." In A. Morris and C. McClurg, eds., *Frontiers in Social Movement Theory,* 53–76. New Haven: Yale University Press.

———. 1992b. *Talking Politics.* New York: Cambridge University Press.

———. 1995. "Constructing Social Protest." In Hank Johnston and Bert Klandermans, eds., *Social Movements and Culture,* 85–106. Minneapolis: University of Minnesota Press.

Gamson, William A., David Croteau, W. Hoynes, and T. Sasson. 1992. "Media Images and the Social Construction of Reality." *Annual Review of Sociology* 18: 373–93.

Gamson, William A., and David S. Meyer. 1992. "The Framing of Political Opportunity." Paper presented at the Annual Meetings of the American Sociological Association, Pittsburgh, August.

Gamson, William A. and G. Wolfsfeld. 1993. "Movements and Media as Interacting Systems." *Annals of the American Academy of Political and Social Science* 528: 114–25.

Garofalo, Reebee. 1997. *Rockin' Out: Popular Music in the USA.* Boston: Allyn and Bacon.

Gellhorn, Martha. 1934. Letter to Harry Hopkins, Director of the Federal Emergency Relief Administration (November 11, 1934), http://newdeal.feri.org/hopkins/hop08.htm. New Deal Network, http://newdeal.feri.org (April 23, 1999).

Giddens, Anthony. 1982. "Class Structuration and Class Consciousness." In Anthony Giddens and David Held, eds., *Classes, Power, and Conflict: Classical and Contemporary Debates,* 157–74. Berkeley: University of California Press.

Goffman, Erving. 1961. *Asylums: Essays on the Social Situation of Mental Patients and Other Inmates.* Garden City, N.Y.: Anchor Books.

———. 1981. *Forms of Talk.* Philadelphia: University of Pennsylvania Press.

Green, Archie. 1961. *Rough Information on and Interview from Dave McCarn.* File 654 of the Archie Green Papers, Southern Folklife Collection, Library of the University of North Carolina at Chapel Hill.

———. 1963. *Correspondence, Interview, and Biographical Material on Dorsey Dixon.* Files 795–825 of the Archie Green Papers, Southern Folklife Collection, Library of the University of North Carolina at Chapel Hill.

———. 1966. "Dorsey Dixon: Minstrel of the Mills," *Sing Out!* 6 (July): 10–12.

———. 1993. "A Southern Cotton Mill Rhyme." In *Wobblies, Pile Butts, and Other Heroes: Laborlore Explorations,* 275–320. Chicago: University of Illinois Press.

Greenway, John. 1953. *American Folksongs of Protest.* Philadelphia: University of Pennsylvania Press.

Griffin, Larry, Michael Wallace, and Beth Rubin. 1986. "Capitalist Resistance to the Organization of Labor before the New Deal: Why? How? Success?" *American Sociological Review* 51: 147–67.

Griffith, Barbara S. 1988. *The Crisis of American Labor: Operation Dixie and the Defeat of the CIO.* Philadelphia: Temple University Press.

Grundy, Pamela. 1991. "From Il Trovatore to Crazy Mountaineers: WBT-Charlotte and Changing Musical Culture in the Carolina Piedmont: 1922–1935." Master's thesis, University of North Carolina at Chapel Hill.

———. 1995. "We Always Tried to Be Good People—Respectability, Crazy Water Crystals, and Hillbilly Music on the Air, 1933–1935." *Journal of American History* 81: 1591–1620.

Gurlach, Luther P. 1999. "The Structure of Social Movements: Environmental Activism and Its Opponents." In Jo Freeman and Victoria Johnson, eds., *Waves of Protest: Social Movements since the Sixties,* 85–97. New York: Rowman and Littlefield.

Haessly, Lynn. 1987. "Mill Mother's Lament: Ella May, Working Women's Militancy and the 1929 Gaston County Strikes." Master's thesis, University of North Carolina at Chapel Hill.

Hall, Jacquelyn Dowd, James Leloudis, Robert Korstad, Mary Murphy, Lu Ann Jones, and Christopher B. Daly. 1987. *Like a Family: The Making of a Southern Cotton Mill World.* Chapel Hill: University of North Carolina Press.

Hall, Jacquelyn Dowd, Robert Korstad, and James Leloudis. 1986. "Cotton Mill People: Work, Community, and Protest in the Textile South, 1880–1940." *American Historical Review* 91: 245–86.

Hampton, Francis. 1935. "New Leisure: How Is It Spent? A Study of What One Hundred Twenty-Two Textile Workers of Leaksville, Spray, and Draper Are Doing with the New Leisure Created by the N.R.A., as Applied to Certain Types of Activities." Master's thesis, Department of Sociology, University of North Carolina at Chapel Hill.

Hayes, Jack Irby, Jr. 2001. *South Carolina and the New Deal.* Columbia: University of South Carolina Press.

Hille, Waldemar. 1948. *The People's Song Book.* New York: Boni and Gaer.

Hilliard, Robert L., and Michael C. Keith. 1992. *The Broadcast Century: A Biography of American Broadcasting.* Stoneham, Mass.: Butterworth-Heinemann.

Hodges, James A. 1986. *New Deal Labor Policy and the Southern Cotton Textile Industry, 1933–1941.* Knoxville: University of Tennessee Press.

Hodson, Randy. 1999. "Management Citizenship Behavior: A New Concept and an Empirical Test." *Social Problems* 46: 460–78.

———. 2001. *Dignity at Work.* Cambridge: Cambridge University Press.

Hogan, John W. L. 1971 [1930]. "How Radio Works." In Martin Codel, ed., *Radio and Its Future*, 267–74. New York: Arno Press.

Hodson, Randy, Deborah Ziegler, and Barbara Bump. 1987. "Who Crosses the Picket Line: An Analysis of the CWA Strike of 1983." *Labor Studies Journal* 12(2): 19–38.

Holt, George, ed. 1985. *The Charlotte Music Story*. Charlotte: North Carolina Arts Council.

Huber, Patrick. 1998. "Battle Songs of the Southern Class Struggle: Songs of the Gastonia Textile Strike of 1929." *Southern Cultures* 4: 109–25.

Irons, Janet. 2000. *Testing the New Deal: The General Textile Strike of 1934 in the American South*. Urbana: University of Illinois Press.

James, David R. 1988. "The Transformation of the Southern Racial State: Class and Race Determinants of Local-State Structures." *American Sociological Review* 53: 191–208.

Jenkins, J. Craig. 1985. *The Politics of Insurgency*. New York: Columbia University Press.

Jenkins, J. Craig, and Charles Perrow. 1977. "Insurgency of the Powerless: Farm Worker Movements (1946–1972)." *American Sociological Review* 42: 249–68.

Kahan, Michael. 1999. *Media as Politics: Theory, Behavior and Change in America*. Englewood Cliffs, N.J.: Prentice Hall.

Kimeldorf, Howard. 1999. *Battling for American Labor: Wobblies, Craft Workers, and the Making of the Union Movement*. Berkeley: University of California Press.

Kittross, John, ed. 1977. *Documents in American Telecommunications Policy*. New York: Arno Press.

Kizer, Elizabeth J. 1983. "Protest Song Lyrics as Rhetoric." *Popular Music and Society* 9: 3–11.

Kleinman, Sherryl, and Gary Alan Fine. 1979. "Rethinking Subculture: An Interactionist Analysis. *American Journal of Sociology* 85: 1–20.

Koon, Henry. 1975. "Dave McCarn." *John Edwards Memorial Foundation Quarterly* (winter): 167–76.

Kurzman, Charles. 1996. "Structural Opportunity and Perceived Opportunity in Social Movement Theory: The Iranian Revolution of 1979." *American Sociological Review* 61: 153–70.

Lachmann, Richard. 1990. "Class Formation without Class Struggle: An Elite Conflict Theory of the Transition to Capitalism." *American Sociological Review* 55: 398–414.

Larkin, Margaret. 1929. "Ella May's Songs." *Nation* 29: 382–83.

Lazersfeld, Paul F. 1971. *History of Broadcasting: Radio to Television*. New York: Arno Press.

Leiter, Jeffrey, Michael Schulman, and Rhonda Zingraff. 1991. *Hanging by a Thread: Social Change in Southern Textiles*. New York: ILR Press.

Levine, Rhonda F. 1988. *Class Struggle and the New Deal: Industrial Labor, Industrial Capital, and the State*. Lawrence: University of Kansas Press.

Lewis, Sinclair. 1929. *Cheap and Contented Labor: The Picture of a Southern Mill Town in 1929*. New York: United Features Syndicate.

Lichterman, Paul. 1999. "Talking Identity in the Public Sphere: Broad Visions and Small Spaces in Sexual Identity Politics." *Theory and Society* 28: 101–41.

Lieberman, Robbie. 1989. *My Song Is My Weapon: People's Songs, American Communism, and the Politics of Culture, 1930–1950*. Urbana: University of Illinois Press.

Lomax, Alan. 1960. *The Folk Songs of North America*. New York: Doubleday.

———. 1991. *Appalachian Journey Videorecording*. Alexandria, Va.: PBS Video.

———. 1993. *The Land Where the Blues Began*. New York: New Press.

Lomax, Alan, Woody Guthrie, and Pete Seeger. 1967. *Hard-Hitting Songs for Hard-Hit People*. New York: Oak Publications.

Luebke, Paul. 1990. *Tar Heel Politics*. Chapel Hill: University of North Carolina Press.

Lynch, Timothy P. 2001. *Strike Songs of the Great Depression*. Jackson: University of Mississippi Press.

Malone, Bill C. 1979. *Southern Music, American Music*. Lexington: University of Kentucky Press.

———. 1985. *Country Music USA*. 2d ed. Austin: University of Texas Press.

———. 1993. *Singing Cowboys and Musical Mountaineers: Southern Culture and the Roots of Country Music*. Athens: University of Georgia Press.

———. 2002. "I'm a Small-Time Laboring Man." In *Don't Get above Your Raisin': Country Music and the Southern Working Class*. Chicago: University of Illinois Press.

Mann, Michael. 1973. *Consciousness and Action among the Western Working Class*. London: Macmillan.

Mansbridge, Jane, and Aldon Morris, eds. 2001. *Oppositional Consciousness: The Subjective Roots of Social Protest*. Chicago: University of Chicago Press.

Marshall, F. Ray. 1967. *Labor in the South*. Cambridge: Harvard University Press.

Mathews, Jane De Hart. 1982. "The New Feminism and the Dynamics of Social Change." In Linda K. Kerber and Jane De Hart Mathews, eds., *Women's America: Refocusing the Past*, 397–425. New York: Oxford University Press.

Mattern, Mark. 1998. *Acting in Concert: Music Community, and Political Action*. New Brunswick, N.J.: Rutgers University Press.

McAdam, Doug. 1982. *Political Process and the Development of Black Insurgency, 1930–1970*. Chicago: University of Chicago Press.

———. 1983. "Tactical Innovation and the Pace of Insurgency." *American Sociological Review* 48: 735–54.

McCarthy, John D., and Meyer N. Zald. 1977. "Resource Mobilization and Social Movements: A Partial Theory." *American Journal of Sociology* 82: 1212–41.

McChesney, Robert W. 1993. *Telecommunications, Mass Media, and Democracy: The Battle for the Control of Broadcasting, 1928–1935.* New York: Oxford University Press.

———. 1999. *Rich Media, Poor Democracy: Communication Politics in Dubious Times.* New York: New Press.

McElvaine, Robert S. 1983. *Down & Out in the Great Depression: Letters from the "Forgotten Man."* Chapel Hill: University of North Carolina Press.

McLaurin, Meltin A. 1971. *Paternalism and Protest: Southern Cotton Mill Workers and Organized Labor, 1875–1905.* Westport, Conn.: Greenwood Press.

McLaurin, Meltin A., and Richard A. Peterson. 1992. *You Wrote My Life: Lyrical Themes in Country Music.* Philadelphia: Gordon and Breach.

McNeil, W. K. 1993. *Southern Mountain Folksongs: Folk Songs from the Appalachians and the Ozarks.* Little Rock: August House Publishers.

Melucci, Alberto. 1985. "The Symbolic Challenge of Contemporary Movements." *Social Research* 52: 781–816.

Meyer, David S., and Nancy E. Whittier. 1994. "Social Movement Spillover." *Social Problems* 41: 277–98.

Meyer, David S., and Suzanne Staggenborg. 1996. "Movements, Counter-movements, and the Structure of Political Opportunity." *American Journal of Sociology* 101: 1628–60.

Miller, Marc, ed. 1980. *Working Lives: The "Southern Exposure" History of Labor in the South.* New York: Random House.

Mills, C. Wright. 1939. "Language, Logic, and Culture." *American Sociological Review* 4: 670–80.

———. 1940. "Situated Actions and Vocabularies of Motive." *American Sociological Review* 5: 904–13.

Minchin, Timothy J. 1997. *What Do We Need a Union For? The TWUA in the South, 1945–1955.* Chapel Hill: University of North Carolina Press.

Mitchell, Broadus, and George Sinclair Mitchell. 1968. *The Industrial Revolution in the South.* New York: Greenwood Press.

Monroe, Bill, and Charlie Monroe. 2000 [1937]. "The Monroe Brothers." In Tom Ewing, ed., *The Bill Monroe Reader,* 7–9. Chicago: University of Illinois Press.

Montgomery, David. 1987. *The Fall of the House of Labor.* New York: Cambridge University Press.

Morris, Aldon D. 1984. *Origins of the Civil Rights Movement: Black Communities Organizing for Change.* New York: Free Press.

Morris, John. 1987. *The Dixon Brothers.* Vol. 4. Liner notes. Old Homestead Records, Brighton, Michigan.

Myers, Daniel J. 2000. "The Diffusion of Collective Violence: Infectiousness, Susceptibility, and Mass Media Networks. *American Journal of Sociology* 106: 173–208.

Nagel, Joane. 1994. "Constructing Ethnicity: Creating and Recreating Ethnic Identity and Culture." *Social Problems* 41: 152–76.

Natale, Doug, and Glenn Hinson. 1993. "The Southern Textile Song Tradition Reconsidered." In Archie Green, ed., *Songs about Work: Essays in Occupational Culture for Richard A. Reuss,* 77–107. Bloomington: Indiana University & Folklore Institute.

National Organization for Women. 1979. *Let's Stand Together: The Story of Ella May Wiggins.* Ed. Dorsett Edmunds, Laurie Greybeal, Eileen Hanson, Ann Horne, Charlie Thomas, and Julie Vaughan. Charlotte, N.C.: Metrolina Chapter of NOW.

Nolan, Dennis R., and Donald E. Jones. 1976. "Textile Unionism in the Piedmont, 1901–1932," In Gary M. Fink and Merl E. Reed, eds., *Essays in Southern Labor History: Selected Papers, Southern Labor History Conference, 1976,* 48–69. Westport, Conn.: Greenwood Press.

Oberschall, Anthony. 1989. "The 1960 Sit-ins: Protest Diffusion and Movement Take-off." *Research in Social Movements, Conflict and Change* 11: 31–53.

Oliver, Pamela E. 1989. "Bringing the Crowd Back In: The Nonorganizational Elements of Social Movements." *Research in Social Movements, Conflict and Change* 11: 1–30.

Oliver, Pamela E., and Hank Johnston. 1999. "What a Good Idea! Frames and Ideologies in Social Movement Research." Paper presented at the Annual Meetings of the American Sociological Association, Chicago, August.

Olzak, Susan. 1992. *The Dynamics of Ethnic Competition and Conflict.* Stanford, Calif.: Stanford University Press.

Paris, Mike. 1970. *Liner Notes for "Singers of the Piedmont."* Folk Variety/Bear Family Record 15505.

———. 1973. "The Dixons of South Carolina." *Old Time Music* 10 (autumn): 13.

Parkin, Frank. 1979. *The Marxist Theory of Class: A Bourgeois Critique.* London: Tavistock.

Pattillo-McCoy, Mary. 1998. "Church Culture as a Strategy of Action in the Black Community." *American Sociological Review* 63: 767–84.

Peterson, Florence. 1971. *Strikes in the United States: 1880–1936.* St. Claire Shores, Mich.: Scholarly Press.

Peterson, Richard A. 1992. "Class Unconsciousness." In Melton A. McLaurin and Richard A. Peterson, eds., *You Wrote My Life: Lyrical Themes in Country Music,* 35–62. Philadelphia: Gordon and Breach.

———. 1997. *Creating Country Music: Fabricating Authenticity.* Chicago: University of Chicago Press.

Pichardo, Nelson A. 1995. "The Power Elite and Elite-Driven Countermovements: The Associated Farmers of California during the 1930s." *Sociological Forum* 10: 21–49.

Piven, Frances Fox, and Richard A. Cloward. 1977. *Poor People's Movements: Why They Succeed, How They Fail.* New York: Pantheon.

Pope, Liston. 1942. *Millhands and Preachers: A Study of Gastonia.* New Haven: Yale University Press.

Preis, Art. 1964. *Labor's Giant Step: Twenty Years of the CIO.* New York: Pioneer Publishers.

Pratt, Ray. 1990. *Rhythm and Resistance.* New York: Praeger.

Pula, James S., and Eugene E. Dziedzic. 1990. *United We Stand: The Role of Polish Workers in the New York Mills Textile Strikes, 1912 and 1916.* Boulder, Colo.: East European Monographs; New York: Columbia University Press.

Purcel, Kristin. 1997. "Towards a Communication Dialectic: Imbedded Technology and the Enhancement of Place." *Sociological Inquiry* 67: 101–12.

Redding, Kent. 1992. "Failed Populism: Movement-Party Disjuncture in North Carolina, 1890 to 1900." *American Sociological Review* 57: 340–52.

Rogers, Everett M. 1995. *Diffusion of Innovations.* New York: Free Press.

Roosevelt, Franklin Delano. 1933. "On the Purposes and Foundations of the Recovery Program." From Fireside Chats of FDR, Mid-Hudson Regional Information Center. http://www.mhrcc.org/fdr/fdr.html.

Rorrer, Kinney. 1982. *Rambling Blues: The Life and Songs of Charlie Poole.* London: Old Time Music.

Roscigno, Vincent J., and M. Keith Kimble. 1995. "Elite Power, Race, and the Persistence of Low Unionization in the South." *Work and Occupations* 22: 271–300.

Roscigno, Vincent J., and Randy Hodson. 2004. "The Organizational and Social Foundations of Worker Resistance." *American Sociological Review* 69: 14–39.

Roscigno, Vincent J., and William F. Danaher. 2001. "Media and Mobilization: The Case of Radio and Southern Textile Worker Insurgency, 1929–1934." *American Sociological Review* 66: 21–48.

Roscigno, Vincent J., William F. Danaher, and Erika Summers-Effler. 2002.

"Music, Culture, and Social Movements: Song and Southern Textile Worker Mobilization, 1929–1934." *International Journal of Sociology and Social Policy* 22: 141–74.

Rupp, Leila J., and Verta Taylor. 2003. *Drag Queens at the 801 Cabaret.* Chicago: University of Chicago Press.

Russell, Tony. 1970. *Blacks, Whites, and Blues.* New York: Stein and Day.

Salmond, John A. 1995. *Gastonia 1929: The Story of the Loray Mill Strike.* Chapel Hill: University of North Carolina Press.

Saposs, David J. 1930. "Labor." *American Journal of Sociology* 35: 924–25.

Scott, Emmett J. 1969. *Negro Migration during the War.* New York: Arno Press.

Seeger, Pete. 1992. *American Industrial Ballads.* Washington, D.C.: Smithsonian Folkways Recordings.

Simon, Bryant. 1998. *The Fabric of Defeat: The Politics of South Carolina Mill-hands, 1910–1948.* Chapel Hill: University of North Carolina Press.

Snow, David A. 2001. "Collective Identity." In Neil J. Smelser and Paul B. Baltes, eds., *International Encyclopedia of the Social and Behavior Sciences,* 141–74. London: Elsevier Science.

Snow, David A., and Robert D. Benford. 1992. "Master Frames and Cycles of Protest." In Aldon Morris and Carol Mueller, eds., *Frontiers of Social Movement Theory,* 133–55. New Haven: Yale University Press.

Snow, David A., E. Burke Rochford, Steven K. Worden, and Robert D. Benford. 1986. "Frame Alignment Process, Micromobilization, and Movement Participation." *American Sociological Review* 51: 464–81.

Soule, Sarah A., and Yvonne Zylan. 1997. "Runaway Train? The Diffusion of State-Level Reform in ADC/AFDC Eligibility Requirements, 1950–1967." *American Journal of Sociology* 103: 733–62.

Spilerman, Seymour. 1970. "The Causes of Racial Disturbances: A Comparison of Alternative Explanations." *American Sociological Review* 3: 627–49.

Stoney, George, Judith Helfand, and Susanne Rostock. 1995. *The Uprising of '34.* Video Documentary. Brooklyn, N.Y.: First Run/Icarus Films.

Stotik, Jeffrey, Thoman E. Shriver, and Sherry Cable. 1994. "Social Control and Movement Outcome: The Case of AIM." *Sociological Focus* 27: 53–66.

Strang, David, and John W. Meyer. 1993. "Institutional Conditions for Diffusion." *Theory and Society* 22: 487–511.

Summers, Harrison B. 1958. *A Thirty-Year History of Programs Carried on National Radio Networks in the United States, 1926–1956.* New York: Arno Press.

Summers-Effler, Erika. 2001. "The Micro Potential for Social Change: Emotion, Consciousness, and Social Movement Formation." *Sociological Theory* 20: 41–60.

Sussman, Leila A. 1963. *Dear FDR: A Study of Political Letter-Writing.* Totowa, N.J.: Bedminster Press.

Swidler, Ann. 1986. "Culture in Action: Symbols and Strategies." *American Sociological Review* 51: 273–86.

Tarrow, Sidney. 1988. "National Politics and Collective Action: Recent Theory and Research in Western Europe and the United States." *Annual Review of Sociology* 14: 421–40.

Taylor, Verta. 1996. *Rock-a-By Baby: Feminism, Self Help, and Postpartum Depression.* New York: Routledge.

Taylor, Verta, and Nancy E. Whittier. 1992. "Collective Identity in Social Movement Communities: Lesbian Feminist Mobilization." In Aldon Morris and Carol McClurg, eds., *Frontiers in Social Movement Theory,* 104–29. New Haven: Yale University Press.

———. 1995. "Analytical Approaches to Social Movement Culture: The Culture of the Women's Movement." In Hank Johnston and Bert Klandermans, eds., *Social Movements and Culture,* 163–86. Minneapolis: University of Minnesota Press.

Tilly, Charles. 1976. *From Mobilization to Revolution.* Englewood Ciffs, N.J.: Prentice Hall.

Tippett, Thomas. 1931. *When Southern Labor Stirs.* New York: Jonathan Cape & Harrison Smith.

Tomaskovic-Devey, Donald, and Vincent J. Roscigno. 1996. "Racial Economic Subordination and White Gain in the U.S. South." *American Sociological Review* 61: 565–89.

Tribe, Ivan M. 1983. *The Tobacco Tags.* Vol. 1. Liner notes. Old Homestead Records, Brighton, Michigan.

Tribe, Ivan M., and John W. Morris. 1975. "J. E. and Wade Mainer." *Bluegrass Unlimited* 10: 12–21.

Tullos, Allen. 1989. *Habits of Industry: White Culture and the Transformation of the Carolina Piedmont.* Chapel Hill: University of North Carolina Press.

Uhlenberg, Peter. 1973. "Non-Economic Determinants of Non-Migration: Sociological Considerations for Migration Theory." *Rural Sociology* 38(3): 297–311.

Vallas, Stephen P. 1987. "The Labor Process as a Source of Class Consciousness: A Critical Examination." *Sociological Forum* 2: 237–56.

Waldrep, George Calvin. 2000. *Southern Workers and the Search for Community: Spartanburg County, South Carolina.* Urbana: University of Illinois Press.

Weisbord, Vera Buch. 1974. "Gastonia, 1929: Strike at the Loray Mill," *Southern Exposure* 1(3/4): 1–23.

Wiggins, Gene. 1987. *Fiddlin' Georgia Crazy: Fiddlin' John Carson, His Real World, and the World of His Songs.* Chicago: University of Illinois Press.

Williams, Robert L., and Elizabeth W. Williams. 1984. *Thirteenth Juror: The Story of the Nineteen Twenty-Nine Loray Strike.* Bronxville, N.Y.: Herald Books.

Wingerd, Mary Lether. 1996. "Rethinking Paternalism: Power and Parochialism in a Southern Mill Village." *Journal of American History* 83: 872–902.

Wolfe, Charles. 1977. *Tennessee Strings: The Story of Country Music in Tennessee.* Knoxville: University of Tennessee Press.

Wood, Philip. 1986. *Southern Capitalism: The Political Economy of North Carolina, 1880–1980.* Durham, N.C.: Duke University Press.

Wright, Annette C. 1994. "The Aftermath of the General Textile Strike: Managers and the Workplace at Burlington Mills." *Journal of Southern History* 60: 81–112.

Yellen, Samuel. 1936. "The Southern Textile Strikes and Gastonia." In *American Labor Struggles,* 292–326. New York: S. A. Russell.

Zeiger, Robert H. 1997. "From Primordial Folk to Redundant Workers: Southern Textile Workers and Social Observers: 1920–1990." In *Southern Labor in Transition, 1940–1995.* Knoxville: University of Tennessee Press.

Interviews and Correspondence

Asbury, Abner Darden, Jr. 1976. Interview by Brent Glass of Abner Darden Asbury Jr. on April 6, 1976, at Greenville, South Carolina. From the Southern Oral History Program #4007, Southern Historical Collection, Wilson Library, University of North Carolina at Chapel Hill.

Auton, Mary Ruth. 1976. Interview with Jacquelyn Dowd Hall in 1976 at Catawba, North Carolina. From the Southern Oral History Program #4007, Southern Historical Collection, Wilson Library, University of North Carolina at Chapel Hill.

Barkin, Solomn. 1995. Transcribed interview from the film *The Uprising of '34,* produced by George Stoney, Judith Helfand, and Susanne Rostock. Brooklyn, New York: First Run/Icarus Films.

Beard, Laura. 1995. Transcribed interview from the film *The Uprising of '34,* produced by George Stoney, Judith Helfand, and Susanne Rostock. Brooklyn, New York: First Run/Icarus Films.

Brown, Marion "Peanut." 1995. Transcribed interview from the film *The Uprising of '34,* produced by George Stoney, Judith Helfand, and Susanne Rostock. Brooklyn, New York: First Run/Icarus Films.

Carter, Jessie Lee. 1980. Interview by Allen Tullos of Jesse Lee Carter on May 5,

1980, at Greenville, South Carolina. From the Southern Oral History Program #4007, Southern Historical Collection, Wilson Library, University of North Carolina at Chapel Hill.

Chapman, Ernest E. 1979. Interview by Mary Murphy of Ernest E. Chapman on June 4, 1979, at Burlington, North Carolina. From the Southern Oral History Program #4007, Southern Historical Collection, Wilson Library, University of North Carolina at Chapel Hill.

Davidson, Lloyd. 1979. Interview by Allen Tullos of Betty and Lloyd Davidson on February 2 and 15, 1979, at Burlington, North Carolina. From the Southern Oral History Program #4007, Southern Historical Collection, Wilson Library, University of North Carolina at Chapel Hill.

Dewey, Woody. 2000. Interview with William F. Danaher in Mount Pleasant, South Carolina.

Dixon, Dorsey. 1948. *Early Life of Dorsey M. Dixon, Songwriter and Composer and Author of the Famous Wreck of the Highway and Many Others. Correspondence, Interview, and Biographical Material on Dorsey Dixon.* Files 795 and 2002 of the Archie Green Papers, Southern Folklife Collection, Library of the University of North Carolina at Chapel Hill.

———. 1962. "Letter to Archie Green." In *Correspondence, Interview, and Biographical Material on Dorsey Dixon.* Files 795–825 of the Archie Green Papers, Southern Folklife Collection, Library of the University of North Carolina at Chapel Hill.

Duncan, Mack Fretwell. 1979. Interview by Allen Tullos of Mack Duncan on June 7 and August 30, 1979, at Greenville, South Carolina. From the Southern Oral History Program #4007, Southern Historical Collection, Wilson Library, University of North Carolina at Chapel Hill.

Durham, Eula. 1979. Interview by Jim Leloudis of Eula and Vernon Durham on November 29, 1978, at Bynum, North Carolina. From the Southern Oral History Program #4007, Southern Historical Collection, Wilson Library, University of North Carolina at Chapel Hill.

———. 1995. Transcribed interview from the film *The Uprising of '34,* produced by George Stoney, Judith Helfand, and Susanne Rostock. Brooklyn, New York: First Run/Icarus Films.

Durham, Vernon. 1979. Interview by Jim Leloudis of Eula and Vernon Durham on November 29, 1978, at Bynum, North Carolina. From the Southern Oral History Program #4007, Southern Historical Collection, Wilson Library, University of North Carolina at Chapel Hill.

Ellington, Harvey. 1979. Interview by Allen Tullos of Harvey Ellington and Sam Pridgen on March 1 and April 5, 1979, at Oxford, North Carolina. From the Southern Oral History Program #4007, Southern Historical Collection, Wilson Library, University of North Carolina at Chapel Hill.

Elmore, George R. 1976. Interview by Brent Glass of George R. Elmore on March 11, 1976, at Durham, North Carolina. From the Southern Oral History Program #4007, Southern Historical Collection, Wilson Library, University of North Carolina at Chapel Hill.

Evitt, Alice P. 1979. Interview by Jim Leloudis of Alice P. Evitt on July 18, 1979, at Charlotte, North Carolina. From the Southern Oral History Program #4007, Southern Historical Collection, Wilson Library, University of North Carolina at Chapel Hill.

———. 1995. Transcribed interview from the film *The Uprising of '34,* produced by George Stoney, Judith Helfand, and Susanne Rostock. Brooklyn, New York: First Run/Icarus Films.

Finley, Sam. 1975. Interview by Mary Frederickson and Marion Roydhouse of Vesta and Sam Finley on July 22, 1975, at Marion, North Carolina. From the Southern Oral History Program #4007, Southern Historical Collection, Wilson Library, University of North Carolina at Chapel Hill.

Finley, Vesta. 1975. Interview by Mary Frederickson and Marion Roydhouse of Vesta and Sam Finley on July 22, 1975 at Marion, North Carolina. From the Southern Oral History Program #4007, Southern Historical Collection, Wilson Library, University of North Carolina at Chapel Hill.

Grant, Roy "Whitey," and Polly Grant. 2001. Interview with William F. Danaher and Vincent Roscigno in Charlotte, North Carolina.

Hall, Red. 2001. Interview with William F. Danaher and Vincent Roscigno in Marion, North Carolina.

Ham, Roy. 1977. Interview by Pat Dilley of Roy Ham in summer 1977 at Catawba, North Carolina. From the Southern Oral History Program #4007, Southern Historical Collection, Wilson Library, University of North Carolina at Chapel Hill.

———. 1995. Transcribed interview from the film *The Uprising of '34,* produced by George Stoney, Judith Helfand, and Susanne Rostock. Brooklyn, New York: First Run/Icarus Films.

Hardin, Grover. 1980. Interview by Allen Tullos of Grover Hardin on May 2, 1980, at Greenville, South Carolina. From the Southern Oral History Program #4007, Southern Historical Collection, Wilson Library, University of North Carolina at Chapel Hill.

Hill, Sue. 1995. Transcribed interview from the film *The Uprising of '34,* produced by George Stoney, Judith Helfand, and Susanne Rostock. Brooklyn, New York: First Run/Icarus Films.

Hopkins, Eva B. 1980. Interview by Lu Ann Jones of Eva B. Hopkins on March 5, 1980, at Charlotte, North Carolina. From the Southern Oral History Program #4007, Southern Historical Collection, Wilson Library, University of North Carolina at Chapel Hill.

Jacobs, Joe. 1995. Transcribed interview from the film *The Uprising of '34,* produced by George Stoney, Judith Helfand, and Susanne Rostock. Brooklyn, New York: First Run/Icarus Films.

James, M. S. and R. S. Kirby. 1933. Letter to Franklin Delano Roosevelt, October 23, 1933. NRA, RG9, Series 398, Box 25. United States National Archives, College Park, Maryland.

Jenks, Esther. 1977. Interview by Dolores Janiewski of Esther Jenks on April 26, 1977, at Durham, North Carolina. From the Southern Oral History Program #4007, Southern Historical Collection, Wilson Library, University of North Carolina at Chapel Hill.

Jones, Louise. 1976. Interview by Mary Frederickson of Louise Jones on October 13, 1976, at Bynum, North Carolina. From the Southern Oral History Program #4007, Southern Historical Collection, Wilson Library, University of North Carolina at Chapel Hill.

Kilgro, Grady. 1995. Transcribed interview from the film *The Uprising of '34,* produced by George Stoney, Judith Helfand, and Susanne Rostock. Brooklyn, New York: First Run/Icarus Films.

Kirby, Lloyd. 1995. Transcribed interview from the film *The Uprising of '34,* produced by George Stoney, Judith Helfand, and Susanne Rostock. Brooklyn, New York: First Run/Icarus Films.

Kloster, Father. 1995. Transcribed interview from the film *The Uprising of '34,* produced by George Stoney, Judith Helfand, and Susanne Rostock. Brooklyn, New York: First Run/Icarus Films.

Lamb, Kathy. 1995. Transcribed interview from the film *The Uprising of '34,* produced by George Stoney, Judith Helfand, and Susanne Rostock. Brooklyn, New York: First Run/Icarus Films.

Mainer, J. E. 1965. Letter Correspondence of J. E. Mainer to Archie Green, August 17, 1965. Files, Series 1 of the Archie Green Papers, Southern Folklife Collection, Library of the University of North Carolina at Chapel Hill.

Mainer, Wade. 2000. Telephone interview with William F. Danaher.

Martin, Carl. 2001. Interview with William F. Danaher and Vincent Roscigno in Marion, North Carolina.

McCormick, J. D. 2001. Interview with William F. Danaher and Vincent Roscigno in Marion, North Carolina.

McCoy, W. E. 1934. Letter to Hugh S. Johnson, January 14, 1934. NRA,

RG9, Series 398, Box 33. United States National Archives, College Park, Maryland.

McGill, Eula. 1995. Transcribed interview from the film *The Uprising of '34,* produced by George Stoney, Judith Helfand, and Susanne Rostock. Brooklyn, New York: First Run/Icarus Films.

McMichael, Opal. 1995. Transcribed interview from the film *The Uprising of '34,* produced by George Stoney, Judith Helfand, and Susanne Rostock. Brooklyn, New York: First Run/Icarus Films.

Mooney, P. M. 1933. Letter to Franklin Delano Roosevelt, October 23, 1933. NRA, RG9, Series 398, Box 25. United States National Archives, College Park, Maryland.

Nealy, Mr. 1995. Transcribed interview from the film *The Uprising of '34,* produced by George Stoney, Judith Helfand, and Susanne Rostock. Brooklyn, New York: First Run/Icarus Films.

Norman, Icy. 1979. Interview by Mary Murphy of Icy Norman on April 6 and 30, 1979, at Burlington, North Carolina. From the Southern Oral History Program #4007, Southern Historical Collection, Wilson Library, University of North Carolina at Chapel Hill.

Price, Lillie Morris. 1975. Interview by Mary Frederickson and Marion Boydhouse of Lillie Morris Price on July 22, 1975, at Asheville, North Carolina. From the Southern Oral History Program #4007, Southern Historical Collection, Wilson Library, University of North Carolina at Chapel Hill.

Riddle, Mozelle. 1979. Interview by Doug DeNatale of Mozelle Riddle, November 13, 1978, at Bynum, North Carolina. From the Southern Oral History Program #4007, Southern Historical Collection, Wilson Library, University of North Carolina at Chapel Hill.

Robinette, Jefferson M. 1979. Interview by Cliff Kuhn of Jefferson M. Robinette in July 1977 at Burlington, North Carolina. From the Southern Oral History Program #4007, Southern Historical Collection, Wilson Library, University of North Carolina at Chapel Hill.

Sanders, Albert N. 1980. Interview by Allen Tullos of Albert N. Sanders on May 30, 1980, at Greenville, South Carolina. From the Southern Oral History Program #4007, Southern Historical Collection, Wilson Library, University of North Carolina at Chapel Hill.

Sherrill, Homer "Pappy." 2000. Phone interview with William F. Danaher.

———. 2001a. Interview with William F. Danaher in Chapin, South Carolina.

———. 2001b. Interview with William F. Danaher and Vincent Roscigno in Cypress Gardens, South Carolina.

Stetin, Sol. 1995. Transcribed interview from the film *The Uprising of '34,* produced by George Stoney, Judith Helfand, and Susanne Rostock. Brooklyn, New York: First Run/Icarus Films.

Thornburgh, Lucille. 1995. Transcribed interview from the film *The Uprising of '34*, produced by George Stoney, Judith Helfand, and Susanne Rostock. Brooklyn, New York: First Run/Icarus Films.

Trammel, Naomi Sizemore. 1980. Interview by Allen Tullos of Naomi Sizemore Trammel on March 25, 1980, at Greenville, South Carolina. From the Southern Oral History Program #4007, Southern Historical Collection, Wilson Library, University of North Carolina at Chapel Hill.

Troutman, Fred. 2000. Interview with William F. Danaher in Statesville, North Carolina.

Troutman, Gray. 2000. Interview with William F. Danaher in Statesville, North Carolina.

Wall, Alvin. 2000a. Interview with William F. Danaher and Vincent J. Roscigno in Cypress Gardens, North Carolina.

———. 2000b. Letter correspondence with William F. Danaher.

———. 2001. Telephone interview with William F. Danaher on March 16.

Williams, W. W. 1995. Transcribed interview from the film *The Uprising of '34*, produced by George Stoney, Judith Helfand, and Susanne Rostock. Brooklyn, New York: First Run/Icarus Films.

Wise, Mae. 1933. Letter to Franklin Delano Roosevelt, October 10. NRA, RG9, Series 398, Box 25. United States National Archive, College Park, Maryland.

Wood, Woody. 1995. Transcribed interview from the film *The Uprising of '34*, produced by George Stoney, Judith Helfand, and Susanne Rostock. Brooklyn, New York: First Run/Icarus Films.

INDEX

VINCENT J. ROSCIGNO is associate professor of sociology at The Ohio State University. His research centers on inequality, power, and collective mobilization in the labor process.

WILLIAM F. DANAHER is associate professor of sociology at the College of Charleston, where he teaches and conducts research on inequality and the sociology of music. He spent several years as a traveling musician before his academic career.

Series page continued from page ii.

Volume 9   Cynthia Irvin, *Militant Nationalism: Between Movement and Party in Ireland and the Basque Country*

Volume 8   Raka Ray, *Fields of Protest: Women's Movements in India*

Volume 7   Michael P. Hanagan, Leslie Page Moch, and Wayne te Brake, editors, *Challenging Authority: The Historical Study of Contentious Politics*

Volume 6   Donatella della Porta and Herbert Reiter, editors, *Policing Protest: The Control of Mass Demonstrations in Western Democracies*

Volume 5   Hanspeter Kriesi, Ruud Koopmans, Jan Willem Duyvendak, and Marco G. Giugni, *New Social Movements in Western Europe: A Comparative Analysis*

Volume 4   Hank Johnston and Bert Klandermans, editors, *Social Movements and Culture*

Volume 3   J. Craig Jenkins and Bert Klandermans, editors, *The Politics of Social Protest: Comparative Perspectives on States and Social Movements*

Volume 2   John Foran, editor, *A Century of Revolution: Social Movements in Iran*

Volume 1   Andrew Szasz, *EcoPopulism: Toxic Waste and the Movement for Environmental Justice*